Big Book of ACT® Practice Tests

ISBN: 978-1-5062-0746-9

Table of Contents

Practice Makes Perfect

Don't be scared of the ACT. Why? Because we know what's on the exam, and we know exactly how you should prepare for it. Kaplan has been teaching kids how to succeed on standardized tests for more than 75 years—longer than anyone else, period.

This book contains your four course practice tests. Each exam mirrors the ACT you will see on Test Day and will provide you with plenty of practice as well as opportunities to assess your strengths and weaknesses before you take the real thing. Taking practice tests is important, but just as important is understanding why you got a particular question right or wrong. So when you're done, check out the detailed answers and explanations in your online center. These provide you with thorough explanations for the correct answers as well as strategic advice, all of which will help you practice thinking like an expert! In addition, every explanation includes the difficulty level of each question. All of this practice is geared toward one thing—getting you the most points on Test Day!

HOW TO USE THIS BOOK

This book is filled with over 850 practice questions to help you master the ACT.

Follow these steps to get the most out of these practice tests:

1. Bring this book, a pencil, and a calculator to every class!

2. Follow the proctor's instructions for each test. It's important that your Kaplan test experience be as close to the real thing as possible.

3. Assess your strengths and weaknesses. After you finish each test, go online and check out your score AND read the explanations for questions you missed as well as for questions on which you guessed.

4. Complete the required homework in your Course Book.

5. Log into your online center at least two to three times a week and work on the assignments from your personalized recommendations. These recommendations are based on your strengths and weaknesses and will help you improve your score in the least amount of time.

SCORING YOUR TEST

You gain one point for every question you answer correctly. You lose no points for answering a question wrong OR for leaving a question blank. This means you should ALWAYS answer EVERY question on the ACT—even if you have to guess.

ACT TEST DATES

As a general rule, students take the ACT at least once in their junior year, often taking it for the first time in the early spring. The ACT is administered on select Saturdays during the school year. Sunday testing is also available for students who cannot take the Saturday test because of religious observances. Check the official ACT website at actstudent.org/regist/dates.html for the most up-to-date test dates.

ACT REGISTRATION

To register for the ACT by mail, you'll need to get an ACT Paper Registration Guide from your high school guidance counselor.

- You can register online at actstudent.org/regist/. Note: Not all students are eligible to register online, so read the instructions and requirements carefully.

- Register early to secure the time you want at the test center of your choice and to avoid late registration fees.

- Students with disabilities can go toactstudent.org/regist/disab/ to learn how to apply for accommodations.

- In the United States, the fee for the ACT is $56.50 with the essay, and $39.50 without the essay. This price includes reports for you, your high school, and up to four colleges and scholarship programs. To get the most up-to-date information on test fees, please check actstudent.org/regist/actfees.html

- You will receive an admission ticket at least a week before the test. The ticket confirms your registration on a specified date, at a specified test center. Make sure to bring this, along with proper identification, to the test center. Some acceptable forms of identification include photo IDs such as a driver's license, a school identification card, or a valid passport. (Unacceptable forms of identification include a Social Security card, credit card, or birth certificate.)

- Your ACT scores will be available online approximately three weeks after the test.

- Remember to check actstudent.org for all the latest information on the ACT. Every effort has been made to keep the information in this book as up-to-date as possible, but changes may occur after the book is published.

- Finally, bookmark the ACT's website: actstudent.org.

KAPLAN

TEST PREP AND ADMISSIONS

ACT®
Practice Test 1

For Courses Starting On or After 2/1/2016

PLEASE BE SURE TO RECORD THE FOLLOWING SCAN CODE ON YOUR ANSWER GRID. WITHOUT THIS INFORMATION, WE WILL NOT BE ABLE TO SCAN YOUR TEST OR PROVIDE YOU WITH YOUR TEST SCORES.

SCAN CODE: 8007

ENGLISH TEST

45 Minutes—75 Questions

Directions: In the following five passages, certain words and phrases are underlined and numbered. In the right-hand column are alternatives for each underlined portion. Select the one that best conveys the idea, creates the most grammatically correct sentence, or is most consistent with the style and tone of the passage. If you decide that the original version is best, select NO CHANGE. You may also find questions that ask about the entire passage or a section of the passage. These questions will correspond to small, numbered boxes in the text. For these questions, decide which choice best accomplishes the purpose set out in the question stem. After you've selected the best choice, fill in the corresponding oval on your Answer Grid. For some questions, you'll need to read the context in order to answer correctly. Be sure to read until you have enough information to determine the correct answer choice.

PASSAGE I

MY COUSIN NICOLA

My father and his two younger brothers emigrated

from Italy to New York in the early 1970s. Only their

older sister Lucia, <u>which</u> was already married, remained
₁
behind in their small home

<u>town, this village</u> lies in the shadow of Mount Vesuvius.
₂
Growing up in America, my cousins and I were as close

as brothers and sisters, but we hardly <u>known</u> our family
₃
across the Atlantic. When I was a young child, my par-

ents and I went to Italy to visit Aunt Lucia and her family

for a week. I first met my cousin <u>Nicola however,</u> I
₄
remember that we were not only about the same age,

1. **A.** NO CHANGE
   B. whom
   C. who
   D. she who

2. **F.** NO CHANGE
   G. town, it can be seen where it
   H. town it
   J. town that

3. **A.** NO CHANGE
   B. knew
   C. had knew
   D. been known

4. **F.** NO CHANGE
   G. Nicola, so then
   H. Nicola because
   J. Nicola then.

GO ON TO THE NEXT PAGE

<u>and</u> we also got along well. But because
5

<u>I being</u> so young, I remember little else. I hadn't seen
6
him again up until this last summer.

Nicola decided that he wanted to join the Italian

Air Force after finishing high school. Before beginning

his service, though, he wanted to travel for a bit. <u>He had</u>
7
<u>never been to America, even though so many of his rela-</u>
7
<u>tives live here, but he had been to England already.</u> When
7
the rest of the cousins heard the news, they were

<u>ecstatic</u>. Most of them had never met Nicola or, like me,
8

<u>hadn't seen him, since we were kids;</u> they were eager to
9
get to know him.

Two weeks later, we picked Nicola up at JFK

Airport. Right away, I was surprised by his height. I am

the tallest of all the cousins in America, and Nicola was

easily a couple of inches taller than me. In addition to

5. **A.** NO CHANGE
   B. so
   C. but
   D. then

6. **F.** NO CHANGE
   G. I, who was
   H. I was
   J. I,

7. Assuming that each choice is true, which one provides the most relevant information about Nicola's travel plans?

   A. NO CHANGE
   B. He had never been to America, so he called my father and asked if he could come spend the summer with us in New York.
   C. He had never been to America, which is most easily reached from Italy by plane.
   D. Because it was expensive for his whole family to travel overseas, Nicola had never been to America before.

8. Three of these choices indicate that the cousins looked forward to meeting Nicola. Which choice does NOT do so?

   F. NO CHANGE
   G. excited
   H. apprehensive
   J. thrilled

9. **A.** NO CHANGE
   B. hadn't seen him since we were kids
   C. hadn't seen him since we were kids;
   D. hadn't seen, him since we were kids,

GO ON TO THE NEXT PAGE ▷

our height, he and I had <u>another similarity in common:</u>
　　　　　　　　　　　　　　　　　10
we were both musicians. The moment I saw the acoustic

guitar slung over his shoulder, I knew he and I would

get along just fine. None of my American cousins plays

an instrument, and I always thought that I was the only

musician <u>in the family (even though some relatives have</u>
　　　　　　　　　　　　　　　　11
<u>lovely singing voices).</u> I was happy to find out I was
　　　11

wrong.

　　Throughout that summer, Nicola and I shared the

gift of music. We would sing and play our guitars long

into the night, only stopping when my mother came

downstairs and forced us to quit. We liked many of the

same bands, and we taught each other to play our fa-

vorite songs. <u>Taught to him as a child before she passed</u>
　　　　　　　　　　　　　　　12
<u>away in Italy, I was taught by him the Italian folk songs</u>
　　　　　　　　　　　　　12
<u>of our grandmother more importantly.</u> It was through
　　　　　　　　　12
those songs that I truly connected to the beauty of our

ancestry. On the night before Nicola returned to Italy,

my father <u>would have thrown</u> a big party for all of the
　　　　　　　　13
relatives.

10. F. NO CHANGE
　　G. another similar trait in common:
　　H. another similarity that we shared:
　　J. another similarity:

11. A. NO CHANGE
　　B. in the family, which has at least 20 members that I know of.
　　C. in the family.
　　D. OMIT the underlined portion (ending the sentence with a period).

12. F. NO CHANGE
　　G. Teaching him as a child before she passed away, our grandmother in Italy more importantly taught to me many of the Italian folk songs.
　　H. Teaching him as a child, more importantly, by our grandmother in Italy, I was taught by him many Italian folk songs.
　　J. More importantly, however, he taught me many of the Italian folk songs our grandmother in Italy had taught him as a child before she passed away.

13. A. NO CHANGE
　　B. will have thrown
　　C. threw
　　D. throws

GO ON TO THE NEXT PAGE ▶

Nicola and I played the folk songs of <u>our grand-mothers</u> country for the American side of our family.
14
When we were done, my Uncle Vittorio had a tear in his eye. Since coming to America so long ago, he had never been able to return to Italy. 15

14. **F.** NO CHANGE
    G. our grandmother's
    H. our grandmothers'
    J. are grandmother's

15. Which of the following sentences, if included here, would best conclude the essay as well as maintain the tone established in this paragraph?

    A. In the music and our singing, Nicola and I brought the beautiful country back to Uncle Vittorio.
    B. Uncle Vittorio is the youngest member of his generation of the family, so he probably misses Italy the least.
    C. I had a good time singing in front of an audience.
    D. Nicola is better at playing the guitar than singing.

PASSAGE II

THE HANDSOME BEAN

On the ground floor of the apartment <u>building where, I live,</u> the Handsome Bean coffee shop is
16
almost always bustling with customers. During the warm months, the shop sets up outdoor tables on the sidewalk, and the chatter of conversation mixed with the aroma of coffee often floats in through my window to wake me in the mornings. Next to the Handsome Bean is a used bookstore, and the two shops share many of the same <u>customers who are interested in purchasing items.</u> People come to find a book and stay to enjoy a
17
cup of coffee. Across the street from the building is the neighborhood Little League field. The Handsome Bean

16. **F.** NO CHANGE
    G. building where I live,
    H. building, where I live
    J. building where I live

17. **A.** NO CHANGE
    B. people who express interest in acquiring items by shopping.
    C. customers who shop for items to purchase or consume.
    D. customers.

GO ON TO THE NEXT PAGE ⟶

often <u>sponsors</u> a local team. During the games, the
18

coffee shop offers a discount to parents whose children

are competing across the street. [19] It is a pleasure to

18. F. NO CHANGE
   G. had sponsored
   H. was a sponsor of
   J. supported

19. At this point, the writer wants to add a sentence that provides additional detail about the customers who come to the Handsome Bean. Which of the following sentences would best achieve the writer's purpose?

   A. In addition to this discount, the shop offers all patrons a punch card to receive a tenth coffee for free.

   B. The shop also sells ice cream, so it often gets very crowded with children and parents after the Little League games are over.

   C. The Handsome Bean also provides uniforms for an elementary school soccer team.

   D. The Little League field doesn't have a concession stand, so the coffee shop doesn't have much competition for the parents' business.

have as a neighbor a business that <u>children. And adults</u>
20
enjoy so much.

20. F. NO CHANGE
   G. children and adults
   H. children and that adults
   J. children. Adults

GO ON TO THE NEXT PAGE ⟩

Over the past few years, I have become friends with
21
Mary, the owner of the shop. The store's main counter is
21
a century-old antique that Mary bought and restored

to its originally conditional, and the photos that adorn
22
the back wall

depicts our town during the 1920s and 1930s. My
23
favorite detail of the shop, however, is the original tin

ceiling. One afternoon, while staring at the intricate pat-

terns etched into the tin tiles, I noticed a name camou-

flaged within the ornate design: Harvey. I pointed it out

to Mary, and she said the original owner of the building

was named Harvey Wallaby. Her guess was that he had

probably written it there more than 70 years ago. [24]

That night after the coffee shop had closed, Mary and I

etched our names into the ceiling right next to Harvey's,

hoping that our names would similarly be discovered in

the far-off future.

21. Which choice most effectively leads the reader into the topic of this paragraph?

A. NO CHANGE

B. Mary, the shop's owner, has a great appreciation for history.

C. The Handsome Bean has only been open for a couple of years, but the owner, Mary, has taken great care to make it look like it has been there for decades.

D. Before Mary, the shop's owner, opened the Handsome Bean, the space had been unoccupied for six months.

22. F. NO CHANGE

G. original conditional,

H. original condition,

J. conditionally original,

23. A. NO CHANGE

B. depict

C. has depicted

D. shows

24. The writer is considering deleting the sentence below from the passage:

> Her guess was that he had probably written it there more than 70 years ago.

If the writer were to delete this sentence, the essay would primarily lose:

F. an additional detail about the building that houses the coffee shop.

G. an explanation of the action taken by Mary and the writer.

H. an emphasis on the original owner's influence.

J. a description of the shop's interior.

GO ON TO THE NEXT PAGE ⟩

On Friday nights, the Handsome Bean has live entertainment, usually in the <u>form of, a</u> band or a poetry read-
                                    25
ing. For a small town coffee shop, the HandsomeBean

attracts a <u>good amount</u> of talented musicians and poets.
              26

<u>It being that I am amazed by the performances, they</u> tran-
                              27
spire within its cozy walls.

    [1] The clientele of the coffee shop is as varied as
the selection of flavored brews. [2] In the mornings, the
Handsome Bean is abuzz with the 9-to-5 crowd stopping
in for some java before heading off to work. [3] During
the days, the tables are home to local artists lost in their
thoughts and cappuccinos. [4] The evening finds the
Handsome Bean filled with bleary-eyed college students
loading up on caffeine so they can cram all night for their
upcoming exams or <u>finishing</u> their research papers with
                        28
looming due dates. [5] Then there's me, sitting in the
corner, maybe talking to Mary or reading the paper,
smiling at the thought that the best cup of coffee in town
is found right beneath my bedroom window. [6] In the
afternoons, a group of high school <u>students who</u> stops
                                        29

25. **A.** NO CHANGE
     B. form; of a
     C. form, of a
     D. form of a

26. **F.** NO CHANGE
     G. better amount
     H. better number
     J. good number

27. **A.** NO CHANGE
     B. Amazing the performances, it is that I
        know they
     C. I am amazed by the performances that
     D. Amazing the performances, they

28. **F.** NO CHANGE
     G. finish
     H. finishes
     J. finalizing

29. **A.** NO CHANGE
     B. students that
     C. students, and they
     D. students

GO ON TO THE NEXT PAGE ▷

by to have an ice cream cone or an egg cream. 30

30. For the sake of logic and coherence, Sentence 6 should be placed:

    F. where it is now.

    G. before Sentence 2.

    H. before Sentence 4.

    J. before Sentence 5.

PASSAGE III

MR. MIDSHIPMAN MARRYAT

The paragraphs below may or may not be in the most logical order. A number in brackets appears above each paragraph. At the end of the passage, Question 45 will ask you to determine the most logical place for Paragraph 1.

[1]

Born to an upper-class English family in 1792, Marryat had a thirst for <u>naval adventure</u> and exploration very early in his childhood. As a young boy at private school, he tried to run away to sea a number of times.

<u>Finally, his exasperated parents</u> at last granted him his wish in 1806; <u>they were</u> enlisted in the British Navy as a midshipman. Marryat had the luck to be assigned to sail upon the frigate *HMS Imperieuse* under the command of Lord Cochrane. Cochrane, <u>that's</u> naval exploits are

31. **A.** NO CHANGE

    B. naval, adventure,

    C. naval, adventure

    D. naval adventure;

32. **F.** NO CHANGE

    G. His exasperated parents

    H. In the end, his exasperated parents

    J. Ultimately, the result was that his exasperated parents

33. **A.** NO CHANGE

    B. they

    C. he

    D. and he

34. **F.** NO CHANGE

    G. who's

    H. whose

    J. who the

GO ON TO THE NEXT PAGE

legendary, would later serve as the inspiration for

<u>a number of</u> Marryat's fictional characters. 36
35

35. The writer is considering deleting the phrase "a number of." If the writer decided to delete the phrase, would the meaning of the sentence change?

   A. Yes, because without this phrase, the reader would think that all of Marryat's fictional characters were based on Cochrane.

   B. Yes, because without this phrase, the reader would not understand that Marryat used Cochrane as a model for more than one fictional character.

   C. No, because this phrase is an example of wordiness that should be eliminated from the sentence.

   D. No; although the phrase adds a detail about Marryat's character, this detail is not essential to the meaning of the sentence.

36. At this point, the writer is considering adding the sentence below:

   > The well-known writer Patrick O'Brian also modeled his Captain Jack Aubrey after Cochrane.

   Should the writer make this addition?

   F. Yes, because if readers know that other writers were inspired by Cochrane, they will better understand that Cochrane was an impressive person.

   G. Yes, because the added detail provides information about a writer who used a style similar to Marryat's.

   H. No, because the essay doesn't reveal the relationship between O'Brian and Marryat.

   J. No, because the detail distracts from the main focus of the essay.

GO ON TO THE NEXT PAGE ⟩

[2]

Unlike most of the other <u>prominently famous</u>
                                      37
authors who have spun tales of brave British naval officers

fighting for king and country on the high seas, Frederick

Marryat actually served as a captain in the British Royal

Navy. While others could only use their imagination and

accounts to describe what life must have been like for a

young man rising through the ranks from lowly mid-

shipman to all-powerful captain <u>from historical records</u>,
                                              38
Marryat needed only to dip into the vast library of adven-

ture stored in his memory.

[3]

Marryat's three years aboard the *Imperieuse* were

filled with experiences that would later serve him well in

his writing career. The *Imperieuse* saw much action off the

coast of Spain, where Marryat took part in capturing a

Spanish castle and numerous vessels in the Mediterrane-

an. Marryat willingly accepted any chance to distinguish

himself in the eyes of his revered <u>captain and literary</u>
                                              39
<u>inspiration, Cochrane.</u> In fact, Marryat once jumped into
          39
the turbulent sea to save the life of another midshipman

who <u>had fallen</u> overboard. Not only did Marryat have the
          40
privilege of knowing first-hand a character as illustrious

as Cochrane, but his own bold experiences as a midship-

man would also be the basis for his most famous novel,

Mr. Midshipman Easy.

37. **A.** NO CHANGE
　　B. prominent famous
　　C. prominent
　　D. prominent and famous

38. The best placement for the underlined
　　portion is:
　　F. where it is now.
　　G. after the word "accounts."
　　H. after the word "others."
　　J. after the word "adventure."

39. **A.** NO CHANGE
　　B. captain, and literary inspiration
　　　　Cochrane.
　　C. captain and literary inspiration
　　　　Cochrane.
　　D. captain and, literary inspiration,
　　　　Cochrane.

40. **F.** NO CHANGE
　　G. would have fallen
　　H. had been falling
　　J. falls

GO ON TO THE NEXT PAGE ⇨

[4]

As Marryat quickly climbed through the ranks of the Royal Navy, <u>many feats were accomplished by him.</u> These

41
included single-handedly saving his ship during a horrific storm and fighting in a number of sea battles against

the United States Navy during the War of 1812. ☐42

41. **A.** NO CHANGE

    B. his accomplishment of many feats occurred.

    C. his many feats were accomplished.

    D. he accomplished many feats.

42. Which of the following true statements would most effectively conclude this paragraph?

    F. The British eventually lost the War of 1812.

    G. He also earned a medal from the Royal Humane Society for inventing a special lifeboat.

    H. The British Navy was considered the world's most powerful navy until the time of World War II.

    J. Marryat considered it a privilege to serve his country.

[5]

<u>Marryat earned his greatest acclaim for his novels</u>

43
<u>and short stories during this time,</u> which were published

43
in England while he was at sea. He retired from the navy shortly after being awarded the rank of post captain

in 1825 to concentrate <u>for writing</u> full-time. Marryat's

44
thrilling stories of sea adventure still live today because, as the old cliché goes, the best stories are the ones that are true.

43. **A.** NO CHANGE

    B. During this time, Marryat earned his greatest acclaim for his novels and short stories,

    C. His greatest acclaim was earned by him, for his novels and short stories during this time,

    D. During this time for his novels and short stories, earned him his greatest acclaim,

44. **F.** NO CHANGE

    G. at writing

    H. on writing

    J. in writing of

GO ON TO THE NEXT PAGE ➡

Question 45 asks about the preceding passage as a whole.

45. The most logical placement of Paragraph 1 is:
   A. where it is now.
   B. after Paragraph 2.
   C. after Paragraph 3.
   D. after Paragraph 4.

PASSAGE IV

THE TOUGHEST TASK IN SPORTS

[1]

I've often heard others make the comment that the hardest single act in all of sports is to hit a major league fastball. I'm not going to deny that hitting a ball traveling at upwards of 95 miles per hour is a daunting task, but I can think of something even tougher than taking a major league at-bat: stopping a crank shot in men's lacrosse. Football quarterbacks facing oncoming defensive linemen are also in a difficult position.
                                    46

[2]

[1] Lacrosse that is often referred to as "the fastest
                    47
sport on two feet," and with good reason. [2] The game is

46. F. NO CHANGE
   G. Also in a challenging position are football quarterbacks facing oncoming defensive linemen.
   H. (Football quarterbacks also face a daunting task when they are rushed by defensive linemen.)
   J. OMIT the underlined portion.

47. A. NO CHANGE
   B. which has been
   C. is
   D. OMIT the underlined portion.

GO ON TO THE NEXT PAGE

often <u>brutally</u>, and the best players normally possess
48

a bit of <u>toughness</u>, a bit of finesse. [3] As in hockey or
49
soccer, the only thing that stands between the ball and

the goal is the goalkeeper. [4] Using sticks known as

"crosses" to pass a hard rubber ball back and forth

through the air, players on two teams sprint around a

<u>field; they then attempted</u> to set up a shot on the
50
opposing team's goal. [5] Using just his body and his

crosse, the keeper must protect the six-foot by six-foot

goal from being penetrated by a ball that is less than

eight inches in circumference. 51

[3]

    This brings me to the heart of my argument. A

regulation lacrosse ball is almost an inch narrower than

a regulation baseball, with an unstitched, smooth rubber

surface. The fastest baseball pitch on record was clocked

at 100.9 mph, though only a handful of major league

pitchers can approach even the upper nineties in speed.

In men's lacrosse, because the crosse acts as a lever, the

fastest "crank shots" on <u>goal, can</u> reach 110 mph. Even at
52
the high school level, crank shots of more than 90 mph

<u>made by high school players</u> are not uncommon. Unlike
53
a baseball pitcher throwing his fastball from a fixed posi-

tion on the mound, a lacrosse player may shoot from

48. **F.** NO CHANGE
    G. brutal
    H. brute
    J. brutality

49. **A.** NO CHANGE
    B. toughness;
    C. toughness
    D. toughness, and,

50. **F.** NO CHANGE
    G. they must attempt
    H. one then attempts
    J. one must attempt

51. The most logical placement of Sentence 3 in Paragraph 2 is:
    A. where it is now.
    B. after Sentence 1.
    C. after Sentence 4.
    D. OMITTED, because the paragraph does not discuss hockey or soccer.

52. **F.** NO CHANGE
    G. goal, can,
    H. goal can
    J. goal can,

53. **A.** NO CHANGE
    B. made by these high school players
    C. shot by high school players
    D. OMIT the underlined portion.

GO ON TO THE NEXT PAGE ⟹

anywhere on the <u>field, which is typically grass.</u> This means
                        54
that a lacrosse goalie may be asked to stop a crank shot

from <u>a distance of only six feet</u> away! To make the goalie's
        55
job even more difficult, a lacrosse player may shoot from

over his shoulder, from his side, or drop his stick down

and wind up from the ground. <u>On top of that,</u> the best
                                        56
players often employ a variety of fakes, and most have

the ability to shoot left-handed or right-handed, de-

pending upon their angle to the goal.

[4]

<u>Like hitting a major league fastball, stopping a crank</u>
                                    57
<u>shot in lacrosse is tough.</u> Both of these endeavors,
        57

however, <u>require</u> the same set of skills. One must possess
            58

54. **F.** NO CHANGE

   G. field, which is covered with natural turf.

   H. field that is covered with grass.

   J. field.

55. **A.** NO CHANGE

   B. merely a length of six feet

   C. just a mere six feet

   D. only six feet

56. Of the following possible replacements for the underlined portion, which would be LEAST acceptable?

   F. In addition,

   G. On the other hand,

   H. Furthermore,

   J. What's more,

57. Which choice is the most effective and logical transition from the topic of Paragraph 3 to the topic of Paragraph 4?

   A. NO CHANGE

   B. The combination of these unknown variables makes stopping a crank shot in lacrosse tougher than hitting a major league fastball.

   C. Though baseball is less challenging than lacrosse, both sports require tremendous skill and dedication from athletes.

   D. There is little question that stopping a crank shot in lacrosse is among the toughest tasks an athlete can face.

58. **F.** NO CHANGE

   G. requires

   H. required

   J. would have required

superlative athleticism, great hand-eye coordination, and

catlike quickness. Above all, <u>you must be</u> fearless.
59

59. **A.** NO CHANGE
    B. one must be
    C. they must be
    D. he must have been

Question 60 asks about the preceding passage as a whole.

60. Suppose that the writer had wanted to write an essay comparing the strategies used by baseball pitchers and lacrosse goalies. Would this essay fulfill the writer's goal?

    F. Yes, because the writer compares both sports throughout the essay.

    G. Yes, because the writer details the challenges that lacrosse goalies face.

    H. No, because the writer does not provide any specific details about baseball pitchers.

    J. No, because the writer focuses on comparing the difficulty of hitting a ball pitched by a major league pitcher to the difficulty of blocking a crank shot in men's lacrosse.

GO ON TO THE NEXT PAGE

PASSAGE V

THOMAS EDISON, TINFOIL CYLINDERS, AND MP3 PLAYERS

[1]

Thomas Edison first recorded sounds on tinfoil cylinders in the 1870s, and since then, <u>formats for recording music have come and gone</u> at a breakneck
                    61
pace. Innovation in recording music has been constant, and the popularity and lifespan of the newest format have always been transitory at best. Those first tinfoil cylinders, which were hailed as a miracle in their day, quickly progressed to wax cylinders, then hard plastic cylinders and, within a decade, were completely replaced by the next "miracle," the gramophone disc record.

[2]

The vinyl phonograph record, which sounded, soon <u>better</u> supplanted the gramophone in the 1940s. This
 62
new-fangled format dominated the music landscape for the next 30 years, but like its predecessors, it would

eventually fall into obsolescence. The vinyl <u>record being</u>
                                              63
no longer mass marketed to the public. For that matter, neither is its successor, the 8-track cartridge of the 1970s.

61. A. NO CHANGE
  B. formats for recording music have come and gone,
  C. formats for recording music, have come and gone
  D. formats, for recording music have come and gone

62. The most logical placement for the underlined word would be:
  F. where it is now.
  G. before the word "vinyl."
  H. after the word "sounded."
  J. before the word "gramophone."

63. A. NO CHANGE
  B. record, having been
  C. record is
  D. record,

GO ON TO THE NEXT PAGE ⟶

[3]

It may seem curious to a 40-year-old man today that the average high-school student is well acquainted with the older vinyl record format, <u>so</u> has never even
64
heard of an 8-track cartridge. DJs and those who mix

popular music still <u>uses and appreciates</u> the vinyl
65

<u>record format cherished by them.</u>
66

They have kept records from <u>potentially vanishing into</u>
67
<u>oblivion,</u> along with the 8-track and the more recent
67
recording format, the cassette tape.

[4]

That same 40-year-old man witnessed the rise and fall of the cassette tape, so he may not be surprised that many in today's recording industry view the compact disc as similarly spiraling towards its own doom. For the first <u>time, though</u> it is not the sound quality of the
68
recording that is ushering in the change. Now the

driving force is something <u>different</u> the quality of the
69
player itself.

64. **F.** NO CHANGE
   G. yet
   H. thus
   J. or

65. **A.** NO CHANGE
   B. use and appreciates
   C. uses and appreciate
   D. use and appreciate

66. **F.** NO CHANGE
   G. record format that they cherish.
   H. format for records they play on turn-tables.
   J. record format.

67. **A.** NO CHANGE
   B. disappearing into oblivion
   C. a disappearance into being oblivious
   D. disappearance toward the oblivion

68. **F.** NO CHANGE
   G. time; though
   H. time, though,
   J. time though,

69. **A.** NO CHANGE
   B. different;
   C. different:
   D. different,

GO ON TO THE NEXT PAGE ▷

[5]

Lack of portability was one of the drawbacks of the
                    70
vinyl record and even of the compact disc. In contrast,
                    70
recently introduced small personal music players, such as

the iPod, can have up to an impressive 60 gigabytes worth

of storage space. For those who are music lovers, this has

completely changed the experience of listening

to their favorite songs. Contrasting by the few hours'
                              71
worth of songs stored on a single CD, a 60-gigabyte MP3

player can store a month's worth of uninterrupted music

on a machine about the size of an old cassette tape.

It's no wonder that MP3 players are among the most
                            72
popular technology purchases for people of all ages.
                            72

[6]

    Has the apex in the climb towards better and better

ways to play recorded music been reached? For those

who believe it has, history teaches that they are wrong;

such a proclamation will surely prove to be shortsighted

when the next "miracle" in music arrives.

70. Which sentence makes the most effective beginning for Paragraph 5?

    F. NO CHANGE

    G. A standard audio compact disc can store only about 700 megabytes worth of digital data, which equates to only a few hours worth of songs.

    H. Most music listeners want a format with a great sound that also provides ample storage space for all of their favorite songs.

    J. Recording devices have become smaller and smaller over the years, from the unwieldy gramophone to the pocket-sized cassette player.

71. A. NO CHANGE

    B. Compared to

    C. While

    D. In contrast of

72. In this paragraph, the writer wants to help readers understand the storage capacity and size of the new personal music players. Which true statement would best help the writer accomplish this goal?

    F. NO CHANGE

    G. It is not unreasonable to expect that technological improvements will soon allow personal music players to have an even more compact size and store twice as many songs.

    H. Experts in the music industry predict that personal music players will quickly replace compact disc players, just as compact disc players so recently replaced vinyl record players.

    J. Entire music libraries once confined to the living room wall can now fit into a music lover's pocket, and be taken and listened to anywhere.

GO ON TO THE NEXT PAGE

Questions 73–75 ask about the preceding passage as a whole.

---

73. Paragraphs 5 and 6 of this essay are written in the third person, using the pronouns *those*, *their*, and *they*. If the writer revised these paragraph using the second-person pronouns *you* and *your*, the essay would primarily:

    A. gain a sense of urgency by suggesting actions to be taken by the reader.

    B. gain a more personal tone by speaking directly to the reader.

    C. lose the formal and removed tone that matches the content and purpose of the essay.

    D. lose a sense of the author's knowledge on the subject by personalizing the essay.

74. After reading the essay, the writer realized that some information had been left out. The writer then composed the sentence below to convey that information:

> Though the gramophone record's disc shape proved to have longevity, the gramophone record itself did not.

The most effective and logical placement of this sentence would be before the first sentence of Paragraph:

    F. 2.

    G. 3.

    H. 4.

    J. 5.

75. Suppose the writer had set out to write an essay explaining the process of recording sounds in a variety of formats. Does this essay meet that purpose?

    A. Yes, because the essay describes the different recording formats used since the 1870s.

    B. Yes, because the writer provides specifics about how each new recording format has improved upon earlier formats.

    C. No, because the essay discusses a limited number of recording formats.

    D. No, because the essay does not discuss the mechanics of how sounds are recorded and played back in different formats.

IF YOU FINISH BEFORE TIME IS CALLED, YOU MAY CHECK YOUR WORK ON THIS SECTION ONLY. DO NOT TURN TO ANY OTHER SECTION IN THE TEST. **STOP**

MATHEMATICS TEST

60 Minutes—60 Questions

Directions: Solve each of the following problems, select the correct answer, and then fill in the corresponding space on your answer sheet.

Don't linger over problems that are too time-consuming. Do as many as you can, then come back to the others in the time you have remaining.

The use of a calculator is permitted on this test. Though you are allowed to use your calculator to solve any questions you choose, some of the questions may be most easily answered without the use of a calculator.

Note: Unless otherwise noted, all of the following should be assumed.

1. Illustrative figures are *not* necessarily drawn to scale.

2. All geometric figures lie in a plane.

3. The term *line* indicates a straight line.

4. The term *average* indicates arithmetic mean.

1. Khristina walked $1\frac{2}{3}$ miles on Sunday and $2\frac{3}{4}$ on Monday. What was the total distance, in miles, that she walked over those two days?

   A. $3\frac{1}{2}$

   B. $3\frac{5}{7}$

   C. $3\frac{11}{12}$

   D. $4\frac{1}{4}$

   E. $4\frac{5}{12}$

2. $2y^3 \cdot 3xy^2 \cdot 6xy^2$ is equivalent to which of the following?

   F. $11x^2y^7$

   G. $11x^2y^{12}$

   H. $36x^2y^7$

   J. $36xy^{12}$

   K. $36x^2y^{12}$

3. Ms. Ruppin is a machinist who works 245 days a year and earns a salary of $51,940. She recently took an unpaid day off from work to attend a bridge tournament. The company pays temporary replacements $140 a day. How much less did the company have to pay in salary by paying the replacement instead of Ms. Ruppin that day?

   A. $ 72

   B. $113

   C. $140

   D. $196

   E. $212

4. On his first four 100-point tests this quarter, a student has earned the following scores: 52, 70, 76, 79. What score must the student earn on the fifth, final 100-point test in order to earn an average test grade of 75 for all five tests?

   F. 69

   G. 70

   H. 71

   J. 98

   K. The student cannot earn an average of 75.

GO ON TO THE NEXT PAGE →

5. Relative humidity is found by dividing the grams of water vapor per cubic meter of air by the maximum possible grams of water vapor per cubic meter of air, then converting to a percentage. If on a given day the air has 6.7 grams of water vapor per cubic meter, and the maximum possible at that temperature is 19.2 grams of water vapor per cubic meter, what is the relative humidity, to the nearest percent?

   A. 19%

   B. 30%

   C. 35%

   D. 67%

   E. 87%

6. A fence completely surrounds a pool that is 30 feet by 10 feet. What is the approximate length, in feet, of the fence?

   F. 20 feet

   G. 40 feet

   H. 60 feet

   J. 80 feet

   K. 160 feet

7. The expression $w[x - (y + z)]$ is equivalent to:

   A. $wx - wy - wz$.

   B. $wx - wy + wz$.

   C. $wx - wy - z$.

   D. $wx - y + z$.

   E. $wx - y - z$.

8. If $2x - 5 = 7x + 3$, then $x = ?$

   F. $-\dfrac{8}{5}$

   G. $-\dfrac{5}{8}$

   H. $-\dfrac{2}{5}$

   J. $\dfrac{2}{5}$

   K. $\dfrac{8}{9}$

9. What two numbers should be placed in the blanks below so that each pair of consecutive numbers has the same difference?

   13, _____, _____, 49

   A. 22, 31

   B. 23, 39

   C. 24, 38

   D. 25, 37

   E. 26, 39

10. If x is a real number such that $x^3 = 729$, then $\sqrt{x} + x^2 = ?$

    F. 9

    G. 21

    H. 53

    J. 84

    K. 90

11. The formula for the volume of a sphere with radius r is $V = \dfrac{4}{3}\pi r^3$. If the radius of a spherical ball is $1\dfrac{1}{3}$ inches, what is its volume to the nearest cubic inch?

    A. 6

    B. 7

    C. 10

    D. 17

    E. 66

12. If a ball is randomly chosen from a bag with exactly 10 purple balls, 10 yellow balls, and 8 green balls, what is the probability that the ball chosen will NOT be green?

    F. $\dfrac{2}{7}$

    G. $\dfrac{2}{5}$

    H. $\dfrac{1}{2}$

    J. $\dfrac{9}{14}$

    K. $\dfrac{5}{7}$

GO ON TO THE NEXT PAGE

13. The number of employees at a company in each division can be shown by the following matrix.

$$\begin{array}{cccc} \text{Marketing} & \text{Public Relations} & \text{Development} & \text{Recruitment} \\ [\;30 & 20 & 60 & 10\;] \end{array}$$

The head of recruitment estimates the proportion of current employees who will leave within the next year with the following matrix.

$$\begin{array}{c} \text{Marketing} \\ \text{Public Relations} \\ \text{Development} \\ \text{Recruitment} \end{array} \begin{bmatrix} 0.3 \\ 0.5 \\ 0.2 \\ 0.4 \end{bmatrix}$$

Given these matrices, what is the head of recruitment's estimate of the number of current employees in these departments who will leave within the next year?

A. 27

B. 35

C. 42

D. 49

E. 53

Use the following information to answer questions 14–15.

The following chart shows the current enrollment in all the English classes offered at King High School.

Course title	Section	Period	Number of students
English I	1	5	29
	2	1	27
	3	2	22
English II	1	3	26
	2	6	25
	3	4	24
British Literature	1	6	23
African-American Literature	1	2	26
	2	5	25

14. What is the average number of students per section in English I?

F. 22

G. 25

H. 26

J. 27

K. 29

15. The school has 2 computer labs with 30 computers each. There are 3 computers in one lab that are broken, and 5 in the other lab that are broken, all of which are not available to be used by students. For which of the following class periods, if any, are there NOT enough computers available for each English student to use a computer without having to share?

A. Period 2 only

B. Period 5 only

C. Period 6 only

D. Periods 5 and 6 only

E. None

GO ON TO THE NEXT PAGE ▷

16. What expression must be in the center cell of the table below so that the sums of each row, each column, and each diagonal are equivalent?

$-3x$	$4x$	$-7x$
$-6x$	?	$2x$
$3x$	$-8x$	$-x$

   F. $-6x$

   G. $-4x$

   H. $-2x$

   J. $2x$

   K. $4x$

17. Point Z is to be graphed in a quadrant, not on an axis, in the standard (x,y) coordinate plane, as shown below.

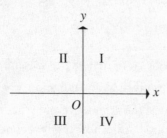

If the x-coordinate and the y-coordinate of point Z have the same sign, then point Z must be located in which of the following?

   A. Quadrant I only

   B. Quadrant III only

   C. Quadrant I or II only

   D. Quadrant I or III only

   E. Quadrant III or IV only

18. Leila has 5 necklaces, 8 pairs of earrings, and 3 hair clips. How many distinct sets of accessories, each consisting of a necklace, a pair of earrings, and a hair clip, can Leila choose?

   F. 16

   G. 55

   H. 64

   J. 120

   K. 360

19. At a factory, 90,000 tons of grain are required to make 150,000 tons of bread. How many tons of grain are required to produce 6,000 tons of bread?

   A. 3,600

   B. 10,000

   C. 25,000

   D. 36,000

   E. 60,000

20. If a rectangle measures 42 meters by 56 meters, what is the length, in meters, of the diagonal of the rectangle?

   F. 48

   G. 49

   H. 70

   J. 98

   K. 196

21. For all positive integers a, b, and c, which of the following is false?

   A. $\dfrac{a \cdot b}{c \cdot b} = \dfrac{a}{c}$

   B. $\dfrac{a \cdot a}{b \cdot b} = \dfrac{a^2}{b^2}$

   C. $\dfrac{a \cdot b}{b \cdot a} = 1$

   D. $\dfrac{a + b}{b} = \dfrac{a}{b} + 1$

   E. $\dfrac{a + b}{c + b} = \dfrac{a}{c} + 1$

GO ON TO THE NEXT PAGE

22. What is the slope-intercept form of
    $-3x - y + 7 = 0$?

    F. $y = 3x - 7$

    G. $y = 3x + 7$

    H. $y = -7x + 3$

    J. $y = -3x - 7$

    K. $y = -3x + 7$

23. Which of the following is a solution to the
    equation $x^2 - 16x = 0$?

    A. 32

    B. 16

    C. 8

    D. 4

    E. -4

24. For right triangle $\triangle ABC$ below, what is tan C ?

    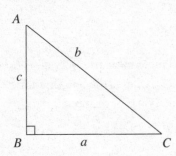

    F. $\dfrac{c}{a}$

    G. $\dfrac{c}{b}$

    H. $\dfrac{a}{c}$

    J. $\dfrac{a}{b}$

    K. $\dfrac{b}{a}$

25. A chord 30 centimeters long is 8 centimeters
    from the center of a circle, as shown below.
    What is the radius of the circle, to the nearest
    tenth of a centimeter?

    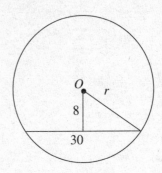

    A. 38.0

    B. 34.0

    C. 31.2

    D. 22.8

    E. 17.0

26. The velocity, in meters per second, of an
    object is given by the equation $V = \dfrac{5}{3}t + 0.05$,
    where t is the amount of time that has passed,
    in seconds. After how many seconds will the
    object be traveling at 0.575 meters per second?

    F. 0.28

    G. 0.315

    H. 0.365

    J. 0.525

    K. 0.57

27. The city has decided to store an estimated 15,000 cubic yards of sand for later distribution to the city's beaches. If this sand were spread evenly over the entire soccer field shown below, about how many yards deep would the sand be?

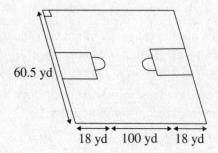

60.5 yd

18 yd   100 yd   18 yd

A. Less than 1

B. Between 1 and 2

C. Between 2 and 3

D. Between 3 and 4

E. More than 4

28. The hypotenuse of the right triangle △ABC shown below is 18 feet long. The cosine of ∠A is $\frac{4}{5}$. About how many feet long is $\overline{AC}$?

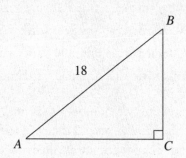

18

A   *C*

B

F. 15.2

G. 14.4

H. 13.9

J. 12.6

K. 10.8

29. The graph below shows the number of beds in each of several hotels, rounded to the nearest 50 beds. According to the graph, what fraction of the beds in these four hotels is at the Bedtime Hotel?

	Key = 100 beds

Hotel	Number of Beds
Comf-E	🛏🛏
Just Like Home	🛏🛏
Budget	🛏🛏🛏🛏
Bedtime	🛏🛏🛏

A. $\frac{1}{4}$

B. $\frac{1}{3}$

C. $\frac{2}{5}$

D. $\frac{5}{11}$

E. $\frac{1}{2}$

30. Points B and C lie on $\overline{AD}$ as shown below. The length of $\overline{AD}$ is 38 units, $\overline{AC}$ is 26 units long, and $\overline{BD}$ is 20 units long. If it can be determined, how many units long is $\overline{BC}$?

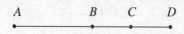

A   *B*   *C*   *D*

F. 6

G. 8

H. 12

J. 18

K. Cannot be determined from the given information

GO ON TO THE NEXT PAGE

31. What is the *x*-coordinate of the point in the standard (*x,y*) coordinate plane at which the two lines $y = 4x + 10$ and $y = 5x + 7$ intersect?

A. 2

B. 3

C. 7

D. 10

E. 22

32. For all pairs of real numbers *V* and *W* where $V = 5W + 4$, $W = ?$

F. $\dfrac{V}{5} - 4$

G. $\dfrac{V}{5} + 4$

H. $\dfrac{V - 4}{5}$

J. $\dfrac{V + 4}{5}$

K. $5V - 4$

33. Parallelogram *FGHJ*, with dimensions in centimeters, is shown in the figure below. What is the area of the parallelogram, in square centimeters?

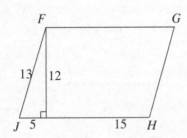

A. 45

B. 130

C. 240

D. 260

E. 480

34. If $s = 4 + t$, then $(t - s)^3 = ?$

F. −64

G. −12

H. −1

J. 12

K. 64

35. A zoo has the shape and dimensions in yards given below. The viewing point for the giraffes is halfway between points *B* and *F*. Which of the following is the location of the viewing point from the entrance at point *A* ?

(Note: The zoo's borders run east/west or north/south.)

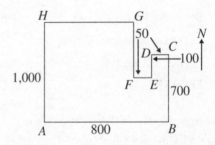

A. 400 yards east and 350 yards north

B. 400 yards east and 500 yards north

C. 600 yards east and 350 yards north

D. 750 yards east and 300 yards north

E. 750 yards east and 350 yards north

36. The larger of two numbers is six less than triple the smaller one. The sum of four times the larger and twice the smaller is 77. If *x* represents the smaller number, which of the following equations determines the correct value for *x* ?

F. $2(3x - 6) + 4x = 77$

G. $2(3x + 6) + 4x = 77$

H. $(12x - 6) + 2x = 77$

J. $4(3x - 6) + 2x = 77$

K. $4(3x + 6) + 2x = 77$

GO ON TO THE NEXT PAGE

37. A painter leans a 35 foot ladder against a house. The side of the house is perpendicular to the level ground, and the base of the ladder is 15 feet away from the base of the house. To the nearest foot, how far up the house will the ladder reach?

   A. 15

   B. 20

   C. 32

   D. 38

   E. 50

38. A circle of radius 6 inches is inscribed in a square, as shown below. What is the area of the square, in square inches?

   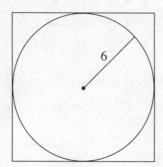

   F.   36

   G.   42

   H.   72

   J.   36π

   K.   144

39. The sides of a triangle are in the ratio of exactly 15:17:20. A second triangle, similar to the first, has a longest side of length 12. To the nearest tenth of a unit, what is the length of the shortest side of the second triangle?

   A. 15.9

   B. 10.2

   C. 9.0

   D. 7.0

   E. Cannot be determined from the given information

40. In the figure below, WXZY is a trapezoid, point X lies on $\overline{WT}$, and the angles are as marked. What is the measure of ∠ZXT ?

   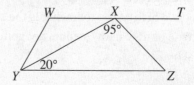

   F.   20°

   G.   30°

   H.   40°

   J.   55°

   K.   65°

41. In the figure below, all angles are right angles, and all lengths are in feet. What is the perimeter, in feet, of the figure?

   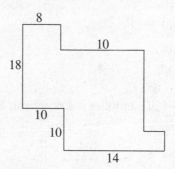

   A.   70

   B.   76

   C.   84

   D.   92

   E.   104

GO ON TO THE NEXT PAGE

42. Of 896 seniors at a certain college, approximately $\frac{1}{3}$ are continuing their studies after graduation, and approximately $\frac{2}{5}$ of those continuing their studies are going to law school. Which of the following is the best estimate of how many seniors are going to law school?

F. 120

G. 180

H. 240

J. 300

K. 360

43. If $a = -2$, $b = 4$, and $c = 7$, what is the value of the expression below?

$$(a + b)(c - a)$$

A. −30

B. −10

C. 10

D. 18

E. 30

44. If 135% of a number is 405, what is 80% of the number?

F. 205

G. 240

H. 270

J. 300

K. 324

45. What is the distance in the standard (x,y) coordinate plane between the points (2,0) and (0,7) ?

A.   5

B.   9

C.   25

D.   81

E. $\sqrt{53}$

46. The ratio of the radii of two circles is 9:16. What is the ratio of their circumferences?

F.   3:4

G.   9:16

H.   81:256

J. $9:18\pi$

K. $16:32\pi$

47. A circle in the standard (x,y) coordinate plane is tangent to the x-axis at 4 and tangent to the y-axis at 4. Which of the following is an equation of the circle?

A. $x^2 + y^2 = 4$

B. $x^2 + y^2 = 16$

C. $(x - 4)^2 + (y - 4)^2 = 4$

D. $(x - 4)^2 + (y - 4)^2 = 16$

E. $(x + 4)^2 + (y + 4)^2 = 16$

48. In complex numbers, where $i^2 = -1, \dfrac{(i+1)(i+1)}{(i-1)(i-1)} = ?$

F. $\dfrac{i+1}{i-1}$

G. $\dfrac{i}{2}$

H. $\dfrac{2}{i}$

J. $2i$

K.   −1

49. One Saturday, an art-museum ticket office sold 120 adult tickets for $10 each and x student tickets for $5 each. Which expression represents the total ticket sales for Saturday, in dollars?

A. $5(120 + x)$

B. $10(120) + 5x$

C. $10x + 5(120)$

D. $10(120 + x)$

E. $10(120 + 5x)$

GO ON TO THE NEXT PAGE ▷

50. In a dance school with 35 students, a poll shows that 12 are studying tap dance and 19 are studying ballet. What is the minimum number of students in the school who are studying both tap dance and ballet?

F.   0
G.   7
H.   9
J.   12
K.   31

51. Which of the following is the solution set for all real numbers x such that $x - 2 < x - 5$?

A.   The empty set
B.   The set containing all real numbers
C.   The set containing all negative real numbers
D.   The set containing all nonnegative real numbers
E.   The set containing only zero

52. Hexagons have 9 diagonals, as illustrated below.

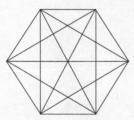

How many diagonals does the octagon below have?

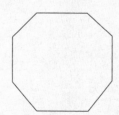

F.   8
G.   11
H.   16
J.   20
K.   40

53. Diane wants to draw a circle graph showing the favorite teachers at her school. When she polled her classmates, 25% said Mr. Green, 15% said Ms. Brown, 35% said Mrs. White, 5% said Mr. Black, and the remaining classmates said teachers other than Mr. Green, Ms. Brown, Mrs. White, or Mr. Black. The teachers other than Mr. Green, Ms. Brown, Mrs. White, or Mr. Black will be grouped together in an Other sector. What will be the degree measure of the Other sector?

A.   144°
B.   72°
C.   36°
D.   20°
E.   15°

54. If $\cos \theta = -\dfrac{12}{13}$ and $\dfrac{\pi}{2} < \theta < \pi$, then $\tan \theta = ?$

F. $-\dfrac{12}{5}$

G. $-\dfrac{12}{13}$

H. $-\dfrac{5}{12}$

J. $\dfrac{5}{13}$

K. $\dfrac{5}{12}$

GO ON TO THE NEXT PAGE

55. Which of the following systems of inequalities is represented by the shaded region of the graph below?

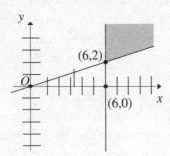

A. $y \geq \frac{1}{3} x$ and $x \geq 6$

B. $y \geq \frac{1}{3} x$ or $x \geq 6$

C. $y \leq \frac{1}{3} x$ and $x \geq 6$

D. $y \leq \frac{1}{3} x$ or $x \geq 6$

E. $y \leq \frac{1}{3} x$ and $x \leq 6$

56. If $f(x) = 1 - x^2$, then $f(x + h) = ?$

F. $1 - x^2 + h$

G. $1 - x^2 - h$

H. $-x^2 - 2xh - h^2$

J. $1 - x^2 - 2xh - h^2$

K. $1 - x^2 + 2xh + h^2$

57. Which of the following is the graph, in the standard (x,y) coordinate plane, of $y = \dfrac{3x^2 + 2x}{x}$?

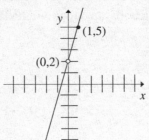

A.

B.

C.

D.

E.

GO ON TO THE NEXT PAGE

58. A triangle, $\triangle ABC$, is reflected across the y-axis to create the image $\triangle A'B'C'$ in the standard (x,y) coordinate plane; for example, A reflects to A'. The coordinates of point A are (v,w). What are the coordinates of point A' ?

F. $(v,-w)$

G. $(-v,w)$

H. $(-v,-w)$

J. (w,v)

K. Cannot be determined from the given information

59. If $a = 6c + 7$ and $b = 3 - 2c$, which of the following expresses a in terms of b ?

A. $a = \dfrac{16 - b}{3}$

B. $a = \dfrac{17 - b}{2}$

C. $a = 16 - 3b$

D. $a = 25 - 12b$

E. $a = 6b + 7$

60. In a contest, the weight of a first-place watermelon is 15 pounds less than 3 times the weight of the second-place watermelon. If w is the weight of the second-place watermelon, which of the following expresses the weight, in pounds, of the first-place watermeon?

F. $w - 5$

G. $w + 15$

H. $w - 15$

J. $3w + 15$

K. $3w - 15$

IF YOU FINISH BEFORE TIME IS CALLED, YOU MAY CHECK YOUR WORK ON THIS SECTION ONLY. DO NOT TURN TO ANY OTHER SECTION IN THE TEST.   **STOP**

READING TEST

35 Minutes—40 Questions

Directions: There are four passages in this test. Each passage is followed by several questions. After reading a passage, choose the best answer to each question and fill in the corresponding oval on your Answer Grid. You may refer to the passages as often as necessary.

PASSAGE I

PROSE FICTION

This passage is an adapted excerpt from Tess of the d'Urbervilles, *by Thomas Hardy. In this excerpt, Tess is working as a milkmaid at a dairy, where she has met and finds herself attracted to a gentleman by the name of Angel Clare.*

They came downstairs yawning next morning; but skimming and milking were proceeded with as usual, and they went indoors to breakfast. Dairy-
Line man Crick was discovered stamping about the
(5) house. He had received a letter, in which a customer had complained that the butter had a twang.

"And begad, so 't have!" said the dairyman, who held in his left hand a wooden slice on which a lump of butter was stuck. "Yes—taste for yourself!"
(10) Several of them gathered round him; and Mr. Clare tasted, Tess tasted, also the other indoor milkmaids, one or two of the milking-men, and last of all Mrs. Crick, who came out from the waiting breakfast-table. There certainly was a twang.
(15) The dairyman, who had thrown himself into abstraction to better realize the taste, and so divine the particular species of noxious weed to which it appertained, suddenly exclaimed, "'Tis garlic! and I thought there wasn't a blade left in that meadow!"
(20) Then all the old hands remembered that a certain dry meadow, into which a few of the cows had been admitted of late, had, in years gone by, spoiled the butter in the same way. The dairyman had not recognized the taste at that time, and thought the
(25) butter bewitched.

"We must overhaul that meadow," he resumed; "this mustn't continue!"

All having armed themselves with old pointed knives, they went out together. As the inimical plant
(30) could only be present in very microscopic dimensions to have escaped ordinary observation, to find it seemed rather a hopeless attempt in the stretch of rich grass before them. However, they formed themselves into line, all assisting, owing to the
(35) importance of the search; the dairyman at the upper end with Mr. Clare, who had volunteered to help; then Tess, Marian, Izz Huett, and Retty; then Bill Lewell, Jonathan, and the married dairywomen— Beck Knibbs, with her woolly black hair and rolling
(40) eyes; and flaxen Frances, consumptive from the winter damps of the water-meads—who lived in their respective cottages.

With eyes fixed upon the ground, they crept slowly across a strip of the field, returning a lit-
(45) tle further down in such a manner that, when they should have finished, not a single inch of the pasture would escape falling under the eye of some one of them. It was a most tedious business, not more than half a dozen shoots of garlic being
(50) discoverable in the whole field; yet such was the herb's pungency that probably one bite of it by one cow had been sufficient to season the whole dairy's produce for the day.

Differing one from another in natures and
(55) moods so greatly as they did, they yet formed, bending, a curiously uniform row—automatic, noiseless. As they crept along, stooping low to discern the plant, a soft yellow gleam was reflected from the buttercups into their shaded faces, giving
(60) them an elfish, moonlit aspect, though the sun was pouring upon their backs in all the strength of noon.

GO ON TO THE NEXT PAGE ⇨

Angel Clare, who communistically stuck to his rule of taking part with the rest in everything, (65) glanced up now and then. It was not, of course, by accident that he walked next to Tess.

"Well, how are you?" he murmured.

"Very well, thank you, sir," she replied demurely. After a moment, she said, "Don't (70) they look pretty?"

"Who?"

"Izzy Huett and Retty."

Tess had moodily decided that either of these maidens would make a good farmer's wife, and that (75) she ought to recommend them, and obscure her own wretched charms.

"Pretty? Well, yes—they are pretty girls. I have often thought so."

"Though, poor dears, prettiness won't last (80) long!"

"Oh no, unfortunately."

"They are excellent dairywomen."

"Yes—though not better than you."

"They skim better than I."

(85) "Do they?"

Clare remained observing them—not without their observing him.

"She is coloring up," continued Tess heroically.

"Who?"

(90) "Retty Priddle."

"Oh! Why is that?"

"Because you are looking at her."

Self-sacrificing as her mood might be, Tess could not well go further and cry, "Marry one of (95) them, if you really do want a dairywoman and not a lady; and don't think of marrying me!" She followed Dairyman Crick, and had the mournful satisfaction of seeing that Clare remained behind.

From this day she forced herself to take pains to (100) avoid him—never allowing herself, as formerly, to remain long in his company, even if their juxtaposition were purely accidental. She gave the other three every chance.

1. At the time of the events of the story, Tess is:

A. reflecting on the qualities required of a good farmer's wife.

B. struggling with conflicting feelings for Clare.

C. frustrated by the tedium of daily life.

D. excited about securing a romantic interest for one of her friends.

2. It can reasonably be inferred that the characters view the search for garlic shoots as a task that is:

F. impossibly monotonous and made more complicated by the number of people participating.

G. relatively simple but made more complicated by the number of people participating.

H. quite dull but something that demands everyone's participation.

J. engaging but something that results in the loss of the dairy's production for the day.

3. It can reasonably be inferred from the passage that garlic presented such a nuisance to the dairy primarily because of which of its following traits?

A. Its status as an unsightly weed

B. Its pungency

C. Its microscopic size

D. Its limited presence in the field

4. The passage states that Tess claims Izzy Huett and Retty Priddle are superior to her in all of the following aspects EXCEPT their:

F. ladylike nature.

G. skills as dairywomen.

H. prettiness.

J. skimming ability.

GO ON TO THE NEXT PAGE

5. It can reasonably be inferred that Tess views her statements and behavior in her conversation with Clare with a mixture of:

   A. sorrow and regret.

   B. confusion and discomfort.

   C. pride and shame.

   D. resolution and sadness.

6. The passage states that Dairyman Crick became aware of the "twang" in the butter as a result of:

   F. the tasting of the butter by the members of the dairy.

   G. discovering the small garlic plants in the meadow that had caused a similar twang years ago.

   H. a letter directly expressing a customer's complaint.

   J. an angry customer's breakfast-time visit to Crick's house.

7. The distinction the author makes between the characters' everyday actions and the characters' actions in the search is that the search:

   A. renders their individual differences less important than their pulling together in the common task.

   B. lets the characters take on an other-worldly aspect that contrasts sharply with their everyday personalities.

   C. makes them more willing to overlook the status differences among the group.

   D. causes them to lose their individual identities.

8. Which of the following statements best describes the way the ninth paragraph (lines 54–62) functions in the passage as a whole?

   F. It sets the stage for a transition from discussion of the "twang" to the conversation between Tess and Clare.

   G. It contrasts the initial disorder of the dairy to the structure and order that emerges after the search.

   H. It emphasizes how the search process transforms the members of the group.

   J. It moves the narrative from a discussion of everyday events to an idealization of the surrounding landscape.

9. The statement "She gave the other three every chance" (lines 102–103) functions in the passage to support Tess' view that:

   A. the other milkmaids are not capable of attracting Clare's attention by themselves.

   B. chance plays an important role in matchmaking.

   C. Clare would never marry Tess, despite her charms.

   D. the other milkmaids are more suitable companions for Clare than she is.

10. The author considers "Marry one of them... don't think of marrying me!" (lines 94–96) to be a statement that:

    F. exposes the high level of competition Tess feels with the other girls.

    G. goes beyond the limits of Tess's commitment to self-sacrifice.

    H. reveals feelings Tess has for Clare that she has put fully behind her.

    J. demonstrates the strength of Tess' wish to have Clare leave her alone.

PASSAGE II

SOCIAL STUDIES

The following two passages were written in the early 1990s and present two viewpoints about the ways that the public responds to the results of scientific research.

PASSAGE A

The way that people in present-day industrial societies think about science in the modern world actually tends to cultivate the very unscientific
Line perception that science supplies us with unques-
(5) tionable facts. If there is one unquestionable fact about science, it is that science is inherently uncertain. Research consists not so much of a search for truth as a search for some degree of certainty in an uncertain world. Every research study,
(10) every experiment, and every survey incorporates an extensive statistical analysis that is meant to be taken as qualifying the probability that the results are consistent and reproducible. Yet policy makers, public relations interests, and so-called experts in
(15) the popular media continue to treat the results of every latest study as if they were surefire truths.

History is filled with examples of the fallibility of scientific certainties. From the medieval monks who believed the sun orbited around Earth and the
(20) world was only 4,000 years old, to the early twentieth-century scientists who thought that X-rays were a hoax and that exploding a nuclear bomb would set off a chain reaction that would destroy all matter in the universe, it has been demonstrated repeatedly
(25) that science deals primarily with possibilities and is subject to the same prejudices as other kinds of opinions and beliefs. Yet statistics are complicated, and in our need to feel that we live in a universe of predictable certainties, it is tempting to place our
(30) faith in the oversimplified generalities of headlines and sound bites rather than the rigorous application of probabilities. Ironically, even though the intent of science is to expand the realm of human knowledge, an unfounded prejudice stemming from a
(35) desire for scientific constancy can actually discourage inquiry.

Science serves an important practical function; predictability and reproducibility are vital to making sure that our bridges remain standing, our
(40) nuclear power plants run smoothly, and our cars start in the morning so we can drive to work. When these practicalities become everyday occurrences, they tend to encourage a complacent faith in the reliability and consistency of science. Yet faced
(45) with so many simple conveniences, it is important to remember that we depend on the advance of science for our very survival. With progress expanding into those gray areas at the boundaries of scientific exploration, caution and prudence are
(50) just as important as open-mindedness and imagination. As technological advances engage increasingly complex moral questions within fields such as pharmaceutical developments, indefinite extension of life, and the potential for inconceivably potent
(55) weapons, an understanding of the limitations of science becomes just as important as an understanding of its strengths.

PASSAGE B

While it is important that scientific knowledge be taken into consideration in significant matters
(60) of public interest, such consideration must be tempered with critical rigor. In the early days during the ascendance of science as a practical discipline, the public was inclined to view every new advance and discovery with a healthy skepticism. In the late
(65) 19th century, when Italian astronomer Giovanni Schiaparelli first detected seas and continents on the planet Mars, many people balked at the idea of Earth-like topography on the Red Planet. Just a few decades later, when fellow Italian astronomer
(70) Vincenzo Cerulli provided evidence that the seas and continents Schiaparelli observed were merely optical illusions, public disbelief proved to be entirely appropriate.

Since then, the historic tendency of the public
(75) to question scientific findings has unfortunately been lost. Yet in present-day industrial societies, and especially where public policy is at issue, response to scientific research needs more than ever to pursue an informed, critical viewpoint. Who

GO ON TO THE NEXT PAGE ▷

(80) performs a research study, what kind of study it is, what kinds of review and scrutiny it comes under, and what interests support it are every bit as important as a study's conclusions.

(85) Studies of mass media and public policy reveal that, all too often, scientific findings presented to the public as objective and conclusive are actually funded at two or three degrees of removal by corporate or political interests with a specific agenda related to the outcome of those findings. For

(90) example, some critics question the issue of whether a study of the effectiveness of a new drug is more likely to produce favorable results when the study is funded by the pharmaceutical company that owns the drug patent. In cases where such findings

(95) conflict with the interests of the funding parties, analysts sometimes wonder if information was repressed, altered, or given a favorable public relations slant in order to de-emphasize dangerous side effects. Some critics of company-funded studies

(100) argue that the level of misrepresentation included in such studies borders on immoral.

Part of the problem grows from the public's willingness to place blind faith in the authority of science without an awareness of the interests that

(105) lie behind the research. Public officials then, in turn, may sometimes be too willing to bend in the face of public or private political pressure rather than pursuing the best interests of the constituency. Issues such as genetics, reproductive health,

(110) and preventative care are particularly fraught with political angst. Where the safety of individuals is at stake, a precautionary principle of allowing for unpredictable, unforeseen negative effects of technological advances should be pursued. It is the

(115) duty of active citizens in a free society to educate themselves about the real-world application of risk-assessment and statistical analysis, and to resist passive acceptance of the reassurances of self-styled scientific authorities. The most favorable approach

(120) to policy decisions based on realistic assessments finds a middle ground between the alarmism of political "Chicken Littles" and the recklessness of profit-seeking risk takers.

Questions 11–13 ask about Passage A.

11. The viewpoint of the author of Passage A toward the results of modern scientific studies can most closely be described as one of:

A. anger.

B. enthusiasm.

C. acceptance.

D. skepticism.

12. The word "probabilities" in line 32 is used to express the author's belief that:

F. scientific theories will eventually be proven true.

G. current scientific findings will be regarded as outdated by future scientists.

H. viewing scientific results as possibly wrong is a wise approach.

J. refusing to question science is unavoidable because people prefer certainty.

13. In lines 46–47, the author of Passage A points out that "we depend on . . . very survival" in order to:

A. strengthen the authority of the central thesis.

B. emphasize an important argument.

C. introduce a new line of reasoning.

D. provide reassurance to the reader.

GO ON TO THE NEXT PAGE →

Questions 14–16 ask about Passage B.

14. The main idea of Passage B is that:

    F. the human desire for stability can lead people to resist scientific inquiry.

    G. scientific findings are always repressed or altered to de-emphasize contradicting results.

    H. citizens should regard scientific advancements with reasonable skepticism.

    J. it is in the best interest of society to embrace new scientific developments without restraint.

15. The author of Passage B uses the first paragraph to explain:

    A. a new scientific hypothesis.

    B. a historical contrast.

    C. a public policy generality.

    D. the underlying cause of an issue.

16. With which of the following statements would the author of Passage B most likely agree?

    F. People should not unquestioningly accept the results of scientific studies.

    G. More government control and regulation are needed to ensure that science serves the best interests of the public.

    H. Society should place less emphasis on modern conveniences and more on understanding the limitations of science.

    J. The results that scientists derive from research are less reliable now than in former times.

Questions 17–20 ask about both passages.

17. What does the author of Passage A believe is the biggest obstacle to reaching the solution described by the author of Passage B in lines 114–119 ("It is the duty...authorities")?

    A. Policymakers are too willing to bend to public pressure when it comes to regulating scientific research.

    B. The interests that fund research are the same interests that stand to profit by favorable results, making impartiality impossible.

    C. Statistics are too abstract when compared with the concrete evidence of technological conveniences.

    D. Unanswered ethical questions are increasingly coming under scrutiny at the forefront of our most advanced scientific research.

18. Both passages refer to which of the following in their introductory paragraphs?

    F. Present-day industrial societies

    G. Early twentieth-century scientists

    H. Critics of company-funded studies

    J. Significant matters of public interest

19. According to Passage B, which of the following is an example of the "fallibility of scientific certainties" (lines 17–18) mentioned in Passage A?

    A. Medieval monks who believed the sun orbited around Earth

    B. People who balked at the idea of Earth-like topography on Mars

    C. Issues such as genetics, reproductive health, and preventative care

    D. Early twentieth-century scientists who thought that X-rays were a hoax

GO ON TO THE NEXT PAGE ⟩

20. The authors of both passages mention the term "pharmaceutical" in order to:

    F. highlight a particular scientific field in which moral questions may arise.

    G. point out an example of the recklessness of profit-seeking risk takers.

    H. identify unfounded prejudice stemming from a desire for scientific constancy.

    J. cite the usefulness of the current approach regarding drug testing and analysis.

PASSAGE III

HUMANITIES

This passage is adapted from an article found on Wikipedia.com.

Born in Edinburgh in 1771, the young Walter Scott survived a childhood bout of polio that would leave him lame in his right leg for the rest of his
Line life. After studying law at Edinburgh University,
(5) he followed in his father's footsteps and became a lawyer in his native Scotland. Beginning at age 25, he started dabbling in writing, first translating works from German, then moving on to poetry. In between these two phases of his literary career, he
(10) published a three-volume set of collected Scottish ballads, *The Minstrelsy of the Scottish Border*. This was the first sign of his interest in Scotland and history in his writings.

After Scott had founded a printing press, his
(15) poetry, beginning with *The Lay of the Last Minstrel* in 1805, brought him great fame. He published a number of other poems over the next ten years, including in 1810 the popular *Lady of the Lake*, portions of which (translated into German) were
(20) set to music by Franz Schubert. Another work from this time period, *Marmion*, produced some of his most quoted (and most often misattributed) lines, such as

    Oh! what a tangled web we weave
(25)   *When first we practise to deceive!*

When Scott's press became embroiled in financial difficulties, Scott set out, in 1814, to write a successful (and profitable) work. The result was *Waverley*, a novel that did not name its author. It
(30) was a tale of the last Jacobite rebellion in the United Kingdom, the "Forty-Five," and the novel met with considerable success. There followed a large number of novels in the next five years, each in the same general vein. Mindful of his reputation as a poet,
(35) he maintained the anonymity he had begun with *Waverley*, always publishing the novels under a name such as "Author of Waverley" or attributed as "Tales of..." with no author. Even when it was clear that there would be no harm in coming out into
(40) the open, he maintained the façade, apparently out of a sense of fun. During this time, the nickname "The Wizard of the North" was popularly applied to the mysterious best-selling writer. His identity as the author of the novels was widely rumored, and
(45) in 1815 Scott was given the honour of dining with George, Prince Regent, who wanted to meet "the author of Waverley."

In 1820, Scott broke away from writing about Scotland with *Ivanhoe*, a historical romance set in
(50) twelfth-century England. It too was a runaway success and, as he did with his first novel, he unleashed a slew of books along the same lines. As his fame grew during this phase of his career, he was granted the title of Baronet, becoming Sir Walter Scott. At
(55) this time he organized the visit of King George IV to Scotland, and when the King visited Edinburgh in 1822, the spectacular pageantry Scott had concocted to portray the King as a rather tubby reincarnation of Bonnie Prince Charlie made
(60) tartans and kilts fashionable and turned them into symbols of national identity.

Beginning in 1825, Scott fell into dire financial straits again, and his company nearly collapsed. That he was the author of his novels became gen-
(65) eral knowledge at this time as well. Rather than declare bankruptcy he placed his home, Abbotsford House, and income into a trust belonging to his creditors, and proceeded to write his way out of debt. He kept up his prodigious output of fiction
(70) (as well as producing a biography of Napoleon Bonaparte) through 1831. By then his health was

GO ON TO THE NEXT PAGE ⟹

failing, and he died at Abbotsford in 1832. Though not in the clear by then, his novels continued to sell, and he made good his debts from beyond the (75) grave. He was buried in Dryburgh Abbey; nearby, fittingly, a large statue can be found of William Wallace—one of Scotland's great historical figures.

Scott was responsible for two major trends that carry on to this day. First, he popularized the (80) historical novel; an enormous number of imitators (and imitators of imitators) would appear in the nineteenth century. It is a measure of Scott's influence that Edinburgh's central railway station, opened in 1854, is called Waverley Station. Second, (85) his Scottish novels rehabilitated Highland culture after years in the shadows following the Jacobite rebellions.

Scott was also responsible, through a series of pseudonymous letters published in the *Edinburgh* (90) *Weekly News* in *1826*, for retaining the right of Scottish banks to issue their own banknotes, which is reflected to this day by his continued appearance on the front of all notes issued by the Bank of Scotland.

21. The main idea of the passage is that:

   A. historical novels can be very successful in rehabilitating a country's culture.

   B. Sir Walter Scott's writings achieved both financial success and cultural impact.

   C. Scott became known more for his financial failures than for his literary talents.

   D. the success of Scott's novels was largely due to the anonymity of the author.

22. According to the passage, Walter Scott turned to writing novels because:

   F. his childhood bout with polio made it difficult for him to continue working as a lawyer.

   G. his printing press business was being sued over copyright violations.

   H. his three-volume set of Scottish ballads did not sell well.

   J. his printing press business was losing money.

23. According to the author, Scott published *Waverly* anonymously because:

   A. he didn't want to damage his reputation as a lawyer.

   B. he had fun watching people try to determine who the author was.

   C. his novels sold faster without an author's name on them.

   D. he was afraid writing fiction would take away from his reputation as a poet.

24. The author would most likely describe Scott's effect on how Scotland was viewed as:

   F. damaging, since Scott degraded Scottish culture by popularizing tartans and kilts.

   G. unimportant, since Scott's novels were no more than popular fiction.

   H. ground-breaking, since Scott was the first to write serious analyses of Scottish history.

   J. positive, since Scott made Scottish culture acceptable again after years of neglect.

GO ON TO THE NEXT PAGE ⟩

25. Based on the passage, it is reasonable to assume that Scott's reputation after his death:

    A. remained favorable.

    B. waned because there were no more of his novels being published.

    C. declined because he died without paying all of his debts.

    D. was debased because of all his imitators.

26. The author describes how Scott influenced Scotland's right to continue issuing its own banknotes in order to:

    F. show a way in which Scott helped overcome his own financial difficulties.

    G. establish the level of Scott's influence with the Prince Regent.

    H. emphasize Scott's continued impact on his native country.

    J. point out a way for the reader to find out what Scott looked like.

27. The author most likely uses "fittingly" (line 76) when describing the presence of a statue of William Wallace near Scott's grave in Dryburgh Abbey because:

    A. Scott's first major novel was about the achievements of William Wallace.

    B. Scott wrote novels about Scottish history and Wallace is a famous historical figure from Scotland.

    C. Scott was a very religious man and deserved to be buried in an abbey.

    D. Wallace was an avid fan of Scott's poetry.

28. The passage suggests that the author's attitude toward Sir Walter Scott is:

    F. restrained and skeptical.

    G. derisive and contemptuous.

    H. interested and appreciative.

    J. passionate and envious.

29. Based on the fifth paragraph (lines 62–77), it is reasonable to infer that Sir Walter Scott's attitude toward his debts was:

    A. irresponsible, since he left them to be taken care of after his death.

    B. resentful, for he believed that they were caused by his partners.

    C. impatient, because he became annoyed that his creditors hounded him so.

    D. accepting, since he acknowledged his responsibility and tried to pay them back.

30. The author's use of "dabbling" in line 7 suggests that:

    F. Scott sought to establish himself in a field in which he had little experience.

    G. the financial losses eventually suffered by Scott's printing press began with this activity.

    H. Scott's inexperience led to the poor quality of his literary work.

    J. Scott's initial work led to his interest in Scottish history.

PASSAGE IV

NATURAL SCIENCE

The following is adapted from Wikipedia articles titled "Lemur" and "Ring-tailed Lemur."

Lemurs are part of a suborder of primates known as prosimians, and make up the infraorder Lemuriformes. This type of primate was the
Line evolutionary predecessor of monkeys and apes
(5) (simians). The term "lemur" is derived from the Latin word *lemures*, which means "spirits of the night." This likely refers to many lemurs' nocturnal behavior and their large, reflective eyes. It is generically used for the members of the four lemuriform
(10) families, but it is also the genus of one of the lemu-

GO ON TO THE NEXT PAGE ⟹

riform species. The two flying lemur species are not lemurs, nor are they even primates.

Lemurs are found naturally only on the island of Madagascar and some smaller surrounding islands,
(15) including the Comoros (where it is likely they were introduced by humans). While they were displaced in the rest of the world by monkeys, apes, and other primates, the lemurs were safe from competition on Madagascar and differentiated into a number of
(20) species. These range in size from the tiny 30-gram pygmy mouse lemur to the 10-kilogram indri. The larger species have all become extinct since humans settled on Madagascar, and since the early twentieth century the largest lemurs reach about seven
(25) kilograms. Typically, the smaller lemurs are active at night (nocturnal), while the larger ones are active during the day (diurnal).

All lemurs are endangered species, due mainly to habitat destruction (deforestation) and hunting.
(30) Although conservation efforts are underway, options are limited because of the lemurs' limited range and because Madagascar is desperately poor. Currently, there are approximately 32 living lemur species.

The ring-tailed lemur is a relatively large pros-
(35) imian, belonging to the family Lemuridae. Ring-tailed lemurs are the only species within the genus *Lemur* and are found only on the island of Mada-gascar. Although threatened by habitat destruction and therefore listed as vulnerable by the IUCN
(40) Red List, ring-tailed lemurs are the most populous lemurs in zoos worldwide; they reproduce readily in captivity.

Mostly grey with white underparts, ring-tailed lemurs have slender frames; their narrow faces are
(45) white with black lozenge-shaped patches around the eyes and black vulpine muzzles. The lemurs' trademark, their long, bushy tails, are ringed in black and white. Like all lemurs, ring-tailed lemurs have hind limbs longer than their forelimbs; their
(50) palms and soles are padded with soft, leathery skin and their fingers are slender and dextrous. On the second toe of their hind limbs, ring-tailed lemurs have claws specialized for grooming purposes.

The very young animals have blue eyes while

(55) the eyes of all adults are a striking yellow. Adults may reach a body length of 46 centimeters (18 inches) and a weight of 5.5 kilograms (12 pounds). Their tails are longer than their bodies, at up to 56 centimeters (22 inches) in length.

(60) Found in the southwest of Madagascar and ranging farther into highland areas than any other lemur, ring-tailed lemurs inhabit deciduous forests with grass floors or forests along riverbanks (gallery forests); some may also inhabit dry, open
(65) brush where few trees grow. Ring-tailed lemurs are thought to require primary forest (that is, forests that have remained undisturbed by human activity) in order to survive; such forests are now being cleared at a troubling rate.

(70) While primarily frugivores (fruit-eating), ring-tailed lemurs will also eat leaves, seeds, and the odd insect. Ring-tailed lemurs are diurnal and primarily arboreal animals, forming troops of up to 25 individuals. Social hierarchies are determined
(75) by sex, with a distinct hierarchy for each gender; females tend to dominate the troop, while males will alternate between troops. Lemurs claim a siz-able territory, which does not overlap with those of other troops; up to 5.6 kilometers (3.5 miles) of this
(80) territory may be covered in a single day's foraging.

Both vocal and olfactory signals are important to ring-tailed lemurs' communication: 15 distinct vocalizations are used. A fatty substance is exuded from the lemurs' glands, which the lemurs run
(85) their tails through; this scent is used by both sexes to mark territory and to challenge would-be rivals amongst males. The males vigorously wave their tails high in the air in an attempt to overpower the scent of others.

(90) The breeding season runs from April to June, with the female fertile period lasting for only a day. Gestation lasts for about 146 days, resulting in a litter of either one or two. The young lemurs begin to eat solid food after two months and are fully
(95) weaned after five months.

GO ON TO THE NEXT PAGE ⇨

31. According to the passage, lemurs survived on the island of Madagascar because:

    A. their large, reflective eyes allowed them to move around at night when predators were asleep.

    B. their ability to mark their territory by scent gave them adequate territory for foraging.

    C. monkeys, apes and other primates were not a threat to them on Madagascar.

    D. their strong social hierarchy allowed them to band together for safety.

32. According to the passage, the social organization of the ring-tailed lemur:

    F. places females at the top of the hierarchy.

    G. functions to ensure adequate food supplies.

    H. has followed the same structure since antiquity.

    J. is notable for its equality of the sexes.

33. The main purpose of the passage is to:

    A. propose a means of preventing the extinction of lemurs.

    B. compare different species of lemurs.

    C. provide information regarding the ring-tailed lemur.

    D. argue that the lemur should not have been introduced into the Comoros Islands.

34. According to the passage, why are ring-tails the most populous species of lemurs in zoos?

    F. They inhabit deciduous forests, which make the lemurs' capture relatively easy.

    G. They have no difficulty giving birth in a zoo environment.

    H. Their attractive appearance makes them popular with patrons.

    J. Their eating preferences are easily accommodated.

35. The passage suggests that the rate at which primary forests are being cleared is "troubling" (line 69) because:

    A. it is causing significant soil erosion in the lemurs' primary habitat.

    B. valuable hardwoods are being destroyed.

    C. lemurs' predators inhabit the cleared area.

    D. lemurs need to live in primary forests to survive.

36. All of the following are given as ways in which ring-tailed lemurs use olfactory signals EXCEPT:

    F. to put male challengers on notice.

    G. to mask the scent of other lemurs.

    H. to signify group identification.

    J. to mark their territory.

37. According to the passage, which of the following describes a characteristic of the infraorder Lemuriformes?

    A. They are nocturnal.

    B. They evolved before monkeys and apes did.

    C. They include two species of flying lemurs.

    D. They are found only on Madagascar.

38. Which of the following can reasonably be inferred from information in the second paragraph (lines 13–27)?

    F. The pygmy mouse lemur is diurnal.

    G. The larger species of lemur were hunted for their fur.

    H. The indri lemur is extinct.

    J. Lemurs are descended from monkeys.

GO ON TO THE NEXT PAGE

39. The primary purpose of the seventh paragraph (lines 60–69) is to:

    A. distinguish between nocturnal and diurnal lemurs.

    B. explain the demise of primary forests.

    C. describe the lemur's habitat.

    D. argue that lemurs inhabit only forested areas.

40. Which of the following questions is NOT answered by the passage?

    F. Will conservationists be able to prevent the extinction of lemurs?

    G. Why did lemurs survive on Madagascar?

    H. How many offspring can a female lemur produce per year?

    J. What makes up the lemur's diet?

IF YOU FINISH BEFORE TIME IS CALLED, YOU MAY CHECK YOUR WORK ON THIS SECTION ONLY. DO NOT TURN TO ANY OTHER SECTION IN THE TEST. **STOP**

SCIENCE TEST

35 Minutes—40 Questions

Directions: There are several passages in this test. Each passage is followed by several questions. After reading a passage, choose the best answer to each question and fill in the corresponding oval on your Answer Grid. You may refer to the passages as often as necessary. You are NOT permitted to use a calculator on this test.

PASSAGE I

Blood samples of equal volumes were collected from five students on one day immediately after waking in the morning and one hour after a breakfast of pancakes and syrup with orange juice. The samples were then analyzed. Tables 1 and 2 show the color, mass, and sugar concentration of the blood samples taken before and after breakfast, respectively. *Sugar concentration* was calculated in milligrams per deciliter (mg/dL) as follows:

$$\text{sugar concentration (mg/dL)} = \frac{\text{mass of sugars (mg)}}{\text{volume of blood (dL)}}$$

The normal range for blood sugar concentration is 90 mg/dL–120 mg/dL.

Table 1

Before-breakfast blood samples			
Student	Color*	Mass(g)	Sugar concentration (mg/dL)
A	9	1.067	116
B	4	1.049	93
C	3	1.051	94
D	6	1.058	108
E	7	1.064	112

*Note: Color values were assigned according to the following scale: 0 = pale red; 10 = dark red

Table 2

After-breakfast blood samples			
Student	Color*	Mass(g)	Sugar concentration (mg/dL)
A	8	1.069	119
B	5	1.051	96
C	4	1.055	102
D	6	1.060	110
E	7	1.066	115

*Note: Color values were assigned according to the following scale: 0 = pale red; 10 = dark red

1. Based on the information presented, which of the following blood samples most likely had the highest water content per milliliter?

   A. The before breakfast blood sample from Student A

   B. The before breakfast blood sample from Student B

   C. The after breakfast blood sample from Student C

   D. The after breakfast blood sample from Student D

GO ON TO THE NEXT PAGE

2. Do the data in Tables 1 and 2 support the conclusion that as the mass of a given volume of blood decreases, blood color darkens?

F. Yes, because blood samples with the lowest masses had lower color values.

G. Yes, because blood samples with the lowest masses had higher color values.

H. No, because blood samples with the lowest masses had lower color values.

J. No, because blood samples with the lowest masses had higher color values.

3. Based on the results provided, as the sugar concentration of a given volume of blood increases, the mass of that volume of blood:

A. increases, then decreases.

B. decreases, then increases.

C. increases only.

D. decreases only.

4. One of the five students had a common cold on the day the blood samples were collected. Given that the sugar concentration of blood tends to increase during periods of illness, the student with a cold was most likely:

F. Student A.

G. Student B.

H. Student C.

J. Student D.

5. A volume of 0.5 mL from which of the following blood samples would weigh the most?

A. The before breakfast blood sample from Student B

B. The before breakfast blood sample from Student D

C. The after breakfast blood sample from Student C

D. The after breakfast blood sample from Student E

6. What is the positive difference in mass, in milligrams, between the before and after samples from Student C?

F. 0.0004

G. 0.004

H. 0.04

J. 4

PASSAGE II

The following experiments were performed to study the effects of adding various amounts of a *solute* (a substance that is dissolved in a solution) on the boiling points and freezing points of two different *solvents* (substances that dissolve other substances). The two solvents, isopropyl alcohol (IPA) and acetone, boil at 108°C and 56°C, respectively, and freeze at –88°C and –95°C, respectively, at standard atmospheric pressure.

EXPERIMENT 1

A student dissolved 0.05 moles of potassium chloride (KCl) in 200 g of IPA. Each mole of KCl produces 2 moles of solute particles (1 mole of potassium ions and 1 mole of chloride ions in solution). After the KCl dissolved, the boiling point of the solution was determined. This procedure was repeated dissolving different amounts of KCl in IPA and acetone. The results are shown in Table 1.

Table 1

Solution	Solvent	Amount of KCl added (moles)	Boiling point (°C)
1	IPA	0.05	109.5
2	IPA	0.1	111.2
3	IPA	0.2	114.4
4	IPA	0.4	119.7
5	acetone	0.05	56.4
6	acetone	0.1	56.8
7	acetone	0.2	57.9
8	acetone	0.4	59.2

Note: Boiling points were measured at standard atmospheric pressure.

GO ON TO THE NEXT PAGE

EXPERIMENT 2

A student dissolved 0.05 moles of KCl in 200 g of IPA. After the KCl dissolved, the freezing point of the solution was determined. The procedure was repeated using various amounts of KCl. The results are shown in Table 2.

Table 2

Solution	Amount of KCl added (moles)	Freezing point (°C)
9	0.05	−88.5
10	0.1	−89.0
11	0.2	−90.0
12	0.4	−92.0

Note: Freezing points were measured at standard atmospheric pressure.

7. A solution containing 200 g of IPA and an unknown amount of KCl freezes at −93.0°C. Based on the results of Experiment 2, the number of moles of KCl dissolved in the solution is closest to:

   A. 0.4.
   B. 0.5.
   C. 0.6.
   D. 0.7.

8. Which of the following factors was NOT directly controlled by the student in Experiment 2?

   F. The substance added to the IPA
   G. The amount of IPA used
   H. The amount of solute added to the IPA
   J. The freezing points of the IPA solutions

9. From the results of Experiment 2, which of the following statements most accurately reflects the effect of the number of solute particles dissolved in IPA on the freezing point of a solution?

   A. The number of solute particles produced does not affect the freezing point.
   B. The more solute particles that are present, the higher the freezing point is.
   C. The more solute particles that are present, the lower the freezing point is.
   D. No hypothesis can be made because only one solute was tested.

10. According to the results of Experiments 1 and 2, which of the following conclusions can be made about the changes in the boiling point and freezing point of IPA solutions when 0.4 moles of KCl are added to 200 g of IPA? The boiling point is:

    F. raised more than the freezing point is lowered.
    G. raised less than the freezing point is raised.
    H. lowered more than the freezing point is lowered.
    J. lowered less than the freezing point is raised.

11. Based on the results of Experiment 1, as the number of potassium particles and chloride particles in 200 g of IPA increases, the boiling point of the solution:

    A. increased only.
    B. decreased only.
    C. increased, then decreased.
    D. remained the same.

GO ON TO THE NEXT PAGE ⇨

12. $MgCl_2$ produces 3 moles of solute particles per mole when dissolved. Experiment 1 was repeated using a solution containing 200 g of IPA and 0.2 moles $MgCl_2$. Assuming that $MgCl_2$ has the same effect on the boiling point of IPA as does KCl per particle produced when dissolved, the boiling point of the solution would most likely be:

    F. between 109.5°C and 111.2°C.

    G. between 111.2°C and 114.4°C.

    H. between 114.4°C and 119.7°C.

    J. above 119.7°C.

13. Based on the relationship between moles and boiling point in Table 1 and the trend with the freezing point of IPA in Table 2, which value is the best approximation of the freezing point for acetone when 0.1 moles of KCl are added?

    A. −88.5

    B. −89

    C. −95

    D. −95.5

PASSAGE III

The study of carbon isotopes present in an archeological sample can help us closely approximate the age of the sample. The ratio of the isotopes ^{14}C and ^{12}C in a sample of formerly living tissue such as skeletal remains is compared to the $^{14}C/^{12}C$ ratio in a sample of air from Earth's *biosphere*. The biosphere is the layer of the atmosphere closest to Earth's surface, where living organisms constantly exchange levels of carbon isotopes with the environment. The comparison of a sample's ratio to that of the biosphere is called the *C-14 index* ($\delta^{14}C$). The $\delta^{14}C$ is calculated using the following formula:

$$\delta^{14}C = \frac{\left(^{14}C/^{12}C\right)_{biosphere} - \left(^{14}C/^{12}C\right)_{sample}}{\left(^{14}C/^{12}C\right)_{biosphere}} \times 100$$

Scientists conducted 3 studies to examine the $\delta^{14}C$ of human remains excavated from tombs in Mexico and Africa and learn about the ancient civilizations that once existed there.

STUDY 1

Human remains from 10 different tombs throughout Mexico were examined and the average $\delta^{14}C$ was calculated for each tomb. Figure 1 shows a comparison between the calculated values of $\delta^{14}C$ and the ages of the remains as determined by other methods.

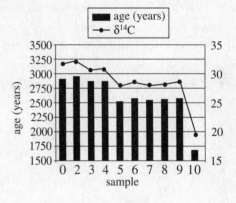

Figure 1

STUDY 2

The remains from one of the largest tombs from Mexico in Study 1 were organized according to the depth beneath the surface from which they were excavated. Since layers of soil and rock were deposited at a known rate at this location, each depth corresponded to a different sample age. In total, 20 m of earth represented the last 4,000 years of soil and rock accumulation. The calculated values of $\delta^{14}C$ for samples taken from different depths are shown in Figure 2.

GO ON TO THE NEXT PAGE ⟹

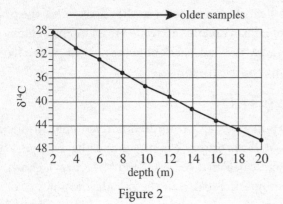

Figure 2

STUDY 3

The procedures of Study 2 were repeated for samples excavated from a large tomb in Africa. The past 4,000 years of soil and rock accumulation was represented by 40 m of depth. The calculated values of $\delta^{14}C$ for the samples are shown in Figure 3.

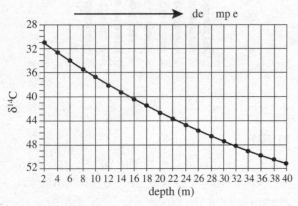

Figure 3

14. According to Study 1, average $\delta^{14}C$ values for the samples from Mexico were closest for which of the following pairs of tombs?

   F. Tomb 2 and Tomb 3

   G. Tomb 4 and Tomb 5

   H. Tomb 5 and Tomb 10

   J. Tomb 6 and Tomb 9

15. According to Study 1, which of the following best describes the relationship between the average $\delta^{14}C$ and the ages of the samples from Mexico? As the ages of the samples increased, the average $\delta^{14}C$ of the samples:

   A. increased only.

   B. decreased only.

   C. increased, then decreased.

   D. decreased, then increased.

16. Which of the following statements best describes why Mexico and Africa were chosen as locations for these studies? These locations had to have:

   F. sample ages greater than 2,000 years for all tomb sites.

   G. tombs over which a significant amount of soil and rock was deposited over the last 4,000 years.

   H. several sites at which little soil and rock was deposited over the last 4,000 years.

   J. large areas of undeveloped land.

17. According to Study 2, a sample excavated from a depth of 25 m under the surface in Mexico most likely had a $\delta^{14}C$ value that was:

   A. less than 30.

   B. between 30 and 40.

   C. between 40 and 50.

   D. greater than 50.

GO ON TO THE NEXT PAGE

18. According to Studies 2 and 3, 4,000 years of soil and rock accumulation was represented by 20 m of earth in Mexico and 40 m of earth in Africa. Which of the following statements best explains why the relationships between time and depth were different? The average rate of soil and rock accumulation over that time period in Africa:

    F. was less than the rate in Mexico.
    G. was the same as the rate in Mexico.
    H. was greater than the rate in Mexico.
    J. could not be determined in comparison with the rate in Mexico.

19. According to the information provided, a sample that has a calculated $\delta^{14}C$ of zero must have a $^{14}C/^{12}C$ ratio that compares in which of the following ways to the $^{14}C/^{12}C$ ratio of the biosphere? The sample's $^{14}C/^{12}C$ ratio is:

    A. 1/4 of the $^{14}C/^{12}C$ ratio of the biosphere.
    B. 1/2 of the $^{14}C/^{12}C$ ratio of the biosphere.
    C. the same as the $^{14}C/^{12}C$ ratio of the biosphere.
    D. twice as large as the $^{14}C/^{12}C$ ratio of the biosphere.

20. What is the approximate age, in years, of a sample from the Mexican tomb that was unearthed 5 meters beneath the surface?

    F. 2,750
    G. 2,850
    H. 3,050
    J. The age can not be determined due to the decomposition of the soil.

PASSAGE IV

Scientists discuss two possible events that may have caused the extinction of dinosaurs approximately 65 million years ago.

SCIENTIST 1

The extinction of the dinosaurs was caused by a meteorite of about 10 km in diameter that struck Earth at a location along what is now the northwestern coast of the Yucatan Peninsula in Mexico. The initial impact incinerated everything on Earth's surface within a radius of approximately 500 km from the point of impact. The resulting shock wave set massive fires and generated tidal waves that caused destruction across much larger distances.

Also, trillions of tons of debris were thrown into the air, blocking light from the sun and causing a significant decrease in global temperatures. The worldwide fires and the large amounts of CO_2 they released later resulted in an equally significant increase in temperatures and chemical reactions leading to downpours of acid rain.

SCIENTIST 2

The extinction of the dinosaurs was caused by an extended period of widespread volcanic activity. Volcanic eruptions around the world introduced large amounts of soot into the atmosphere, causing dramatic climatic changes. Combined with the excess CO_2 released by fires ignited by lava flows, the soot and the change in climate resulted in the production of acid rain. The atmosphere and the sources of food and water became too toxic for the dinosaurs.

The volcanoes also expelled huge amounts of sulfates (SO_4) into the atmosphere, and the mixing of sulfates with water vapor caused more acid rain. Also, SO_4 in the atmosphere led to a breakdown of the ozone layer, allowing high levels of ultraviolet radiation to reach the surface.

GO ON TO THE NEXT PAGE

21. Which of the following statements best explains why Scientist 1 mentioned acid rain?

    A. Acid rain is beneficial to many living things.

    B. Acid rain is harmful to many living things.

    C. Acid rain helps create CO_2 in the atmosphere.

    D. Acid rain results in fires.

22. Sulfates in the atmosphere help to reflect solar radiation back into space, resulting in a reduction of Earth's surface temperature. Based on the information provided, this fact would most likely weaken the viewpoint(s) of:

    F. Scientist 1.

    G. Scientist 2.

    H. both Scientist 1 and Scientist 2.

    J. neither Scientist 1 nor Scientist 2.

23. Scientist 2 would most likely agree that the ozone layer present in today's atmosphere is maintained, at least in part, by:

    A. frequent meteor showers.

    B. periodically active volcanoes.

    C. the high level of CO_2 in the atmosphere.

    D. the low level of SO_4 in the atmosphere.

24. Both scientists would most likely agree that worldwide climate changes occurred partially as a result of:

    F. the impact of a meteorite.

    G. acid rain.

    H. the presence of high levels of CO_2 in the atmosphere.

    J. the presence of high levels of SO_4 in the atmosphere.

25. According to the information provided, radioactive dating of fragments of the meteorite described by Scientist 1 would show the fragments to be about how many million years old?

    A. 2

    B. 10

    C. 50

    D. 65

26. Sulfates are produced in large amounts by a variety of industrial processes. Scientist 2 would most likely predict that in an area of many SO_4-producing industries, if the industries were to alter their processes such that sulfates were no longer produced, the climatic effect in that area would be an increase in the:

    F. average pH of rainfall.

    G. amount of rainfall.

    H. average temperature.

    J. amount of ultraviolet radiation reaching Earth's surface.

27. *Inorganic sulfates* are rocks containing sulfates like barium sulfate ($BaSO_4$) that are formed when minerals combine with sulfates in a high-temperature environment. If scientists found large amounts of inorganic sulfates that had formed about 65 million years ago, this discovery would most likely support the viewpoint(s) of:

    A. Scientist 1.

    B. Scientist 2.

    C. both Scientist 1 and Scientist 2.

    D. neither Scientist 1 nor Scientist 2.

GO ON TO THE NEXT PAGE ⇨

PASSAGE V

Under certain conditions, mixtures of hydrogen and chlorine will form hydrochloric acid (HCl). In their chemistry class, students performed the following experiments to study how HCl forms.

EXPERIMENT 1

A clear, thick-walled gas syringe was filled with 20 mL of hydrogen gas (H_2) and 20 mL of chlorine gas (Cl_2), as shown in Figure 1.

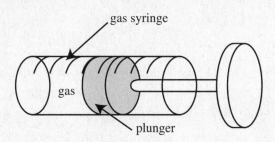

gas syringe

gas

plunger

Figure 1

The syringe plunger was then locked into place, and the syringe was covered in a black cloth. After a few minutes, the cloth was removed and an ultra-violet light bulb was flashed to briefly illuminate the gas from close range. A reaction occurred, forming droplets of HCl. The plunger was then released, and the final volume of gas was recorded after the system was allowed to adjust to room temperature. The composition of the remaining gas, if any, was analyzed. The procedure was repeated with different gas volumes, and the results were recorded in Table 1.

Table 1

Trial	Volume (mL)			
	Initial H_2	Initial Cl_2	Final H_2	Final Cl_2
1	20	20	0	0
2	20	30	0	10
3	20	40	0	20
4	10	40	0	30
5	40	40	0	0
6	30	20	10	0

Since equal numbers of different gas molecules are known to occupy equal volumes at the same pressure and temperature, the students proposed the following equation:

$$H_2 + Cl_2 \rightarrow 2\ HCl$$

EXPERIMENT 2

As shown in Figure 2, streams of silicon tetrachloride ($SiCl_4$) and hydrogen (H_2) gases were allowed to mix in a high-temperature furnace, producing HCl vapor and solid Si. The vapor was released into a cooler chamber, where it condensed to form liquid HCl.

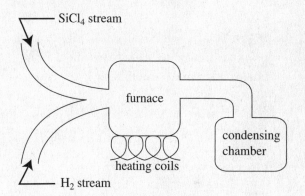

$SiCl_4$ stream

furnace

condensing chamber

heating coils

H_2 stream

Figure 2

The changes in mass of the contents of the furnace and condensing chamber were used to calculate the mass of $SiCl_4$ reacted and the mass of HCl formed. It was determined that 4 molecules of HCl were produced for every 1 molecule of $SiCl_4$ reacted:

$$SiCl_4 + 2\ H_2 \rightarrow Si + 4\ HCl$$

28. When sodium hydroxide (NaOH) and HCl are combined, both compounds decompose, and sodium chloride (NaCl) and H_2O are formed. Which of the following correctly represents this reaction?

F. $NaCl + H_2O \rightarrow NaOH + HCl$

G. $NaCl + 2\ H_2O \rightarrow NaOH + HCl$

H. $NaOH + HCl \rightarrow NaCl + H_2O$

J. $NaOH + HCl \rightarrow NaCl + 2\ H_2O$

GO ON TO THE NEXT PAGE

29. In Trial 5 of Experiment 1, immediately after the reaction began but before the syringe plunger was released, one would predict that, compared to the pressure in the syringe before the flash, the pressure in the syringe after the flash was:

    A. lower, because the total amount of gas increased.

    B. lower, because the total amount of gas decreased.

    C. higher, because the total amount of gas increased.

    D. higher, because the total amount of gas decreased.

30. If 10 mL of H_2 and 20 mL of Cl_2 were reacted using the procedure from Experiment 1, the final volume of Cl_2 would most likely be:

    F. 0 mL.

    G. 5 mL.

    H. 10 mL.

    J. 20 mL.

31. In Experiment 1, which of the following assumptions about the chemical reactions were made before the final measurements were taken?

    A. Each reaction had run to completion.

    B. Excess Cl_2 must be present for HCl to form.

    C. HCl vapor is not absorbed by solid Si.

    D. $SiCl_4$ and H_2 will only react when heated.

32. When oxygen gas (O_2) is reacted with H_2 under certain conditions, the following reaction occurs:

$$2 H_2 + O_2 \rightarrow 2 H_2O$$

Based on the results of Experiment 1, if 10 mL of O_2 were completely reacted with 25 mL of H_2 at the same pressure and temperature, what volume of H_2 would remain unreacted?

    F. 0 mL

    G. 5 mL

    H. 10 mL

    J. 15 mL

33. Which of the following events would NOT cause an error in interpreting the results of Experiment 2?

    A. Other reactions occurring between $SiCl_4$ and H_2 that produced different products

    B. HCl condensing before it reached the condensing chamber

    C. Using $SiCl_4$ contaminated with nonreactive impurities

    D. Using H_2 contaminated with reactive impurities

34. In which trial is Cl_2 a limiting reagent?

    F. Trial 1

    G. Trial 4

    H. Trial 5

    J. Trial 6

GO ON TO THE NEXT PAGE ▷

PASSAGE VI

A wooden box was held in place on a plastic track a distance, d_0, from one end of the track, which was inclined at an angle, θ, above the floor, as shown in Figure 1.

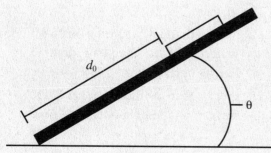

Figure 1

When the box was released it slid down the plane, as shown in Figure 2.

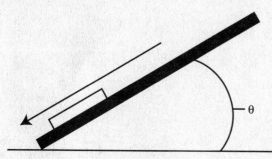

Figure 2

The *slide time* was the time required for the leading face of the box to reach the end of the track. The slide time is graphed in Figure 3 for a fixed θ and various d_0 on the surfaces of Neptune, Earth, and Mercury. The slide time is graphed in Figure 4 for $d_0 = 60$ cm and various θ on the same three surfaces. The acceleration due to gravity on these surfaces is shown in Table 1.

Table 1

Planet	Acceleration due to gravity on surface of planet (m/sec²)
Neptune	13.3
Earth	9.8
Mercury	3.6

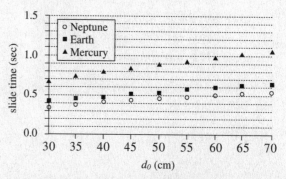

Figure 3

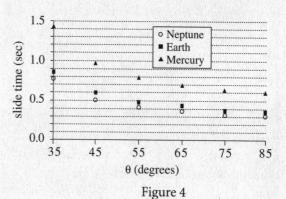

Figure 4

35. Which pair of values for θ produce slide times that are equal for Earth and Mercury, respectively?

   A. 45° and 85°

   B. 35° and 65°

   C. 45° and 55°

   D. 35° and 55°

36. Based on Figure 3, if d_0 were 25 cm, the slide time on Mercury would be closest to:

   F. 0.3 sec.

   G. 0.4 sec.

   H. 0.6 sec.

   J. 1.1 sec.

GO ON TO THE NEXT PAGE

37. According to Figure 4, the box with $d_0 =$ 60 cm will have a slide time on Mercury of 1.2 sec if θ is approximately:

    A. 27°.

    B. 30°.

    C. 38°.

    D. 51°.

38. After the box traveled a distance, x, down the track, the distance from the leading face of the box to the end of the track equaled:

    F. $d_0 - x$.

    G. $d_0 + x$.

    H. d_0.

    J. x.

39. Suppose the box represented in Figure 4 has a 0.8 sec slide time on Mercury's surface. For the same box released from the same d_0 to have a 0.8 sec slide time on Earth's surface, θ on Earth's surface would have to be approximately:

    A. 23° greater than on Mercury's surface.

    B. 23° less than on Mercury's surface.

    C. 17° greater than on Mercury's surface.

    D. 17° less than on Mercury's surface.

40. The acceleration due to gravity on the surface of the planet Jupiter is approximately 24.9 m/sec^2. Based on Figure 3, a box's slide time, calculated for Jupiter's surface and a given θ, would be:

    F. less than its slide time on Neptune's surface.

    G. greater than its slide time on Neptune's surface, and less than its slide time on Earth's surface.

    H. greater than its slide time on Earth's surface, and less than its slide time on Mercury's surface.

    J. greater than its slide time on Mercury's surface.

WRITING TEST

40 Minutes

Directions: This is a test of your writing skills. You will have forty (40) minutes to write an essay in English. Before you begin planning and writing your essay, read the writing prompt carefully to understand exactly what you are being asked to do. Your essay will be evaluated on the evidence it provides of your ability to do the following:

- Express judgments by evaluating the three perspectives given in the prompt, taking a position on an issue, and explaining the relationship among all four ideas
- Develop a position by using logical reasoning and by supporting your ideas
- Maintain a focus on the topic throughout the essay
- Organize ideas in a logical way
- Use language clearly and effectively according to the conventions of standard written English

You may use the unlined pages in this test booklet to plan your essay. These pages will not be scored. *You must write your essay in pencil on the lined pages in the answer folder.* Your writing on those lined pages will be scored. You may not need all the lined pages, but to ensure you have enough room to finish, do NOT skip lines. You may write corrections or additions neatly between the lines of your essay, but do NOT write in the margins of the lined pages. *Illegible essays cannot be scored, so you must write (or print) clearly.*

If you finish before time is called you may review your work. Lay your pencil down immediately when time is called.

DO NOT OPEN THIS BOOKLET UNTIL TOLD TO DO SO.

GO ON TO THE NEXT PAGE ⟶

STUDENT LOANS

Despite the rising cost of higher education, financial experts agree that a college diploma is worth the investment. As students enroll in college to increase their life-time earning potential, broaden their opportunities, and pursue careers, many worry about the challenge of paying off student loans once they graduate. Student loan repayment includes both the original amount borrowed as well as interest accrued over time, which often takes students years to repay. Should colleges and financial institutions be expected to develop programs and policies to address student concern regarding loans? Given the fact that affording college is a primary factor in deciding whether or not to pursue higher education, it is prudent for institutions to develop practices to better assist students in financing their degrees.

Read and carefully consider these perspectives. Each suggests a particular way of thinking about student loans.

Perspective One	Perspective Two	Perspective Three
Student loans should not be subject to interest rates if a student is able to pay off the loan within a reasonable amount of time. Financial lenders, including the United States government, should not be making a profit on loans that students need to complete their degrees. Should a student request additional time to repay the loan beyond the agreed-upon repayment schedule, interest or a penalty fee can then be applied to the remaining balance.	Higher education is a commodity and is subject to supply and demand principles inherent in a capitalist market. Colleges, financial institutions, and the United States government should not make special accommodations for college students. All loans should be held to the same standard and should not differ according to a borrower's intended use.	The amount of money students can borrow should be proportional to the annual salary they are projected to earn once they graduate. Students should not be allowed to borrow more money than they can pay back in a reasonable amount of time. Reducing or eliminating interest rates does not address the more concerning issue of disproportionate debt and future earning potential.

ESSAY TASK

Write a unified, coherent essay in which you evaluate multiple perspectives regarding student loans. In your essay, be sure to:

- analyze and evaluate the perspectives given
- state and develop your own perspective on the issue
- explain the relationship between your perspective and those given

Your perspective may be in full agreement with any of the others, in partial agreement, or wholly different. Whatever the case, support your ideas with logical reasoning and detailed, persuasive examples.

GO ON TO THE NEXT PAGE ⇒

PLANNING YOUR ESSAY

You may wish to consider the following as you think critically about the task:

Strengths and weaknesses of the three given perspectives

- What insights do they offer, and what do they fail to consider?
- Why might they be persuasive to others, or why might they fail to persuade?

Your own knowledge, experience, and values

- What is your perspective on this issue, and what are its strengths and weaknesses?
- How will you support your perspective in your essay?

_____

_____

_____

_____

_____

_____

_____

_____

_____

_____

_____

_____

_____

_____

_____

_____

_____

GO ON TO THE NEXT PAGE

_____

_____

_____

_____

_____

_____

_____

_____

_____

_____

_____

_____

_____

_____

_____

_____

_____

_____

_____

_____

_____

TEST PREP AND
ADMISSIONS

ACT®
Practice Test 2
For Courses Starting On or After 2/1/2016

PLEASE BE SURE TO RECORD THE FOLLOWING SCAN CODE ON YOUR ANSWER
GRID. WITHOUT THIS INFORMATION, WE WILL NOT BE ABLE TO SCAN YOUR
TEST OR PROVIDE YOU WITH YOUR TEST SCORES.

SCAN CODE: 8008

ENGLISH TEST

45 Minutes—75 Questions

Directions: In the following five passages, certain words and phrases are underlined and numbered. In the right-hand column are alternatives for each underlined portion. Select the one that best conveys the idea, creates the most grammatically correct sentence, or is most consistent with the style and tone of the passage. If you decide that the original version is best, select NO CHANGE. You may also find questions that ask about the entire passage or a section of the passage. These questions will correspond to small, numbered boxes in the text. For these questions, decide which choice best accomplishes the purpose set out in the question stem. After you've selected the best choice, fill in the corresponding oval on your Answer Grid. For some questions, you'll need to read the context in order to answer correctly. Be sure to read until you have enough information to determine the correct answer choice.

PASSAGE I

A SCREENWRITING CAREER

[1]

Wanting to have success as a Hollywood screenwriter, if
    1
you do, you should be aware of the difficulties that come
  1
along

with this career and its development. Very less budding
                                          2
screenwriters attain success by selling, let alone producing, their screenplays. Furthermore, even successful
screenwriters report living stressful and dissatisfied,
though wealthy, lives.

[2]

The first difficulty encountered by budding screenwriters is the lack of a formal career path. A recent college graduate cannot approach the career center at his

1. A. NO CHANGE
    B. If you want to succeed as a Hollywood screenwriter,
    C. Whether or not wanting to succeed as a Hollywood screenwriter,
    D. Having decided if you want to or not succeed as a Hollywood screenwriter,

2. F. NO CHANGE
    G. little less
    H. many few
    J. few

GO ON TO THE NEXT PAGE

or her school or <u>find time for extracurricular activities.</u>
3
While several successful screenwriters have written

guides that outline possibilities for success, their

<u>proposed suggestions only highlight and draw attention</u>
4
<u>to the</u> disparity of their experiences.
4

[3]

Unlike its value in other professional pursuits,

<u>a college education are</u> not necessarily a career boost for
5
a budding screenwriter. In fact, a college education can

have the reverse effect on a screenwriter. The academic

study of literature or film may help a budding screen-

writer to produce higher quality work, but such an edu-

cation delays its recipient from competing in the film

industry. <u>This also tends to hold true for actors.</u> While
6
a college graduate spends his or her late teens and early

twenties studying, the budding screenwriters

who do not attend college <u>begins honing</u> their craft and
7
competing for work several years earlier. In a career

3. Assuming that all are true, which choice is the most logical and appropriate in context?

  A. NO CHANGE

  B. read the classified ads in order to find screenwriting opportunities.

  C. understand the difficulties of his or her chosen career.

  D. stumble into an opportunity to work in the field.

4. **F.** NO CHANGE

  G. proposed suggestions only draw attention to the noteworthy

  H. proposed plans merely highlight the emphasized

  J. suggestions only highlight the

5. **A.** NO CHANGE

  B. a college education, is

  C. a college education is

  D. it is, a college education

6. **F.** NO CHANGE

  G. Actors also find this to be true for themselves.

  H. This has similar repercussions for actors.

  J. OMIT the underlined portion.

7. **A.** NO CHANGE

  B. begins to hone

  C. begin honing

  D. has begun honing

GO ON TO THE NEXT PAGE

path that usually requires years to develop, <u>you can see</u>
<u>that education is relevant.</u>
8

[4]

Moreover, <u>the debt of a college education</u>
9
<u>acquired at a prestigious school</u> may lead many young
9
screenwriters to surrender early to the allure of steady, if
not glamorous, work and pay. Those without college

educations often cannot escape to "fallback" <u>careers; this</u>
10
lack of options bolsters their drive to succeed. Furthermore, those without college educations are less averse to

the low-wage <u>jobs, aspiring screenwriters</u> are forced to
11
take in order to pay living expenses while saving blocks
of time to hone their craft.

[5]

The very few screenwriters who succeed often
find <u>that's the realities of their</u> day-to-day lives are far
12
different from their glamorous preconceptions and the
media's idealistic portrayals. While they can earn very
high salaries, successful Hollywood screenwriters often
feel more stressed and powerless than they did when
they struggled. A <u>Hollywood screenwriters reputation</u>
13
always hinges on the success of his or her last screen-
play. This volatile situation produces a high level of

8. Which choice provides the clearest and most logical transition to Paragraph 4?
   F. NO CHANGE
   G. late entry can create a substantial disadvantage.
   H. the months in school add up quickly.
   J. one can recognize that delayed entry may be disadvantageous.

9. A. NO CHANGE
   B. though universities offer work-study programs to help students pay for school, many graduate with debt; this burden
   C. the burden of student loans
   D. student loans which

10. F. NO CHANGE
    G. careers; this,
    H. careers so, this
    J. careers this

11. A. NO CHANGE
    B. jobs, these aspiring screenwriters
    C. jobs these aspiring screenwriters
    D. jobs that aspiring screenwriters

12. F. NO CHANGE
    G. that the realities of there
    H. there the realities of their
    J. that the realities of their

13. A. NO CHANGE
    B. Hollywood screenwriter's reputation
    C. screenwriters Hollywood reputation
    D. reputation of a Hollywood screenwriter's

GO ON TO THE NEXT PAGE

stress and pressure to <u>continually produce more and</u>

<u>better</u> work. Furthermore, the Hollywood hierarchy
14

places studio executives, producers, directors, and star

actors above screenwriters in both pay and importance.

Thus, even the most successful screenwriters must yield

creative power to individuals who often have very little

knowledge of the craft of screenwriting.

[6]

Regardless of the hardships of initially succeed-

ing and then thriving in the screenwriting profession,

young people move to Los Angeles every year to pursue

this career. <u>If they succeed, they will find that studio</u>
15
<u>executives have more decision-making power than they</u>
15
<u>do.</u> If you are one of these people, please research and

learn as much as possible about the vicissitudes as well as

the potential triumphs of this profession.

PASSAGE II

THE SWALLOWS OF SAN JUAN CAPISTRANO

[1]

The oldest building still in use in California is the

Mission at San Juan Capistrano, the seventh in the chain

of California missions built by Spanish priests in the late

eighteenth and early nineteenth centuries. The mission has

gained fame as the <u>well-known summer residence</u> of
16

14. F. NO CHANGE

  G. churn out improving and increasing

  H. be more productive and improved

  J. raising the stakes of

15. A. NO CHANGE

  B. Those who become successful find that
  studio executives have the power to
  make decisions.

  C. The power to make most decisions rests
  with studio executives, not successful
  screenwriters.

  D. OMIT the underlined portion.

16. F. NO CHANGE

  G. seasonal residence for the summer

  H. summer residence

  J. residential summer home

birds.
17

[2]

[1] For centuries, these cliff swallows have migrated to and from California every year in a cloud-like formation. [2] The swallows leave the town of San Juan Capistrano, halfway between San Diego and Los Angeles, around October 23. [3] They then journey 7,000 miles to spend the winter in Argentina. [4] Every spring, the birds faithfully return from Argentina to nest and <u>for bearing</u> their young in the valley near the
18
mission. [5] On March 19, mission bells ring, a fiesta is held, and

a parade <u>snaking</u> through the streets as throngs of locals
19
and tourists celebrate the birds' return.

[3]

According to legend, the swallows were seeking refuge from an innkeeper who had destroyed their muddy <u>nests when they discovered</u> the mission. Biolo-
20
gists have a different explanation for how the birds

<u>might of</u> developed their fondness for the mission. After
21
observing the swallows' behavior and noting that the birds build their nests out of mud, biologists have

postulated that the swallows <u>real chose</u> the mission due
22
to its proximity to two rivers. These rivers provide the

17. Which choice creates the most specific and logical transition to the following paragraph?
    A. NO CHANGE
    B. migrating animals.
    C. the swallows of San Juan Capistrano.
    D. Argentinean species.

18. F. NO CHANGE
    G. with bearing
    H. bearing
    J. bear

19. A. NO CHANGE
    B. snaked
    C. snakes
    D. is snaking

20. F. NO CHANGE
    G. nests when discovering
    H. nests, when
    J. nests, when finding

21. A. NO CHANGE
    B. might have
    C. may of
    D. may

22. F. NO CHANGE
    G. really chosened
    H. really chose
    J. real choosing

GO ON TO THE NEXT PAGE

swallows with ample mud for building their funnel-like

nests <u>of which</u>
23

they return year after year. 24

[4]

[1] One aspect of the legend, however, rings

true. [2] The swallows, sensing that they will be pro-

tected within the mission walls, return to the compound

every spring. [3] In fact, beyond the church walls, the

entire city has sought toprotect the swallows. 25

[5]

[1] Although the <u>community clearly</u> sees the
26
importance of providing a home for the swallows, some

problems have arisen in recent years. [2] Due to the

23. **A.** NO CHANGE
    B. to which
    C. by which
    D. which

24. Of the following true statements, which is
    the best choice to insert here in order to
    further support the biologists' explanation
    that the swallows chose the mission because
    of its proximity to two rivers?

    F. The swallows will repair a damaged
    nest instead of building an entirely new
    nest.

    G. The rivers also supply insects upon
    which the swallows feed.

    H. Both rivers are also home to a wide
    variety of fish.

    J. The location of the mission near the
    rivers also provides other advantages for
    the swallows.

25. Which of the following true sentences, if
    added here, would make the most logical
    transition from Paragraph 4 to Paragraph 5?

    A. The crowds that welcome the swallows
    back each spring reveal the delight that
    people take in the swallows.

    B. The birds have benefited from the
    community's interest in them.

    C. San Juan Capistrano municipal ordi-
    nances declare the city a bird sanctuary
    and outlaw the destruction or damaging
    of swallow nests.

    D. However, these protections do not
    extend to other migrating species.

26. **F.** NO CHANGE
    G. community, clearly
    H. community clearly,
    J. community clear

GO ON TO THE NEXT PAGE ⟹

city's growth and development, the number of insects

has declined, causing many of the swallows to locate

farther from the mission in the town center and closer

to the open areas where their food source thrives. [3]

Large groups of swallows have found other nesting sites

in the area, usually in the hills due to
                    27
disruptions from recent restorations of the historic

buildings at the mission. [4] Fortunately, city and mis-
                                                28
sion officials have started, to respond to these prob-
        28
lems.

[5] For example, to attempt at enticing the birds back
                            29
home, mission workers have strewn insects about the

mission's grounds.

27. **A.** NO CHANGE
    B. area; usually in the hills,
    C. area—usually in the hills—
    D. area, having been usual in the hills,

28. **F.** NO CHANGE
    G. Fortunately city and mission officials
        have started,
    H. Fortunately, city and mission officials
        have started
    J. Fortunately, city and mission officials,
        have started

29. **A.** NO CHANGE
    B. in an attempt to entice
    C. in an attempt's enticement
    D. in an attempt of enticing

Question 30 asks about the preceding passage as a whole.

30. The writer is considering adding the following sentence to further explain how residents of San Juan Capistrano feel about the swallows:

> Many residents and visitors miss the huge clouds of swallows descending upon the mission as in the past decades.

The most logical place to insert this sentence would be directly after:

F. Sentence 5 in Paragraph 2.
G. Sentence 3 in Paragraph 4.
H. Sentence 1 in Paragraph 5.
J. Sentence 3 in Paragraph 5.

GO ON TO THE NEXT PAGE

PASSAGE III

ROOT FOR THE HOME TEAM?

If you are young and love football, it is advantageous to live near a large sporting-goods store that carries a wide variety of paraphernalia from different teams. My daughter and I visit our local store at least once a year to buy another new football jersey for yet another team. Although my daughter is a fan of our <u>city</u> professional team, she frequently changes her jersey to match that of her favorite player.

      A free agent is a professional football player who is no longer under contract with a team, which means he can choose the team <u>which</u> he wants to play.

In the NFL today, players can become free agents <u>easy,</u> so they often switch teams several times during their careers. Things were much different when I was growing up. My favorite player was on the same team for his entire <u>career I had</u> one jersey. My daughter has bought over eight team jerseys in the past six years! At seventy-five dollars a shirt, this is not a sustainable trend.

      There are many disadvantages to <u>free agency.</u> <u>When my</u> daughter and I went to pre-season training practice to get a preview of this year's home team, we constantly consulted the team roster to figure out the new line-up, because there were so many new players. At one point, a number of fans even started to cheer for

31. **A.** NO CHANGE
    B. city's
    C. cities
    D. cities'

32. **F.** NO CHANGE
    G. at which
    H. for which
    J. OMIT the underlined portion.

33. **A.** NO CHANGE
    B. easily
    C. easiest
    D. easier

34. **F.** NO CHANGE
    G. career, so I had
    H. career, because I had
    J. career, and then I had

35. **A.** NO CHANGE
    B. free agency: for when my
    C. free agency, when my
    D. free agency when my

GO ON TO THE NEXT PAGE

a <u>player who, was no longer with the team,</u> because they
                      36
did not realize someone new was wearing his number.

<u>A second disadvantage of</u> free agency is lack of camara-
            37
derie and cohesion.

Football is the ultimate team sport, in which

players must depend <u>upon each other to win.</u> A team
                              38

<u>trains strategizes and plays</u> together for months. The
            39
players learn each other's strengths and weaknesses.

Eleven players are on the field <u>at one time, and their goal</u>
                                              40
is to stop the other team from progressing down the

field. If any one of those eleven players leaves the team,

it <u>disrupt</u> the dynamics and cohesion that the entire
     41
team has worked together to build.

        <u>A third disadvantage is the loss</u> of team dynas-
                          42
ties. When I was a teenager, my home team made the

playoffs for three years in a row. Since free agency was

introduced, our team has not made it back to the playoffs

for ten years. When we did return <u>10 years later,</u> my
                                              43
daughter fell in love with the team and our star quarter-

back.

36. F. NO CHANGE
    G. player who was no longer with the team,
    H. player, who was no longer, with the team
    J. player who was no longer, with the team

37. A. NO CHANGE
    B. (Begin new paragraph) A second disad-
        vantage of
    C. (Begin new paragraph) Secondly
    D. (Do NOT begin new paragraph) A final
        disadvantage of

38. F. NO CHANGE
    G. to win on each other
    H. upon winning with each other
    J. OMIT the underlined portion.

39. A. NO CHANGE
    B. trains, strategizes, and plays,
    C. trains strategizes, and plays
    D. trains, strategizes, and plays

40. F. NO CHANGE
    G. at one time, because their goal
    H. at one time, yet their goal
    J. at one time, or their goal

41. A. NO CHANGE
    B. disrupted
    C. disrupts
    D. disrupting

42. F. NO CHANGE
    G. A loss is the third disadvantage
    H. A disadvantage is the third loss
    J. The third loss is a disadvantage

43. A. NO CHANGE
    B. to the Super Bowl
    C. 10 years' later
    D. OMIT the underlined portion.

GO ON TO THE NEXT PAGE ➤

That player moved to another team; <u>because</u> our home
                                        44
team has not had a winning season since he left, his new

team has won the

Superbowl for the last two years. 45

PASSAGE IV

THE RIGHT TO WRITE

[1]

Going to see a play is a cultural tradition that

has been passed on for thousands of years. Although

theater is a form of art and entertainment, it is also a

highly competitive business, especially for playwrights.

Many plays are written, but <u>it is only</u> a select few are
                                      46
produced and seen by the public, and often with strings

attached. Playwright José Rivera is an example of a

contemporary playwright <u>that</u> has fought for the right
                                47
to have his work produced and seen in the way he

intended it.

[2]

Rivera was born in San Juan, Puerto Rico, in

1955, but his family moved to New York when he was

four years old. <u>Yet</u> many of Rivera's relatives had already
                      48
moved to the Bronx, a bustling neighborhood in

New York, Rivera's father wanted to live in a place that

felt more like a small town. So they moved to a quarter

acre of land in Long Island, New York, which at the time

had dirt roads and woods.

44. **F.** NO CHANGE
    G. however
    H. therefore
    J. while

45. Which of the following sentences, if added,
    would best conclude the essay?

    A. Football is a great sport that will never
    decrease in popularity.

    B. Free agency has a variety of benefits,
    but the negatives outweigh the positives.

    C. Free agency allows players to change
    teams frequently, which has made it
    increasingly difficult to root for a home
    team that never stays the same.

    D. One thing will never change, and that is
    the home team.

46. **F.** NO CHANGE
    G. there are only
    H. only
    J. there only is

47. **A.** NO CHANGE
    B. who
    C. which
    D. whom

48. **F.** NO CHANGE
    G. Meanwhile,
    H. However,
    J. Although

GO ON TO THE NEXT PAGE

[3]

[49] From an early age, Rivera knew that he
wanted to be a writer. As a kid, he wrote comic strips, a

novel about baseball, <u>and essays in response to photo-</u>
                                            50
<u>graphs, from</u> *Life* magazine. When he was in middle
      50
school, he saw a play

that inspired him <u>when he saw the play that he wanted</u>
                                    51

to become a playwright. He <u>writes</u> several plays during
                                            52
high school and in college.

[4]

<u>Rivera, after graduating, returned to New York,</u>
                          53
<u>from college</u> determined to continue writing. He
  53
worked at a bookstore

and became <u>then</u> a copy editor at a publishing company.
                    54
Eventually, Rivera found an artistic home in a

playwriting group called the Theater Matrix; the group

---

49. The most logical placement of Paragraph 3 is
    A. where it is now.
    B. after Paragraph 1.
    C. after Paragraph 4.
    D. after Paragraph 5.

50. F. NO CHANGE
    G. and essays in response to photographs
       from
    H. and essays in response to photographs
       from:
    J. and essays in response to photographs;
       from

51. A. NO CHANGE
    B. that when he saw the play he wanted
    C. that he wanted when he saw that play
    D. OMIT the underlined portion.

52. F. NO CHANGE
    G. is writing
    H. has written
    J. wrote

53. A. NO CHANGE
    B. Rivera returned from college after
       graduating, to New York,
    C. After graduating from college, Rivera
       returned to New York,
    D. Rivera, from graduating, returned to
       New York,

54. F. NO CHANGE
    G. (Place before *became*)
    H. (Place before *publishing*)
    J. (Place after *company*)

GO ON TO THE NEXT PAGE ▷

met on Monday nights to share their work. One of the
plays he wrote and <u>produced, *The House of Roman*</u>
                                                    55
<u>*Iglesia, received*</u> a good review by *The New York Times.*
       55
This was an important step

in Rivera's <u>career receiving</u> a good review from a major
                    56
publication led to more work. The famous television
producer Norman Lear read the review and immediately offered Rivera a job writing for Embassy Television
in California.

[5]

In order to make a living, Rivera accepted the job. He
learned a lot from the process of writing for television
shows, but there were sacrifices he had to make. He
missed writing plays and living in New York. 57 Rivera
also discovered that in the entertainment business, he
was often labeled and identified by his ethnicity. Rivera
was proud of his cultural heritage but wanted to be
acknowledged for his talent.

[5]

After many years of hard work and perseverance,
Rivera has received the recognition he deserves through
countless productions of his plays and the numerous awards he has won for playwriting. Despite the

55. A. NO CHANGE
  B. produced *The House of Roman Iglesia,*
       received
  C. produced, *The House of Roman Iglesia*
       received
  D. produced *The House of Roman Iglesia*
       received

56. F. NO CHANGE
  G. career, receiving
  H. career; receiving
  J. career receiving.

57. If the writer wanted to reinforce the main
  point made in Paragraph 5, which sentence
  would she add here?

  A. He also missed the reward of owning
       his work, because his writing became
       the property of the television shows.
  B. California is a beautiful state with a
       variety of places to visit, from beaches
       to major cities.
  C. He had the opportunity to write for
       television shows such as *Family Matters*
       and *Eerie, Indiana.*
  D. While in California, he became a
       founding member of a theater company
       in the city of Los Angeles.

GO ON TO THE NEXT PAGE ⇒

challenges of show business, José Rivera <u>has became</u>
                                              58
an important playwright whose work has an impact on

audiences worldwide.

58. F. NO CHANGE
G. is became
H. has become
J. have become

Questions 59 and 60 ask about the preceding passage as a whole.

---

59. Does this essay successfully describe the challenges faced by playwrights in the entertainment business?

A. The essay is not successful; it is a biography of the playwright José Rivera.

B. The essay is not successful; it portrays playwriting as a fun and rewarding career.

C. The essay is successful; it describes playwriting as an impossible dream for only the very lucky.

D. The essay is successful; it demonstrates the challenges through the life and work of José Rivera.

60. The writer is considering adding the following sentence:

The contrast between small-town and city life became an influence on Rivera's work.

The best placement for this detail is in:

F. Paragraph 1.
G. Paragraph 2.
H. Paragraph 5.
J. Paragraph 6.

GO ON TO THE NEXT PAGE

PASSAGE V

SIGNATURE OF THE TIME

[1] The home of Tyler Gregory looks like an abandoned bureaucratic archive. [2] Almost all of the available space <u>being crammed with old books</u> or
₆₁
covered with folios and documents. [3] Dr. Gregory, a psychologist, first began collecting old documents as a hobby.

[4] What was initially a <u>hobby quickly became a life's</u>
₆₂
passion and devotion. [5] Predictably, several papers in Dr. Gregory's collection, which includes a faded but detailed inn receipt, <u>is</u> signed by John Hancock.
₆₃
[6] Proudly displayed, the John Hancock documents <u>had represented</u> Dr. Gregory's work: graphology. [7]
₆₄
Unlike other rare and vintage document enthusiasts, Dr. Gregory collects only documents that bear famous signatures. [65]

61. **A.** NO CHANGE
    B. was crammed with old books or is
    C. is crammed with old books or
    D. crammed with old books or

62. **F.** NO CHANGE
    G. hobby, quickly became a life's
    H. hobby quickly became a life's,
    J. hobby: quickly became a life's

63. **A.** NO CHANGE
    B. are
    C. was
    D. OMIT the underlined portion.

64. **F.** NO CHANGE
    G. represent
    H. represented
    J. would have represented

65. To maintain the logic and coherence of this paragraph, Sentence 7 should be placed:

    A. where it is now.
    B. after Sentence 1.
    C. after Sentence 3.
    D. after Sentence 4.

GO ON TO THE NEXT PAGE ⟶

Graphology, <u>a growing field,</u> is used to authenticate

66

documents in court trials and other legal proceedings,

but it has other, less familiar uses as well. Psychologists

can use graphology to analyze a patient's psyche. Many

patients

cannot explain their problems, <u>but psychologists have</u>

67

<u>techniques to help patients learn to express themselves.</u>

67

Psychologists and graphologists have noted that hand-

writing

is a subconscious expression of inner thoughts. Many

of the issues involuntarily revealed <u>of</u> a subject's

68

handwriting remain unknown to the subject herself.

Unlike the patients of most psychologists who use

graphology, however, Dr. Gregory's subjects are dead.

Dr. Gregory once practiced clinical <u>psychology in the</u>

69

<u>past,</u> but his interest in graphology is a more historical

one. He studies the handwriting of

66. Which of the following true choices provides information that is most relevant and meaningful to the essay in its entirety?

   F. NO CHANGE

   G. or handwriting analysis,

   H. which has been practiced for decades,

   J. as a professional endeavor,

67. After reviewing the essay, the writer wants to insert a statement at this point that would lead into the next sentence. Given that all of the choices are true, which one best accomplishes the writer's purpose?

   A. NO CHANGE

   B. and this is one reason they seek help from professionals.

   C. but their handwriting often can.

   D. so analyzing the psyche can be challenging.

68. F. NO CHANGE

   G. from

   H. by

   J. as

69. A. NO CHANGE

   B. psychology for a time,

   C. psychology at an earlier period in his life,

   D. psychology,

GO ON TO THE NEXT PAGE ▷

historical <u>figures, hoping to</u> better understand their
70
personalities. Dr. Gregory's interest in historical

personalities stems from an interdisciplinary desire

to apply psychological theories to the explanation of

historical events. Historians and political scientists have

long sought to apply psychology and its theories to

their work, but they have not always met with success.

While such theories as organizational psychology and

cognitive dissonance have illuminated some historical

decisions, they have done so neither definitively nor

broadly. 71

70. Of the following alternatives to the underlined portion, which choice would NOT be
acceptable?

F. figures in order to

G. figures since hoping to

H. figures with the hope that he will

J. figures. He hopes to

71. If added here, which of the following
sentences would be the best choice to
conclude this paragraph and create an
effective transition to the next one?

A. This lack of widespread success has
discouraged many in the field, but not
Dr. Gregory.

B. The scarcity of information regarding
the personalities of historical figures has
been the biggest obstacle.

C. However, these theories are likely to
gain ground as more historians and
political scientists study their subjects
through a psychological lens.

D. These theories have most frequently
been applied to events from the 18th
and 19th centuries.

GO ON TO THE NEXT PAGE

Unlike current in-depth information from multiple media sources, scarcely any record exists of the private personalities and lives of history's greatest figures. The records that do exist paint skewed <u>pictures, for they</u> come almost entirely from friends, enemies, or the historical figures themselves. Thus, Dr. Gregory uses graphology to study and understand the personalities and inner lives of important men and women who lived so long ago.

Dr. Gregory, along with most graphologists, believes that a person's signature reveals more about that person's personality than normal handwriting. The signature legally and traditionally conveys the mark of an individual. This supports Dr. Gregory's <u>belief that</u> the shape of a signature also serves as a psychological

stamp. According to Dr. Gregory, a person <u>has been</u> both consciously and unconsciously imprinting key aspects of his personality while he forms a signature. Those aspects have led Dr. Gregory to infer many personal details about historical figures. Such details are now being used by historians in their analysis of historical decisions.

72. Of the following alternatives to the underlined portion, which choice would NOT be acceptable?

  F. pictures; they
  G. pictures. They
  H. pictures, as they
  J. pictures they

73. A. NO CHANGE
  B. belief, that
  C. belief that,
  D. belief: that

74. F. NO CHANGE
  G. had been
  H. will be
  J. is

GO ON TO THE NEXT PAGE

Question 75 asks about the preceding passage as a whole.

75. Suppose the writer had intended to write a short essay about an example of one area of study influencing another area of study. Would this essay achieve the writer's goal?

  A. Yes, because the essay explains how personality traits determined through analyzing a historical individual's handwriting can be used to form a psychological study of such figures and their roles in historical events.

  B. Yes, because the essay compares the research process of graphologists to the research process of historians.

  C. No, because the essay focuses on Dr. Gregory, who turned his hobby into an intellectual pursuit.

  D. No, because the essay does not discuss the findings of historians who have applied psychological theories to historical figures and events.

MATHEMATICS TEST

60 Minutes—60 Questions

Directions: Solve each of the following problems, select the correct answer, and then fill in the corresponding oval on your Answer Grid.

Don't linger over problems that are too time-consuming. Do as many as you can, then come back to the others in the time permitted.

You may use a calculator on this test. Some questions, however, may be easier to answer without the use of a calculator.

Note: Unless the question says otherwise, assume all of the following:

1. Illustrative figures are *not* necessarily drawn to scale.

2. All geometric figures lie in a plane.

3. The term *line* indicates a straight line.

4. The term *average* indicates arithmetic mean.

---

1. If $2x - 6 = 18$, then $x = $?

    A. 1.5
    B. 3.0
    C. 6.0
    D. 12.0
    E. 24.0

2. Consider the following two logical statements relating to triangle *RST*.

    If the length of side $\overline{RS}$ is 5, then the length of side $\overline{ST}$ is 8.

    The length of side $\overline{ST}$ is not 8.

    If both of these statements are true, then it follows that the length of:

    F. $\overline{RS}$ is NOT 5.
    G. $\overline{RS}$ is 5.
    H. $\overline{RS}$ is 8.
    J. $\overline{ST}$ is 5.
    K. $\overline{ST}$ is NOT 5.

3. In a raffle, Mark must draw a ticket at random from a bag. The probability that he will draw a winning ticket is 0.3. What is the probability that he will draw a losing ticket?

    A. 0.0
    B. 0.1
    C. 0.7
    D. 1.0
    E. 1.3

4. On the last geometry test, Anna's score was 94. Two of her friends each scored 89. What is the average score of these three students?

    F. $94 + \dfrac{89}{2}$

    G. $\dfrac{94}{3} + \dfrac{89}{2}$

    H. $\dfrac{94 + 89}{2}$

    J. $\dfrac{94 + 89}{3}$

    K. $\dfrac{94 + 2(89)}{3}$

GO ON TO THE NEXT PAGE

5. On Monday Tom received a bag of candy for his birthday and ate half of it. On Tuesday he ate half of the remaining candy, and on Wednesday he ate half of what remained from Tuesday. If 6 pieces of candy then remained, how many pieces of candy did he receive originally?

   A. 18
   B. 24
   C. 36
   D. 48
   E. 96

6. If $R = 4x$ and $S = 3y - x$, then what is the value of $R + S$?

   F. $3x + 3y$
   G. $3x - 3y$
   H. $4x + 3y$
   J. $4x - 3y$
   K. $5x + 3y$

7. In the figure below, l_1 is parallel to l_2, l_3 is parallel to l_4, and the lines intersect as shown. What is the measure of angle y?

   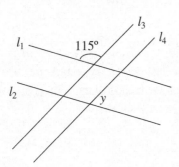

   A. 60°
   B. 65°
   C. 70°
   D. 75°
   E. Cannot be determined from the given information

8. If $x = -3$, then $-x^2 - 7x + 5 = ?$

   F. −25
   G. −7
   H. 14
   J. 17
   K. 35

9. The average of five numbers is 85. If each of the numbers is increased by 4, what is the average of the five new numbers?

   A. 80
   B. 81
   C. 85
   D. 87
   E. 89

10. The expression $3x + 9y$ is equivalent to which of the following?

    F. $3(x + y)$
    G. $12(x + y)$
    H. $3(x + 3y)$
    J. $3xy$
    K. $12xy$

11. For each month on your phone bill you pay $20 plus a fixed amount for every minute of long distance calls. In May you used 80 long distance minutes and your bill was $28. In June you used 20 more long distance minutes than in May. What was the charge on your phone bill in June?

    A. $20.00
    B. $28.20
    C. $29.00
    D. $30.00
    E. $32.50

GO ON TO THE NEXT PAGE ⟩

12. If $\dfrac{6}{x} \geq \dfrac{3}{4}$, what is the largest possible value for x?

   F. $\dfrac{1}{2}$

   G. 2

   H. 4

   J. 7

   K. 8

13. The hands of a clock are both pointing to 12 at noon. By 8 PM, what is the number of degrees the *hour* hand has moved?

   A. 80°

   B. 96°

   C. 120°

   D. 160°

   E. 240°

14. In the standard (x,y) coordinate plane below, $\triangle LMN$ and $\triangle NOP$ are right isosceles triangles with equal areas. Points M, N, O, and P are located on the axes as shown. Which of the following could be the coordinates of point L?

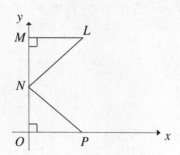

   F. $(0,6)$

   G. $(6,0)$

   H. $(6,12)$

   J. $(12,0)$

   K. $(12,6)$

15. Which of the following equations has both $x = 5$ and $x = -7$ as solutions?

   A. $(x - 5)(x + 7) = 0$

   B. $(x - 5)(-x + 7) = 0$

   C. $(x + 5)(x + 7) = 0$

   D. $(x + 5)(x - 7) = 0$

   E. $x - 5 = x + 7$

16. The grocery store opens each day with $(r + s)$ dollars in each cash register. If the store has t cash registers, which of the following is an expression for the total amount of money, in dollars, in the grocery store?

   F. $(t \cdot r) + s$

   G. $(t \cdot r) + (t \cdot s)$

   H. $(t \cdot s) + r$

   J. $(t \cdot r \cdot s)$

   K. $t + r + s$

17. If 30% of x equals 60, then $x = $?

   A.　　2

   B.　　18

   C.　　200

   D.　1,800

   E.　2,000

18. A school is selling t-shirts as a fund raiser. For the first 100 t-shirts that are sold, the school will earn 7 dollars per shirt. For each additional shirt that is sold, the school will earn 10 dollars. How much will the school earn if 350 t-shirts are sold?

   F. $ 245

   G. $ 250

   H. $2,450

   J. $3,200

   K. $4,200

GO ON TO THE NEXT PAGE ⟩

19. You want to buy a salad for lunch. The price on the menu is $3.99, and the cashier is going to add a sales tax of 7% of the $3.99 (rounded to the nearest cent) to the price of the salad. You are going to pay with a five-dollar bill. How much change should the cashier return to you?

A. 7¢

B. 27¢

C. 28¢

D. 73¢

E. 93¢

20. For which nonnegative value of x is the expression $\dfrac{1}{x^2 - 4}$ undefined?

F. 0

G. 2

H. 4

J. 8

K. 16

21. What is the correct ordering of π, $3\frac{1}{4}$, and 3.5, from greatest to least?

A. $\pi > 3\frac{1}{4} > 3.5\pi$

B. $\pi > 3.5 > 3\frac{1}{4}$

C. $3.5 > 3\frac{1}{4} > \pi$

D. $3.5 > \pi > 3\frac{1}{4}$

E. $3\frac{1}{4} > 3.5 > \pi$

22. Ashley has wrapped a box that measures 20 inches (in) wide, 15 in long, and 4 in tall, as shown below. She wants to tie a single piece of string around the box. If Ashley needs 4 additional inches of string to tie a bow, what is the minimum length, in inches, of string she will need to wrap around the box in both directions, as shown below?

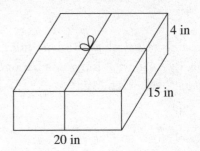

F. 39

G. 43

H. 47

J. 82

K. 90

23. To make the color you want to paint your house, you have to mix 5 parts white paint with 3 parts blue paint. How many quarts of blue paint will you need to make 24 quarts of this color?

A. 3

B. 5

C. 8

D. 9

E. 15

24. Which of the following gives all of the solutions of $x^2 + x = 30$?

F. −6 and 5

G. −5 and 6

H. −2 and 15

J.   2 and 15

K. 15 only

GO ON TO THE NEXT PAGE

25. If $(a - b)^2 = 36$ and $ab = 24$, then $a^2 + b^2 = ?$

    A. −12

    B. 12

    C. 60

    D. 84

    E. 96

26. If, for all x, $(x^{3b - 1})^2 = x^{16}$, then $b = ?$

    F. 1

    G. $\dfrac{5}{3}$

    H. $\dfrac{5}{4}$

    J. 3

    K. $\dfrac{16}{3}$

27. Given the complex number i such that $i^2 = -1$, what is the value of $i^2 - i^4$?

    A. −2

    B. −1

    C. 0

    D. 1

    E. 2

28. $\overline{AB}$ is a line segment in the standard (x,y) coordinate plane with endpoints A and B. If point A has the coordinates $(5,-4)$ and the midpoint of $\overline{AB}$ has coordinates $(-2,4)$ what are the coordinates of point B?

    F. (−9,12)

    G. (−3,−16)

    H. (3,−16)

    J. (3,−1)

    K. (9,12)

29. A circle in the standard (x,y) coordinate plane has the equation $(x + 2)^2 + (y - 2)^2 = 5$. What is the radius of the circle?

    A. −2

    B. $\sqrt{2}$

    C. 2

    D. $\sqrt{5}$

    E. 5

30. The right triangle pictured below has side lengths a, b, and c. What is the value of $\sin \beta$?

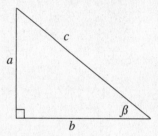

    F. $\dfrac{a}{b}$

    G. $\dfrac{a}{c}$

    H. $\dfrac{b}{a}$

    J. $\dfrac{b}{c}$

    K. $\dfrac{c}{a}$

31. For all nonzero x and y, $\dfrac{(16x^2y^2)(6x^2y^4)}{-8x^2y^3} = ?$

    A. $-12y^3$

    B. $-12x^2y^2$

    C. $-12x^2y^3$

    D. $\dfrac{x^2y^2}{12}$

    E. $\dfrac{12}{y}$

GO ON TO THE NEXT PAGE

32. Three parallel lines are intersected by transversals, as shown below. The points of intersection are labeled. $\overline{QR}$ measures 3 inches, $\overline{RS}$ measures 5 inches, and $\overline{UV}$ measures 7 inches. What is the length of $\overline{TU}$, in inches?

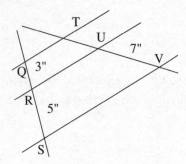

F. 3

G. 4

H. 5

J. $\dfrac{21}{5}$

K. $\dfrac{16}{5}$

33. In the figure below, the circle centered at O has radii $\overline{OA}$ and $\overline{OB}$. $\triangle AOB$ is a right isosceles triangle. If the area of $\triangle AOB$ is 18 square units, what is the area of the circle, in units?

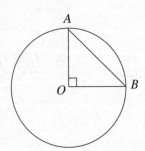

A. 12π

B. 18π

C. 36π

D. 72π

E. 81π

34. Which of the following represents the same set as the figure shown below?

F. $x \le -5$ or $x > 4$

G. $x > -5$ or $x \le 4$

H. $x \ge -5$ or $x < 4$

J. $x > -5$ and $x \le 4$

K. $x \ge -5$ and $x < 4$

35. Jen has built a straight slide from her tree house to her sand box. The top of the slide, directly above the base of the tree house, is 9 feet from the ground. The slide touches the ground 12 feet from the base of the tree house. What is the length of the slide, in feet?

A. $3\sqrt{7}$

B. $6\sqrt{3}$

C. 15

D. 25

E. 108

36. If a and b are real numbers, and $\sqrt{3\left(\dfrac{a^2}{b}\right)} = 2$, then what must be true of b?

F. b must be positive

G. b must be negative

H. b must equal $\dfrac{2}{3}$

J. b must equal 3

K. b may have any value

37. The numbers 84 and 96 are both divisible by n, a real positive integer. Neither 18 nor 16 is divisible by n. What is the sum of the digits of n?

   A. 1

   B. 3

   C. 4

   D. 5

   E. 6

38. In the standard (x,y) coordinate plane, line R is parallel to the x-axis. What is the slope of R?

   F. –1

   G. 0

   H. 1

   J. Undefined

   K. Cannot be determined from the given information

39. Which of the following lines has the same slope as $y = 2x - 1$?

   A. $-y = 2x - 1$

   B. $y = 3x - 1$

   C. $y = 4x + 2$

   D. $4y = 2x + 6$

   E. $5y = 10x + 2$

40. The two triangles in the figure below share a common side. What is $\sin (x + y)$?

(Note: For all x and y, $\sin (x + y) = \sin x \cos y + \sin y \cos x$.)

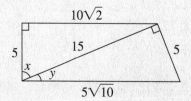

   F. $\dfrac{1}{5\sqrt{10}}$

   G. $\dfrac{12\sqrt{5} + \sqrt{10}}{30}$

   H. $\dfrac{6\sqrt{5} + 3\sqrt{10}}{20}$

   J. $\dfrac{2\sqrt{2} + \sqrt{10}}{3}$

   K. $5\sqrt{10}$

41. Julie can type 3 pages in x minutes. How many minutes will it take her to type 11 pages?

   A. $33x$

   B. $\dfrac{3}{11x}$

   C. $\dfrac{11}{3x}$

   D. $\dfrac{3x}{11}$

   E. $\dfrac{11x}{3}$

GO ON TO THE NEXT PAGE

42. Which of the following will result in an odd integer for any integer a?

F. a^2

G. $3a^2$

H. $4a^2$

J. $3a^2 + 1$

K. $4a^2 + 1$

43. In $\triangle RST$, $\angle R$ is a right angle and $\angle S$ measures $60°$. If $\overline{ST}$ is 8 inches long, what is the area of $\triangle RST$ in square inches?

A. 8

B. $8\sqrt{3}$

C. 16

D. 32

E. $32\sqrt{3}$

44. Right triangle ABC, below, has lengths as marked. If $\overline{DE}$ is the perpendicular bisector of $\overline{AC}$, what is the ratio of the length of $\overline{AB}$ to the length of $\overline{DE}$?

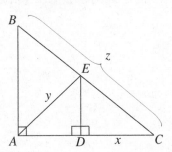

F. $\dfrac{1}{2}$

G. $\dfrac{x}{y}$

H. $\dfrac{y}{x}$

J. $\dfrac{y}{z}$

K. $\dfrac{z}{y}$

45. The figure below is composed of a square and a semicircle. The radius of the semicircle is r and the side of the square is $2r$. Suppose r is doubled. How many times the area of the original figure is the area of the new figure?

A. 2

B. 3

C. 4

D. 8

E. 10

46. For what value of x would the following system of equations have an infinite number of solutions?

$$4a - b = 4$$
$$16a - 4b = 8x$$

F. 2

G. 4

H. 6

J. 16

K. 24

47. Sally and Samir left their camp at the same time. Sally walked at a constant rate of 3 miles per hour. She walked 20 minutes north, then 40 minutes east. Samir walked at a constant rate of 2 miles per hour. He walked 20 minutes south, then 40 minutes east. Which of the following is an expression for the number of miles apart Samir and Sally were one hour after they left camp?

A. $1(3-2)$

B. $\sqrt{\left(1-\dfrac{2}{3}\right)^2+\left(2-\dfrac{4}{3}\right)^2}$

C. $\sqrt{\left(1+\dfrac{2}{3}\right)^2+\left(2-\dfrac{4}{3}\right)^2}$

D. $\sqrt{\left(1+\dfrac{2}{3}\right)^2+\left(2+\dfrac{4}{3}\right)^2}$

E. $\sqrt{\left(1-\dfrac{2}{3}\right)^2\left(2-\dfrac{4}{3}\right)^2}$

48. A golf ball is at a point on the ground that is 20 feet from the base of a flag pole, as shown below. The angle of elevation from this point to the top of the vertical flag pole is 35°. What is the height, in feet, of the flag pole?

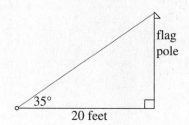

F. 20cos 35°

G. 20cot 35°

H. 20sec 35°

J. 20sin 35°

K. 20tan 35°

49. The shaded portion of the figure below represents a parallelogram. Side lengths are indicated in inches. What is the area of the parallelogram, in square inches?

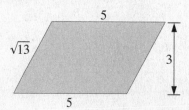

A. 5

B. 15

C. $\sqrt{13}$

D. $\sqrt{26}$

E. $2\sqrt{13}$

50. Three points, A, B, and C, lie on the same line. The length of $\overline{AB}$ is 8 units, and the length of $\overline{BC}$ is 2 units. Which of the following gives all of the possible lengths for $\overline{AC}$?

F. 6 only

G. 10 only

H. 6 and 10 only

J. Any number less than 6 or greater than 10

K. Any number greater than 6 and less than 10

GO ON TO THE NEXT PAGE

51. Given the vertices of $\triangle ABC$ in the standard (x,y) coordinate plane below, what is the area of $\triangle ABC$ in square units?

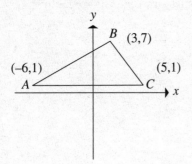

- **A.** 22.0
- **B.** 32.0
- **C.** 33.0
- **D.** 40.0
- **E.** 66.0

52. If $-3x^2y^3 > 0$, which of the following CANNOT be true?

- **F.** $x = y$
- **G.** $x < 0$
- **H.** $x > 0$
- **J.** $y < 0$
- **K.** $y > 0$

53. If the first term in a geometric sequence is x, and the second term is nx, what is the 30th term in the sequence?

- **A.** $n^{29}x$
- **B.** $n^{30}x$
- **C.** $n^{31}x$
- **D.** $(nx)^{29}$
- **E.** $(nx)^{30}$

54. A system of two linear equations in two variables has NO solution. One of the equations is graphed in the (x,y) coordinate plane as shown below. Which of the following could be the equation of the other line?

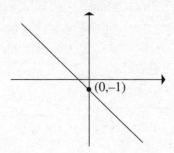

- **F.** $y = x + 1$
- **G.** $y = -x - 1$
- **H.** $y = x + 2$
- **J.** $y = -x + 2$
- **K.** $y = 1$

55. If $0° \leq n \leq 90°$ and $\cos n = \dfrac{15}{17}$, then $\tan n = ?$

- **A.** $\dfrac{8}{17}$
- **B.** $\dfrac{8}{15}$
- **C.** $\dfrac{17}{15}$
- **D.** $\dfrac{15}{8}$
- **E.** $\dfrac{17}{8}$

GO ON TO THE NEXT PAGE

56. For every cent decrease in the price of milk, a grocery sells 10 more gallons of milk per day. Right now, the store is selling 65 gallons of milk per day at $2.25 per gallon. Which of the following expressions represents the number of gallons that will be sold per day if the cost is reduced by c cents?

   F. $65(2.25 - c)$

   G. $2.25(10c + 65)$

   H. $(2.25 - c)(10c + 65)$

   J. $2.25 - c$

   K. $65 + 10c$

57. A group of 100 students are being divided into 10 teams for a relay race. Each student will draw and keep a token from a bag of tokens numbered 00 through 99. Students who draw tokens numbered with the same tens digit will be on the same team. (Students with numbers between 00 and 09, for example, will be on the same team.) Ann is the first student to draw, and she draws 56. If Elizabeth is the second student to draw, what is the probability that she will be on Ann's team?

   A. $\dfrac{1}{8}$

   B. $\dfrac{1}{9}$

   C. $\dfrac{1}{10}$

   D. $\dfrac{1}{11}$

   E. $\dfrac{1}{99}$

58. The figure below shows a cross-section of Dave's room, which is 10 feet long and 8 feet wide. The walls are perfectly vertical, and the floor is horizontal. The ceiling is horizontal for 6 feet, then slopes down as shown. The ceiling is 7 feet from the floor at one end of the room and 4 feet from the floor at the other end. As a prank, Dave's friends are planning to fill his room with packing peanuts. How many cubic feet of packing peanuts will they need to fill Dave's entire room from floor to ceiling (assuming there is nothing in the room)?

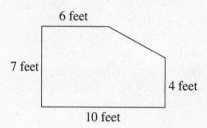

   F. 64

   G. 336

   H. 368

   J. 512

   K. 560

GO ON TO THE NEXT PAGE

59. In the figure below, line *l* has the equation $y = x$. Line *m* is perpendicular to *l* and intercepts the *x*-axis at (3,0). Which of the following is an equation for *m*?

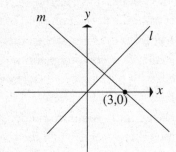

A. $y = x + 3\sqrt{2}$

B. $y = x + 3$

C. $y = -x + 3$

D. $y = -x + 3\sqrt{2}$

E. $y = -3x + 3$

60. What is the smallest possible value for the product of two real numbers that differ by 8?

F. −64

G. −16

H. −8

J. 0

K. 16

READING TEST

35 Minutes—40 Questions

Directions: There are four passages in this test. Each passage is followed by several questions. After reading a passage, choose the best answer to each question and fill in the corresponding oval on your Answer Grid. You may refer to the passages as often as necessary.

PASSAGE I

PROSE FICTION

This passage is adapted from Howard's End, *by E.M. Forster (1910). Two sisters, Helen and Margaret, are attending an orchestra performance with friends and family.*

It will be generally admitted that Beethoven's *Fifth Symphony* is the most sublime noise that has ever penetrated into the ear of man. All sorts and
Line conditions are satisfied by it. Whether you are like
(5) Mrs. Munt, and tap surreptitiously when the tunes come—of course, not so as to disturb the others— or like Helen, who can see heroes and shipwrecks in the music's flood; or like Margaret, who can only see the music; or like Tibby, who is profoundly
(10) versed in counterpoint, and holds the full score of the symphony open on his knee; or like Fraulein Mosebach's young man, who can remember nothing but Fraulein Mosebach: in any case, the passion of your life becomes more vivid, and you
(15) are bound to admit that such a noise is cheap at two shillings. It is cheap, even if you hear it in the Queen's Hall, dreariest music-room in London, though not as dreary as the Free Trade Hall, Manchester; and even if you sit on the extreme left
(20) of that hall, so that the brass bumps at you before the rest of the orchestra arrives, it is still cheap.

"Whom is Margaret talking to?" said Mrs. Munt, at the conclusion of the first movement. She was again in London on a visit to Wickham Place.
(25) Helen looked down the long line of their party, and said that she did not know.

"Would it be some young man or other whom she takes an interest in?"

"I expect so," Helen replied. Music enwrapped
(30) her, and she could not be bothered by the

distinction that divides young men whom one takes an interest in from young men whom one knows.

"You girls are so wonderful in always having—
(35) Oh dear! One mustn't talk."

For the Andante had begun—very beautiful, but bearing a family likeness to all the other beautiful andantes that Beethoven had written, and, to Helen's mind, rather disconnecting the heroes
(40) and shipwrecks of the first movement from the heroes and goblins of the third. She heard the tune through once, and then her attention wandered, and she gazed at the audience, or the organ, or the architecture. Then Beethoven started decorating
(45) his tune, so she heard him through once more, and then she smiled at her Cousin Frieda. But Frieda, listening to classical music, could not respond. Herr Liesecke, too, looked as if wild horses could not make him inattentive; there were lines across his
(50) forehead, his lips were parted, his glasses at right angles to his nose, and he had laid a thick, white hand on either knee. And next to her was Aunt Juley, so British, and wanting to tap. How interesting that row of people was! What diverse influences
(55) had gone into the making of them! Here Beethoven, after humming and hawing with great sweetness, said "Heigho," and the Andante came to an end. Applause ensued, and a round of praise volleying from the audience. Margaret started talking to her
(60) new young man; Helen said to her aunt: "Now comes the wonderful movement: first of all the goblins, and then a trio of elephants dancing"; and Tibby implored the company generally to look out for the transitional passage on the drum.

GO ON TO THE NEXT PAGE ▷

(65)   "On the what, dear?"

"On the drum, Aunt Juley."

"No—look out for the part where you think you are done with the goblins and they come back," breathed Helen, as the music started with a goblin
(70) walking quietly over the universe, from end to end. Others followed him. They were not aggressive creatures; that was what made them so terrible to Helen. They merely observed in passing that there was no such thing as splendor or heroism in the
(75) world. Helen could not contradict them, for once, she had felt the same, and had seen the reliable walls of youth collapse. Panic and emptiness! Panic and emptiness! The goblins were right. Her brother raised his finger; it was the transitional passage on
(80) the drum.

Helen pushed her way out during the applause. She desired to be alone. The music had summed up to her all that had happened or could happen in her life.
(85)   She read it as a tangible statement, which could never be superseded. The notes meant this and that to her, and they could have no other meaning, and life could have no other meaning. She pushed right out of the building and walked slowly down the
(90) outside staircase, breathing the autumnal air, and then she strolled home.

1. Helen would most likely agree with which of the following statements about her relationship with Margaret?

    A. Helen disapproves of Margaret's actions.

    B. Helen's feelings toward Margaret are affected by Helen's jealousy of the attention Margaret receives from suitors.

    C. Helen is not interested in Margaret's actions, at least as long as the music is playing.

    D. They are drawn together principally by their mutual love of music.

2. Helen can most accurately be characterized as:

    F. creative and effervescent.

    G. analytical yet optimistic.

    H. imaginative and introspective.

    J. curt and insensitive.

3. Which of the following statements does NOT describe one of Helen's reactions to the goblins?

    A. She feels that their presence is a denial of the good in the world.

    B. She is frightened by the goblins' aggressive nature.

    C. She cannot deny the viewpoint that the goblins seem to represent.

    D. She believes that the goblins will return after they appear to have left.

4. The main point of the first paragraph is that:

    F. the characters in the story react to the performance in different ways.

    G. Beethoven's *Fifth Symphony* is an outstanding musical accomplishment.

    H. musicians are not being paid in proportion to their talents.

    J. the poor quality of the auditorium keeps Helen's party from enjoying the concert.

5. The main point of the last paragraph is that Helen believes that:

    A. peace can only be found through acceptance of her fate.

    B. life is a meaningless endeavor that must be endured alone.

    C. the music has foretold her future.

    D. the music has told her unchangeable truths about life.

GO ON TO THE NEXT PAGE

6. According to the passage, when Tibby listens to the symphony he is:

   F. most interested in the technical aspects of the music.

   G. caught up in imagery that the music conveys to him.

   H. distracted from the performance as a whole because of his focus on the drum.

   J. depressed by his dreary surroundings.

7. Which of the following statements most accurately expresses Helen's feelings as she leaves after the symphony?

   A. Helen feels alienated by the indifference of her companions.

   B. Helen is meditative, pondering the music's immutable meaning.

   C. Helen is upset with Tibby's constant focus on the technical aspects of the music.

   D. Helen is relieved to have escaped the crowding and discomfort of the performance hall.

8. It can most reasonably be inferred from the passage that the reason Aunt Juley refrains from tapping along with the music is because:

   F. Aunt Juley is concentrating instead on the drum.

   G. Aunt Juley does not want to distract Helen.

   H. British custom only permits snapping one's fingers along with the music.

   J. Aunt Juley feels it would not be appropriate.

9. Based on the passage, it can be inferred that each of the following characters is deeply interested in the music being played EXCEPT:

   A. Herr Liesecke.

   B. Margaret.

   C. Fraulein Mosebach's young man.

   D. Tibby.

10. According to the passage, the reason why Helen's attention returns to the Andante after it had wandered is because she:

    F. hears changes in the tune.

    G. is directed to do so by Tibby.

    H. no longer wishes to speak with Mrs. Munt.

    J. believes the Andante is nearing its end.

PASSAGE II

SOCIAL SCIENCE

The following passage is adapted from the article "What Causes Overweight and Obesity" released by the National Heart, Lung and Blood Institute.

The past 10 years have seen a dramatic rise in "diseases of affluence" in the United States. Americans suffer from type II diabetes, obesity, and cardiovascular disease in epidemic proportions.
Line
(5) Indeed, American culture is often perceived to be entrenched in fast-food, excessive consumption, and minimal physical exertion. Supermarkets and restaurants in the United States serve a panoply of processed foods loaded with sugar, preservatives,
(10) trans-fats and cholesterol. Children develop poor eating habits—from sugar-laden cereals to school lunches drenched in saturated fat—that, unfortunately, last into adulthood. While changes in diet are partly responsible for American obesity, the
(15) primary cause of obesity is the sedentary lifestyle that 40 percent of Americans currently lead.

GO ON TO THE NEXT PAGE ▷

For most of human history, people worked as farmers, hunters, laborers, and tradesmen—all physically demanding occupations. Blacksmiths (20) hammered metal, servants washed dirty linen, and farmers lifted hay bails by hand. At the time, the only sources of work energy were animals or man power. However, these lifestyles afforded people vast stretches of idle time—winter (25) months, religious holidays, and festivals—to rest and recover. Furthermore, routine and leisure activities also required more physical exertion. For all but the wealthy, everyday life was similar to a balanced gym routine. Despite high mortality (30) from infectious diseases and malnutrition (and debilitating physical injuries suffered in far more hazardous working environments than today's workplace), physical fitness was standard.

Urbanization and industrialization during the (35) 19th and 20th centuries drastically changed people's life-styles. Agricultural advances have led to increasingly larger farms manned by fewer workers. Machines are used for most aspects of farming, from sowing seeds to harvesting. Manufacturing, (40) meanwhile, transformed into a system of mass production facilitated by machines—a process that does not require the range or degree of physical exertion from workers as was necessitated by pre-industrial fabrication. People began to move less (45) and sit more. During the 20th century, increasingly elaborate systems of government and finance brought about the most sedentary workplace of all: the office building. Suddenly massive complexes peopled by legions of clerks, salespeople, analysts, (50) and secretaries manning telephones, computers, and typewriters began to fill the American city. Urbanization condensed all aspects of living into a few square blocks. The conveniences of the modern urban environment are also conducive to inactivity. (55) Transportation has also exacerbated the problem by offering city dwellers numerous options for travel, none of which require any real physical exertion. Therefore, the average 9-to-5 worker can go to work, run errands, and seek entertainment with (60) little more effort than what is required to walk to and from a car or a mass transit station.

Leisure has likewise contributed to the obesity epidemic. Watching television and playing video games have supplanted sports, leisurely strolls, (65) and horse-riding as popular pastimes. Pre-studies have revealed a positive correlation between hours of television viewing and levels of obesity. In fact, video games are found to play an especially significant role in childhood obesity.

(70) Despite the proliferation of gimmick diets and fancy gadgets, losing weight is actually a simple matter of burning more calories than one consumes. Active living initiatives are working hard to bring more movement into the average (75) American's life. Urban planners are designing cities that include more sidewalks, crosswalks, parks, and bicycle trails. Education programs and advertising campaigns seek to reform the deleterious habits of adults and create more active lifestyles in children. (80) Parents and nutritionists are working together to banish some of the more egregious offenders— fries, pizza, and soda—from public school cafeterias.

In the 21st century, the stakes for combating (85) obesity in the United States are increasingly high. As an overweight baby boom generation enters its twilight, insurance providers and health care professionals are encountering alarming rates of diabetes and heart disease. American life (90) expectancy has begun to drop from all-time highs during the late 1990s. Even more concerning is the earlier onset of obesity in younger generations. Given that the World Health Organization has estimated 60 percent of the global population get (95) insufficient exercise, finding a way to get people back in shape is perhaps the greatest health care issue that the world currently faces.

GO ON TO THE NEXT PAGE ⟶

11. The main purpose of the first paragraph in relation to the passage as a whole is to:

   A. emphasize the role of overeating in America's health problems.

   B. undermine the theory that Americans don't get enough exercise.

   C. discuss the factors at play in America's obesity pandemic.

   D. criticize the lifestyles of pre-industrial Americans.

12. According to the passage, all of the following are aspects of pre-industrial culture responsible for promoting physical fitness EXCEPT:

   F. the hazardous conditions of the 19th century workplace.

   G. the variation of physical activity required by most occupations.

   H. the absence of alternative energy source for performing tasks.

   J. the vigor of pastime activities.

13. The author most likely included lines 17–33 to:

   A. provide examples of typical pre-industrial occupations that have been rendered obsolete.

   B. cite occupations that necessitated human energy for successful completion.

   C. recommend jobs that modern Americans should pursue to counter obesity.

   D. explain why consuming foods rich in calories was more acceptable in past eras.

14. The third paragraph details the effects of industrialization on the workplace by:

   F. citing the hazards of the modern workplace.

   G. lamenting the working conditions in office buildings.

   H. praising the efficiency of modern farming and manufacturing.

   J. indicating specific ways in which modern workers do less physical work.

15. The author's attitude toward the 9-to-5 worker mentioned in lines 58–61 can best be described as:

   A. dismayed.

   B. envious.

   C. judgmental.

   D. objective.

16. The passage suggests which of the following about television?

   F. There is an inverse relationship between television viewing and obesity.

   G. Watching television directly causes obesity in viewers.

   H. People who watch more television are more likely to be obese.

   J. The obese enjoy television more than fit viewers.

17. According to the passage, losing weight:

   A. is essential to avoiding health problems in later life.

   B. can be achieved only through excessive levels of physical exertion.

   C. is possible when caloric intake exceeds energy burned through activity.

   D. requires a deficit between consumption and metabolism.

GO ON TO THE NEXT PAGE

18. The author most likely mentions diets and exercise machines to:

    F. contrast public opinion with the simplicity of losing weight.

    G. give examples of effective weight loss techniques.

    H. critique nontraditional methods of combating obesity.

    J. emphasize the ease of using modern exercise machines.

19. Based on the passage, health-conscious families and experts' attitudes toward public school lunches can best be described as:

    A. ambivalent.

    B. inimical.

    C. apathetic.

    D. enthralled.

20. The author most likely mentions *life expectancy* in lines 89–90 in order to:

    F. emphasize the longevity of Americans during the 1990s.

    G. indicate that obesity has innocuous effects on older Americans.

    H. illustrate long-term effects of obesity in the U.S. population.

    J. contrast American health with the health of people in other countries.

PASSAGE III

HUMANITIES

This passage is excerpted from "Mr. Bennett and Mrs. Woolf," by Irving Howe. Reprinted by permission of The New Republic, © *1990, The New Republic, LLC.*

Literary polemics come and go, sparking a season of anger and gossip, and then turning to dust. A handful survive their moment:
Line Dr. Johnson's demolition of Soames Jenyn, Hazlitt's
(5) attack on Coleridge. But few literary polemics can have been so damaging, or so lasting in consequences, as Virginia Woolf's 1924 essay "Mr. Bennett and Mrs. Brown," about the once widely read English novelists Arnold Bennett,
(10) H. G. Wells, and John Galsworthy. For several literary generations now, Woolf's essay has been taken as the definitive word finishing off an old-fashioned school of fiction and thereby clearing the way for literary modernism. Writing with her glistening
(15) charm, and casting herself as the voice of the new (always a shrewd strategy in literary debate), Woolf quickly seized the high ground in her battle with Bennett. Against her needling thrusts, the old fellow never had a chance.
(20) The debate has been nicely laid out by Samuel Hynes in *Edwardian Occasions*, and I owe to him some of the following details. It all began in 1917, with Woolf's review of a collection of Bennett's literary pieces, a rather favorable review marred
(25) by the stylish snobbism that was becoming a trademark of the Bloomsbury circle. Bennett, wrote Woolf, had a materialistic view of the world—"he had been worrying himself to achieve infantile realisms." A catchy phrase, though exactly what
(30) "infantile realisms" meant Woolf did not trouble to say. During the next few years she kept returning to the attack, as if to prepare for "Mr. Bennett and Mrs. Brown." More than personal sensibilities or rivalries of status was involved here, though
(35) both were quite visible; Woolf was intent upon discrediting, if not simply dismissing, a group of literary predecessors who enjoyed a large readership.

GO ON TO THE NEXT PAGE ⇨

In 1923 Bennett reviewed Woolf's novel *Jacob's Room*, praising its "originality" and "exquisite" prose
(40) but concluding that "the characters do not vitally survive in the mind." For Bennett, this was a fatal flaw. And for his readers, too—though not for the advanced literary public that by now was learning to suspect this kind of talk about "characters
(45) surviving" as a lazy apology for the shapeless and perhaps even mindless Victorian novel.

A year later Woolf published her famous essay, brilliantly sketching an imaginary old lady named Mrs. Brown whom she supplied with anecdotes
(50) and reflections as tokens of inner being. These released the sort of insights, suggested Woolf, that would not occur to someone like Bennett, a writer obsessed with dull particulars of setting (weather, town, clothing, furniture, and so on). Were Bennett
(55) to write about a Mrs. Brown, he would describe her house in conscientious detail but never penetrate her essential life, for—what a keen polemicist!— "he is trying to hypnotize us into the belief that, because he has made a house, there must be a
(60) person living there." (Herself sensitive to the need for a room with a view, Woolf seemed indifferent to what a house might mean for people who had risen somewhat in the world. For a writer like Bennett, however, imagining a house was part of the way to
(65) locate "a person living there.") And in a quiet put-down of Bennett's novel *Hilda Lessways* (not one of his best), Woolf gave a turn of the knife: "One line of insight would have done more than all those lines of description."
(70) From the suave but deadly attack of "Mr. Bennett and Mrs. Brown" Bennett's literary reputation never quite recovered. He remained popular with the general public, but among literary readers, the sort that became the public for the emerging modernists,
(75) the standard view has long been that he was a middling, plodding sort of Edwardian writer whose work has been pushed aside by the revolutionary achievements of Lawrence, Joyce, and to a smaller extent Woolf herself.
(80) When Bennett died in 1930, Woolf noted in her diary that "he had some real understand-ing power, as well as a gigantic absorbing power [and] direct contact with life"—all attributes, you

might suppose, handy for a novelist but for her
(85) evidently not sufficient. In saying this, remarks Hynes, "Woolf gave Bennett, perhaps, the 'reality gift' that [she] doubted in herself, the gift that she despised and envied." Yes; in much of her fiction Woolf resembles Stevens's man with the blue guitar
(90) who "cannot bring a world quite round/Although I patch it as I can." Still, none of this kept Woolf from steadily sniping at Bennett's "shopkeeping view of literature." Bennett was a provincial from the Five Towns; Bennett was commercially successful;
(95) Bennett was an elder to be pulled down, as elders must always be pulled down even if they are also admired a little.

21. Which of the following statements best char-acterizes the author's view of Virginia Woolf?

   A. Woolf criticized others only in areas where she felt strong, leaving her own weaknesses out of the discussion.

   B. Woolf only disparaged Bennett and his school of authors because she envied the strides they had made.

   C. Woolf almost single-handedly changed the prevailing opinion about a partic-ular writer and laid the path for a new school of literature.

   D. Woolf's views toward the venerated authors of the day were abusive, and her reputation has rightly suffered as a result of those attacks.

GO ON TO THE NEXT PAGE ⟶

22. In lines 58–60, the phrase "he is trying to hypnotize us into the belief that, because he has made a house, there must be a person living there" is an example of which of the following general ideas in the passage?

    F. Woolf's dismissal of the social and economic differences between herself and Bennett, and the effect of that difference on their priorities in writing

    G. Woolf's view that Bennett fails to address the elements necessary to portray fully developed characters

    H. Woolf's recognition of Bennett's obsession with material goods

    J. The author's belief that Woolf revolutionized the view of literary polemics

23. In the first paragraph, the author compares Woolf's polemic against Bennett to other literary attacks. This comparison supports the author's view that:

    A. Bennett's dull style of writing would soon have fallen out of fashion anyway.

    B. many such attacks are remembered as turning points for the arts.

    C. Woolf fought with other authors often.

    D. Woolf's criticisms of Bennett were especially important and memorable.

24. According to the passage, Bennett's literary output was marked by:

    F. description of the scene rather than insight into the characters.

    G. the use of colorful characters who frequently reveal their deepest emotions.

    H. fewer essays than Woolf wrote.

    J. exhaustive description of minute details.

25. It can be reasonably inferred from the passage that the author means to:

    A. demonstrate an effective strategy for writing a literary polemic.

    B. suggest a new interpretation of a well-known literary polemic.

    C. analyze one literary polemic and its effect on the literature of its era.

    D. assess the significance of a literary polemic in the context of similar works.

26. Based on the passage, it is most reasonable to infer that Woolf's phrase *infantile realisms* (line 30) means:

    F. a focus on things rather than on people.

    G. the values of the Bloomsbury Circle.

    H. the type of writing that doesn't survive in the reader's mind.

    J. the superficial details of Mrs. Brown's house.

27. In the final sentence of the passage, the author suggests that Woolf believed that "elders must always be pulled down." This same sentiment is most closely exemplified by which of the following examples from the passage?

    A. The author's view of Woolf's novel *Jacob's Room*

    B. The author's view of *Edwardian Occasions* by Samuel Hynes

    C. The author's comparison of Woolf to "Stevens's man with the blue guitar"

    D. The author's reference to Bennett's *Hilda Lessways* as "not one of his best"

GO ON TO THE NEXT PAGE

28. Bennett's general opinion of Woolf's novel *Jacob's Room* was that it was:

    F. inferior to other novels published at that time.

    G. a keen example of a new style of literature.

    H. a success, despite one or two minor failings.

    J. generally original and inspired, but with significant problems.

29. It is Woolf's opinion that the thoughts and feelings of characters are more important than the details of a scene because:

    A. scenic descriptions were part of a literary style that she disliked.

    B. scenic details cannot convey a sense of the character within.

    C. good authors know to include at least one line of insight into a character.

    D. scenic details create characters that are easily forgettable.

30. Without the last paragraph, the passage as a whole would not include an example of:

    F. Woolf criticizing Bennett.

    G. Woolf praising Bennett.

    H. Bennett praising Woolf.

    J. the author of the passage criticizing Woolf.

PASSAGE IV

NATURAL SCIENCE

Fossil fuels are energy-rich substances formed from the remains of organisms. Both coal and petroleum help power commercial energy throughout the world.

PASSAGE A

Coal is a solid fossil fuel formed from the remains of land plants that flourished 300 to 400 million years ago. It is composed primarily of
Line carbon but also contains small amounts of sulfur.
(5) When the sulfur is released into the atmosphere as a result of burning, it can form SO_2, a corrosive gas that can damage plants and animals. When it combines with H_2O in the atmosphere, it can form sulfuric acid, one of the main components of acid
(10) rain, which has been demonstrated to be an environmental hazard. Burning coal has also been shown to contain trace amounts of mercury and radioactive materials, similarly dangerous substances. The type of coal that is burned directly affects the amount of
(15) sulfur that is released into the atmosphere.

The formation of coal goes through discrete stages as, over millions of years, heat and pressure act on decomposing plants. Coal begins as peat, partially decayed plant matter, which is still found
(20) today in swamps and bogs, and can be burned, but produces little heat. As the decayed plant material is compressed over time, lignite is formed. Lignite is a sedimentary rock with low sulfur content and, like peat, also produces a small amount of heat
(25) when burned. With further compaction, lignite loses moisture, methane, and carbon dioxide, and becomes bituminous coal, the form of coal most widely used. Bituminous coal is also a sedimentary rock, but it has a high sulfur content.
(30) Anthracite, or hard coal, is a metamorphic rock formed when heat and pressure are added to bituminous coal. Anthracite coal is most desirable because it burns very hot and also contains a much smaller amount of sulfur, meaning that it burns
(35) cleaner.

However, the supplies of anthracite on Earth are limited. In the United States, most anthracite

GO ON TO THE NEXT PAGE

is extracted from the valleys of northeastern Pennsylvania, which is known as the Coal Region.

(40) The major American reserve of bituminous coal is in West Virginia, while the largest coal producer in the world is The People's Republic of China. The United States and China are also foremost among the world's coal consumers. There are many other

(45) coal-producing areas throughout the world, though in some cases, the coal is essentially tapped out, or other, cleaner sources of coal are preferred.

Coal is extracted from mines. For subsurface mines, machines dig shafts and tunnels underground

(50) to allow the miners to remove the material. Buildup of poisonous gases, explosions, and collapses are all dangers that underground miners must face. The Sago Mine disaster of January 2006 in West Virginia—where only 1 of 13 trapped miners

(55) survived an explosion—shows how extracting these underground deposits of solid material is still a very dangerous process. Strip mining, or surface mining, is cheaper and less hazardous than underground mining. However, it often leaves the land scarred and

(60) unsuitable for other uses.

PASSAGE B

Petroleum, or crude oil, is a thick liquid that contains organic compounds of hydrogen and carbon, called hydrocarbons. The term "crude oil" refers to both the unprocessed petroleum and the

(65) products refined from it, such as gasoline, heating oil, and asphalt. Petroleum contains many types of hydrocarbons in liquid, solid and gaseous forms, as well as sulfur, oxygen, and nitrogen.

When organic material such as zooplankton

(70) and algae settled on the bottom of oceans millions of years ago, the material mixed with mud and was covered in sediment more quickly than it could decay. Thousands of years later, the sediments that contained the organic material were subjected to

(75) intense amounts of heat and pressure, changing it into a waxy material called kerogen. From this substance, liquid hydrocarbons can be produced to create oil shale. When more heat was added to the kerogen, it liquefied into the substance we know

(80) as oil. Since hydrocarbons are usually lighter than rock or water, they migrate upward through the

permeable rock layers until they reach impermeable rocks. The areas where oil remains in the porous rocks are called reservoirs.

(85) Oil is traditionally pumped out of the layer of reserves found under the surface of Earth. In order to penetrate the earth, an oil well is created using an oil rig, which turns a drill bit. After the hole is drilled, a casing—a metal pipe with a slightly

(90) smaller diameter than the hole—is inserted and bonded to its surroundings, usually with cement. This strengthens the sides of the hole, or wellbore, and keeps dangerous pressure zones isolated. This process is repeated with smaller bits and thinner

(95) casings, going deeper into the surface to reach the reservoir. Drilling fluid is pushed through the casings to break up the rock in front of the bit and to clean away debris and lower the temperature of the bit, which grows very hot. Once the reservoir is

(100) reached, the top of the wellbore is usually equipped with a set of valves encased in a pyramidal iron cage called a Christmas Tree.

The natural pressure within the reservoir is usually high enough to push the oil or gas up to the

(105) surface. But sometimes, additional measures, called secondary recovery, are required. This is especially true in depleted fields. Installing thinner tubing is one solution, as are surface pump jacks—the structures that look like horses repeatedly dipping their heads.

(110) It is impossible to remove all of the oil in a single reservoir. In fact, a 30 percent to 40 percent yield is typical. However, technology has provided a few ways to increase drilling yield, including forcing water or steam into the rock to "push" out more of the oil.

(115) Even with this technique, only about 50 percent of the deposit will be extracted.

There are also more unconventional sources of oil, including oil shale and tar sands. The hydrocarbons obtained from these sources require

(120) extensive processing to be useable, reducing their value. The extraction process also has a particularly large environmental footprint.

GO ON TO THE NEXT PAGE ⟹

Questions 31–33 ask about Passage A.

31. The author would be most likely to support:

  A. the use of oil over that of coal.

  B. the continued use of fossil fuels.

  C. the use of lignite for fuel.

  D. secondary recovery.

32. The passage suggests that which of the following has the smallest amount of moisture, methane, and carbon dioxide?

  F. Lignite

  G. Peat

  H. Bituminous coal

  J. Kerogen

33. It can be inferred that the author believes that:

  A. acid rain is a direct contrast to carbon in coal.

  B. acid rain provides proof that burning coal is dangerous.

  C. acid rain is a direct result of decaying plant matter.

  D. the amount of acid rain produced can be reduced by burning anthracite coal instead of bituminous coal.

Questions 34–36 ask about Passage B.

34. As used in the passage, the phrase "environmental footprint" (line 122) most likely means:

  F. indentations in the surface of the earth.

  G. the positive environmental results of extracting oil.

  H. the effect that a person or activity has on the environment.

  J. irreversible damage to the earth.

35. According to the passage, the second step in extracting the oil is:

  A. drilling a hole.

  B. pushing in draining fluid.

  C. topping with valves.

  D. inserting a pipe.

36. What is most likely true about an oil field in which a pump jack is installed?

  F. Oil is being extracted in the safest way.

  G. The oil reserves in the field are greatly diminished.

  H. About 50 percent of the available oil is recovered.

  J. The wellbore is strengthened.

Questions 37–40 ask about both passages.

37. Both passages include details regarding all of the following EXCEPT:

  A. the transformation of organic material into usable energy sources.

  B. the lengthy nature of converting organic material into fossil fuel.

  C. the limited supply of fossil fuels.

  D. evidence to support the claim that solar power is a safer energy source than oil or coal.

38. The formation of both coal and oil requires all of the following EXCEPT:

  F. proper extraction techniques

  G. pressure.

  H. heat.

  J. organic material.

GO ON TO THE NEXT PAGE ⟩

39. Fossil fuel is formed in a multi-step process, as stated in Passage A where the author writes that "The formation of coal goes through discrete stages. . ." Which sentence in Passage B confirms a similar step process for the formation of oil?

A. The areas where oil remains in the porous rocks are called reservoirs.

B. The natural pressure within the reservoir is usually high enough to push the oil or gas up to the surface.

C. When more heat was added to the kerogen, it liquefied into the subtance we know as oil.

D. Petroleum contains many different types of hydrocarbons in liquid, solid, and gaseous forms, as well as sulfur, oxygen, and nitrogen.

40. The final sentence in each passage conveys which of the following?

F. The land cannot recover after fossil fuels have been extracted.

G. The process of extracting coal and oil present environmental repercussions.

H. New technology can reduce the amount of sulfur released into the air.

J. Lead is as equally hazardous to people as are coal and oil.

SCIENCE TEST

35 Minutes—40 Questions

Directions: There are several passages in this test. Each passage is followed by several questions. After reading a passage, choose the best answer to each question and fill in the corresponding oval on your Answer Grid. You may refer to the passages as often as necessary. You are NOT permitted to use a calculator on this test.

PASSAGE I

The growth of flowering plants and trees can depend on a number of factors, including the type of plant and the latitude where it is grown. Table 1 below contains typical adult heights for several different varieties of a particular flowering plant.

The rate of flowering for many plants and trees, such as the pecan tree, depends on the age of the organism. Growth occurs in several distinct phases, which reflect changes in the development of the organism over time. See Figure 1.

Table 1

Variety	Soil type	Latitude (degrees)	Height (meters)
Lagerstroemia Apalachee	Soil alone	28	5.2
Lagerstroemia indica Catawba	Soil and organic compost	28	2.7
Lagerstroemia Chickasaw	Soil alone	28	0.9
Lagerstroemia Choctaw	Soil and mulch	28	7.3
Lagerstroemia indica Conestoga	Soil alone	28	2.4
Lagerstroemia fauriei Kiowa	Soil and organic compost	28	8.3
Lagerstroemia Miami	Soil alone	28	6.4
Lagerstroemia Natchez	Soil and mulch	33	5.8
Lagerstroemia Natchez	Soil and natural fertilizer	28	8.6
Lagerstroemia Natchez	Soil and artificial fertilizer	28	7.6
Lagerstroemia indica Potomac	Soil alone	28	4.6
Lagerstroemia Tuscarora	Soil alone	25	4.9

GO ON TO THE NEXT PAGE ⟩

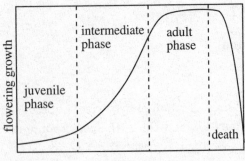

Figure 1

1. Based on the information presented in Table 1, if a young *Lagerstroemia Natchez* was planted at a latitude of 28 degrees, one would predict its adult height to most likely be:

   A. less than 6.0 meters.
   B. between 6.0 and 6.5 meters.
   C. between 6.5 and 7.5 meters.
   D. between 7.5 and 9.0 meters.

2. Flowering growth increases most rapidly during which of the following phases?

   F. Juvenile phase
   G. Intermediate phase
   H. Adult phase
   J. Death

3. Based on the information contained within Table 1, which of the following varieties grown in soil alone reached the greatest adult height?

   A. *Lagerstroemia indica Conestoga*
   B. *Lagerstroemia Miami*
   C. *Lagerstroemia indica Potomac*
   D. *Lagerstroemia Tuscarora*

4. Seedlings of the plant varieties shown in Table 1 were planted in a patch of soil enriched with organic compost at a latitude of 28 degrees. Which of the following varieties would probably come closest to an adult height of 3 meters?

   F. *Lagerstroemia indica Catawba*
   G. *Lagerstroemia Chickasaw*
   H. *Lagerstroemia fauriei Kiowa*
   J. *Lagerstroemia Natchez*

5. Which of the following hypotheses about flowering trees is supported by the information displayed in Figure 1?

   A. Flowering growth increases at a constant rate throughout the life cycle of the tree.
   B. The flowering growth of juvenile trees begins to increase sharply immediately after they are planted.
   C. The flowering growth of juvenile trees begins to decrease immediately after they are planted.
   D. Young trees experience little flowering growth until they reach a certain point in their developmental cycle.

6. If a *Lagerstroemia indica Potomac* shrub that is five meters tall and is located at 28 degrees latitude were observed for one year to determine its flowering rate, what trend would be observed?

   F. The shrub would not produce flowers during that time.
   G. The growth rate would increase slowly.
   H. The growth rate would increase quickly.
   J. The growth rate would remain the same.

GO ON TO THE NEXT PAGE ⟩

PASSAGE II

An isotope is a species of an element character-ized by the number of neutrons it contains. Some isotopes are stable, while others are radioactive. Radioactive isotopes emit particles in radioactive decay. The process of bombardment involves shoot-ing beams of particles at a sample material, often provoking radioactive decay. Scientists performed a series of experiments with 2 different isotopes in order to study 2 different types of radiation. One radiation, called alpha radiation, consists in the release of alpha particles (composed of 2 protons and 2 neutrons). Another radiation, called beta negative radiation, consists in the release of beta negative particles (composed of 1 electron).

EXPERIMENT 1

A sample of Isotope 1 was placed in a chamber and was bombarded with 1 of 4 particles (Particles A–D). The sample was then placed in a cloud chamber, allowing scientists to view the paths traced by any particles emitting from the sample (see Figure 1).

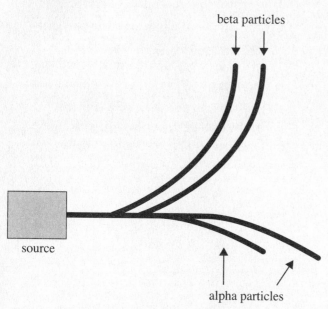

Figure 1

This procedure was repeated for Isotope 2. The particles emitted from the isotopes after bombard-ment were recorded in Table 1:

Table 1

Bombarding particle	Isotope 1		Isotope 2	
	alpha	beta	alpha	beta
A	−	−	+	−
B	+	−	−	+
C	+	+	+	+
D	−	+	−	−
None	−	−	+	−

EXPERIMENT 2

When a radioactive isotope emits particles, its properties change and it can transform into a different radioactive isotope. This decay process, called a decay chain, will continue until a relatively stable isotope is reached. In order to study decay chains, the resulting isotopes (Isotopes 1b and 2b) from Experiment 1 were monitored for their next decay process. The results were recorded in Table 2:

Table 2

Associated particle (from Experiment 1)	Isotope 1b		Isotope 2b	
	alpha	beta	alpha	beta
A	−	−	+	−
B	+	−	−	−
C	−	−	+	+
D	+	−	−	−
None	−	−	+	+

GO ON TO THE NEXT PAGE ▷

7. What is the difference in the number of protons emitted by Isotope 1 before being bombarded with Particle D and after being bombarded with Particle D?

   A. 0

   B. 1

   C. 2

   D. 4

8. In Experiment 1, which of the bombarding particles caused alpha decay in Isotope 1?

   F. Particle B only

   G. Particle D only

   H. Particle B and Particle C only

   J. Particle A and Particle D only

9. Suppose that, after Experiment 2, scientists bombarded Isotopes 1b and 2b again with beams of Particle A. Which of the following could be the decay patterns from the resulting isotopes?

Isotope 1b		Isotope 2b	
alpha	beta	alpha	beta

   A. + − + +

   B. − − − +

   C. + + − −

   D. − + + −

10. Suppose that a scientist randomly selects one of the particle beams from Experiment 1 and bombards both initial isotopes with it. Following this bombardment, Isotope 1 emits only beta particles and Isotope 2 appears relatively stable. Based on the results of Experiment 1, it is most likely that the beam used for this bombardment consists of:

   F. Particle A.

   G. Particle B.

   H. Particle C.

   J. Particle D.

11. What is the evidence from Experiments 1 and 2 that suggests that bombardment by Particle C will trigger a relatively short decay chain in Isotope 1?

   A. No particles were emitted at all from Isotope 1 following bombardment by Particle C.

   B. Alpha particles were emitted from Isotope 1, but only beta particles were emitted in a second stage of decay.

   C. Initially both alpha and beta particles were emitted from Isotope 1, but no particles were emitted in a second stage of decay.

   D. Initially no particles were emitted from Isotope 1, but beta particles were emitted in a second stage of decay.

GO ON TO THE NEXT PAGE ⟹

12. Which of the following figures best represents the results from the bombardment of Isotope 2 with Particle B in Experiment 1?

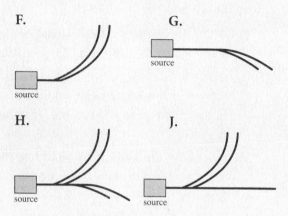

F.

source

G.

source

H.

source

J.

source

13. Is the conclusion that Isotope 2 will become relatively stable upon bombardment by Particle A supported by the results of Experiments 1 and 2?

A. Yes, because alpha particles were emitted in both experiments.

B. Yes, because beta particles were emitted in Experiment 1 and no particles were emitted in Experiment 2.

C. No, because no particles were emitted in either experiment.

D. No, because alpha particles were emitted in both experiments.

PASSAGE III

Ultraviolet (UV) light, a component of natural sunlight, can be damaging to human skin at high doses. UV light occurs in several ranges, including less damaging UV-A light and more damaging UV-B and UV-C light. Scientists designed two experiments to investigate the various factors affecting levels of UV light in a certain region of the United States.

EXPERIMENT 1

Scientists studied how levels of UV-A light vary seasonally and with elevation. They measured UV-A energy over a 10-minute span of time for several days to determine an average daily UV-A value for each site. Three sites were studied at three different elevations, and measurements from each site were obtained once in the winter and once in the summer. UV-A levels for an average 10-minute period beginning 30 minutes after the sun appeared directly overhead were calculated in millijoules per square centimeter (mJ/cm^2). The results are shown in Table 1.

Table 1

Season	Elevation (meters above sea level)	Average UV-A level (mJ/cm^2)
Winter	0	1,270
	1,000	1,400
	2,000	1,530
Summer	0	1,580
	1,000	1,740
	2,000	1,900

EXPERIMENT 2

Next, the levels of UV-A and UV-B were measured at 0, 1, and 2 hours past the time of day at which the sun was directly overhead during the winter at the site with an elevation of 2,000 meters above sea level. The level of UV-A decreased from 1,620 mJ/cm^2 at 0 hours to 1,430 mJ/cm^2 at 2 hours. The level of UV-B decreased from 48 mJ/cm^2 at 0 hours to 42 mJ/cm^2 at 2 hours.

GO ON TO THE NEXT PAGE

EXPERIMENT 3

UV-B light is another component of sunlight that occurs at a lower rate than UV-A but with higher energy. Levels of UV-B light, in millijoules per square centimeter (mJ/cm^2), were measured at various times of day during the summer at the site with an elevation of 2,000 meters above sea level. The results are shown in Table 2.

Table 2

Hours after sun is directly overhead	Average UV-B level (mJ/cm^2)
0	68
1	63
2	57
3	49
4	41

14. Which of the following variables was changed in Experiment 3?

   F. Background levels of UV-A light

   G. Background levels of UV-B light

   H. Time of day

   J. Season of the year

15. According to the results of these experiments, one way to reduce exposure to UV-A light would be to:

   A. spend time in environments with higher levels of UV-B light.

   B. live in an area with shorter summers and longer winters.

   C. live in an area with longer summers and shorter winters.

   D. make sure that all windows are designed to filter out UV-B light.

16. Based on the results of these experiments, if one compared UV-B levels when the sun is directly overhead to those when the sun is low on the horizon, the UV-B levels:

   F. when the sun is overhead would be lower than when the sun is low on the horizon.

   G. when the sun is overhead would be higher than when the sun is low on the horizon.

   H. when the sun is overhead would be the same as when the sun is low on the horizon.

   J. would be measurable only when the sun is overhead.

17. UV-C light is a third type of UV light that was not directly studied in the experiments above. However, if it behaves like the other types of UV light in the experiments, one would expect that UV-C levels:

   A. would decrease from year to year.

   B. would increase from year to year.

   C. are higher when the sun is directly overhead.

   D. are lower when the sun is directly overhead.

18. Based on the experimental results, as the number of hours after the sun is directly overhead increases:

   F. UV-A and UV-B levels both increase.

   G. UV-A levels increase and UV-B levels decrease.

   H. UV-A levels increase and UV-B levels stay the same.

   J. UV-A and UV-B levels both decrease.

GO ON TO THE NEXT PAGE

19. A community near the region studied has an elevation of 3,000 meters above sea level. At a time 30 minutes after the sun is directly overhead, one would predict that UV-A levels during the summer are:

   A. less than 1,580 mJ/cm².

   B. between 1,580 and 1,740 mJ/cm².

   C. between 1,740 and 1,900 mJ/cm².

   D. above 1,900 mJ/cm².

20. Which of the following would best represent the average UV-B level at an altitude of 2,000 meters in winter, one hour after the sun is directly overhead?

   F. 45 mJ/cm²

   G. 48 mJ/cm²

   H. 57 mJ/cm²

   J. 63 mJ/cm²

PASSAGE IV

The following experiments were performed to study the motion of gyroscopes, objects on a surface that spin quickly around an axis of rotation. These experiments focus on the gyroscopes' rate of *precession*, or the rate at which they revolve around the point where the axis of rotation touches a surface (see Figure 1).

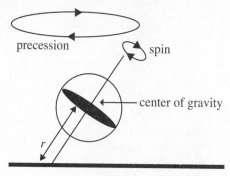

Figure 1

EXPERIMENT 1

A scientist tested several different gyroscopes that differed only in the distance from the gyroscope's center of gravity to the surface (*r*). A mechanical device was used to spin each gyroscope at the exact same rate of spin on the same surface, and the rate of precession was measured for each gyroscope in revolutions per minute (rpm). These rates are given in Table 1.

Table 1

r (centimeters)	Precession rate (rpm)
4	9
6	14
8	19
10	24
12	28

EXPERIMENT 2

Then, the scientist used a gyroscope of fixed size and varied the settings on the mechanical device spinning the gyroscope. The precession rate was measured several times for different spin rates, also measured in revolutions per minute (rpm). The results of this experiment are given in Table 2.

Table 2

Spin rate (rpm)	Precession rate (rpm)
250	41
400	25.5
600	17
750	14
1,200	8.5

GO ON TO THE NEXT PAGE

EXPERIMENT 3

A scientist placed a gyroscope similar to that used in the first two experiments on board a satellite orbiting Earth. It was found that for a gyroscope of fixed size and spin rate, its precession rate on the satellite was about one-eighth of its precession rate on the surface of Earth. For example, a precession rate of approximately 24 rpm would become approximately 3 rpm on the satellite.

21. If, during Experiment 1, the scientists had tested a sixth gyroscope with a center of gravity that was 9 cm from the surface, its precession rate would most likely have been:

    A.   4 rpm.

    B.   9 rpm.

    C.   21.5 rpm.

    D.   23.5 rpm.

22. According to the results of Experiment 1, one can conclude that the gyroscope's precession rate increases as the gyroscope's center of gravity:

    F.   decreases in distance from the surface.

    G.   increases in distance from the surface.

    H.   remains the same distance from the surface.

    J.   changes in mass.

23. Of the following graphs, which best represents how changes in precession rate are related to changes in spin rate, as shown in Experiment 2?

A.
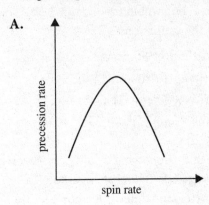

B.
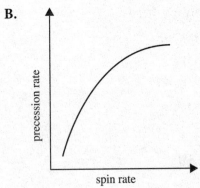

C.
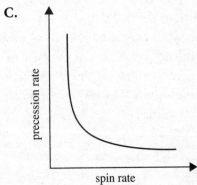

D.
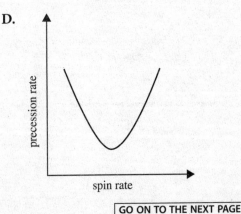

GO ON TO THE NEXT PAGE

24. The hypothesis of the scientist in Experiment 3 was that precession rate is related to gravity, which decreases as one's distance from Earth increases. To confirm this hypothesis, the scientist should repeat this experiment on:

   F. several different satellites at varying distances from Earth.

   G. another satellite at the exact same distance from Earth as the first satellite.

   H. a satellite orbiting in the opposite direction.

   J. Earth's surface while varying the gyroscope's spin rate.

25. If an r of 6 cm was used throughout Experiment 2, what was the most likely spin rate used in Experiment 1?

   A. 400 rpm

   B. 600 rpm

   C. 750 rpm

   D. 1,200 rpm

26. If the effects tested in Experiment 1 had not been known during the design of Experiment 2, how might this have affected Experiment 2?

   F. The scientist might have used gyroscopes with different masses.

   G. The scientist might not have always used the same size gyroscope.

   H. The scientist might have tested the gyroscope on a different surface.

   J. The scientist might have used a different-shaped gyroscope.

27. Which is the best way to investigate the effect of gyroscope mass on precession rate while keeping the spin rate constant?

   A. Use gyroscopes made by different companies.

   B. Use gyroscopes that are the same size and shape, but that are made from different types of metal.

   C. Use several different gyroscopes that are each measured on both Earth and on a satellite.

   D. Use gyroscopes that are all the same mass but that have different sizes.

PASSAGE V

Precipitation is a general term for a form of water, such as rain, snow, sleet, or hail, that falls from the sky to the surface of Earth. There are two theories that attempt to explain how the tiny water droplets in clouds combine to form precipitation.

COLLISION AND COALESCENCE THEORY

As shown in Stage I of Figure I, a cloud is initially composed of numerous droplets of liquid water of varying sizes, but all microscopic. As these droplets move about within the cloud, they can collide with one another. These collisions can either result in the droplets bouncing apart again or sticking together (*coalescence*) to form a larger droplet (see Stage II). The process continues until large drops are formed which are too heavy to remain suspended in the cloud any longer. Some of these drops will then split apart into smaller drops that continue the collision and coalescence process, while others will fall to the ground in the form of precipitation (see Stage III).

GO ON TO THE NEXT PAGE

ICE CRYSTAL THEORY

In this theory, the tiny droplets in clouds rise to a point in Earth's atmosphere where the temperature is lower than the freezing point of water. Initially, the cloud is composed of many supercooled water droplets, still in liquid form (see Stage I of Figure II). Some of these droplets then condense around tiny impurities in the air to form miniature ice crystals (see Stage II). Water vapor in the air can then freeze onto the surface of the crystals, causing some of the droplets to evaporate in order to maintain a constant level of water vapor (see Stage III). The ice crystals quickly become too heavy to remain suspended in the air and fall to the ground, often melting again in the warmer temperatures near the ground to form rain (see Stage IV). The net effect is that the formation of ice crystals takes moisture out of the air, allowing the crystals to grow larger at the expense of the droplets.

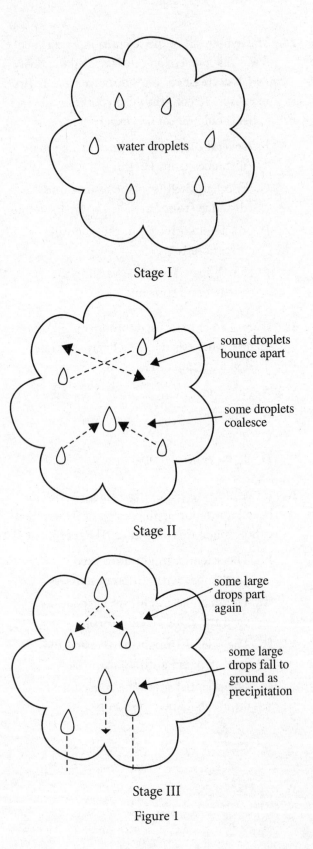

Figure 1

GO ON TO THE NEXT PAGE ⇨

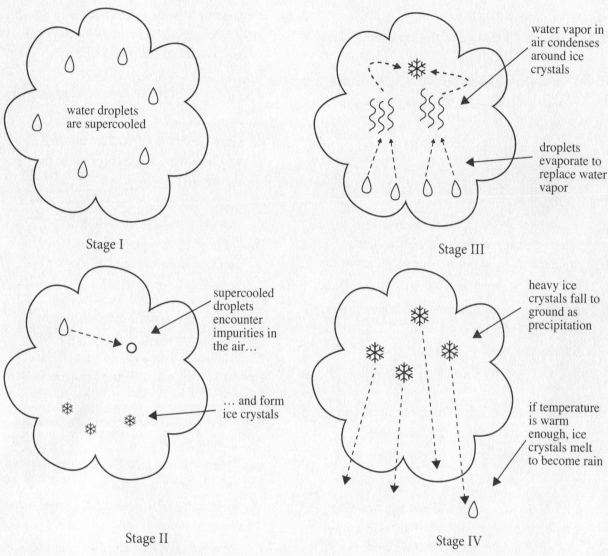

Stage I

Stage III

Stage II

Stage IV

Figure 2

28. In which of the following situations would supporters of both theories agree that precipitation should NOT occur?

F. A cloud with water droplets colliding and coalescing to produce larger droplets

G. A cloud with water droplets forming crystals around impurities in the air

H. A cloud with an insufficient number of water droplets

J. A cloud containing elements too heavy to remain suspended in the air

29. The Collision and Coalescence and Ice Crystal Theories differ on which of the following points?

A. Exterior shape of cloud formation

B. State of matter of precipitation before falling from the cloud

C. Amount of precipitation that reaches the ground

D. Climate required for precipitation to occur

GO ON TO THE NEXT PAGE

30. According to the Collision and Coalescence Theory, the likelihood of producing rainfall is greater:

   F. when the droplets collide at a high rate.

   G. when the droplets collide at a variable rate.

   H. when the temperature causes droplets to freeze.

   J. shortly after the last rainfall occurred.

31. A weather balloon travels through a cloud and detects a high proportion of particles in the cloud too heavy to remain suspended in the air. Both theories would agree that:

   A. there are insufficient impurities in the air to form ice crystals.

   B. the probability of precipitation occurring in the near future is very high.

   C. the water-based particles in the cloud are colliding at a very rapid rate.

   D. the entire cloud is decreasing in altitude.

32. City A has a higher rate of precipitation than City B, despite similar temperatures, humidity, and cloud formations in both locations. The Ice Crystal Theory would suggest that the higher rate of precipitation in City A most likely results from which of the following?

   F. The greater frequency of thunder and lightning storms in City A

   G. Large atmospheric density differences between City A and City B

   H. A greater number of impurities released into the air by factories in City A

   J. The lower rate of air pollution in City A

33. If a cloud initially consisted entirely of liquid water droplets, which of the following statements about the cloud would support the Collision and Coalescence Theory?

   A. The mass of the droplets is too great for them to remain suspended in the air.

   B. Water droplets crystallize around smaller water droplets found in the atmosphere.

   C. Larger water droplets are formed by smaller droplets combining.

   D. Some of the droplets evaporate to make up for lost water vapor in the air.

34. Depending on temperature and other conditions, it is possible for precipitation to change forms on its way to the ground. If precipitation forms according to the Ice Crystal Theory, which of the following is NOT possible?

   F. After ice in the cloud falls, it melts to become rain.

   G. After ice in the cloud falls, it partially melts to become sleet.

   H. After water in the cloud falls, it freezes to become snow.

   J. Some ice crystals formed around impurities in the air first melt and then evaporate before they fall from the cloud.

PASSAGE VI

Elements as shown in the periodic table have a number of different properties which depend on the structure of the element's atoms. For example, these properties might depend on the atom's number of *electrons* (negatively charged particles), which move in patterns called *shells* (see Figure 1).

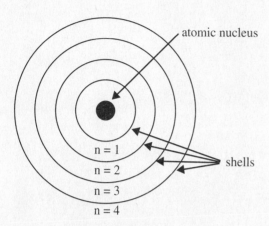

atomic nucleus

n = 1
n = 2
n = 3
n = 4

shells

Figure 1
Note: Drawing is NOT to scale.

Table 1 lists properties for several chemical elements. The table includes the number of shells in the atom (n), the number of electrons in the atom's outer shell (e), the atomic radius (r), the energy (I) required to remove one electron from the atom's outer shell (in electron volts, eV), and a measure of attraction (c) to electrons in a chemical bond (in Pauling units).

Table 1

Element	n	e	r (× 10⁻¹¹ m)	I (eV)	c
C	2	4	9.1	11.2	2.5
N	2	5	7.5	14.5	3.0
O	2	6	6.5	13.6	3.5
F	2	7	5.7	17.4	4.0
Si	3	4	14.6	8.2	1.8
P	3	5	12.6	10.5	2.1
S	3	6	10.9	10.4	2.5
Cl	3	7	9.7	13.0	3.0
Ge	4	4	15.2	7.9	1.8
As	4	5	13.3	9.8	2.0
Se	4	6	12.2	9.8	2.4
Br	4	7	11.2	11.8	2.8

35. For any value of n, Table 1 indicates that as e increases, r:

   A. increases only.

   B. first increases, then decreases.

   C. decreases only.

   D. remains unchanged.

36. According to Table 1, for an element with n = 2 and e = 3, the most likely value of r would be:

   F. 11.7×10^{-11} m.

   G. 8.8×10^{-11} m.

   H. 7.4×10^{-11} m.

   J. 6.2×10^{-11} m.

37. According to the information in the passage, it is possible to decrease an atom's negative charge by:

   A. decreasing the radius of the atom.

   B. forming a chemical bond with the atom.

   C. applying energy to the atom.

   D. changing the number of shells in the atom.

38. The hypothesis that for a given value of n, c increases as the number of electrons in the atom's outer shell increases, is supported by the data in Table 1 when:

   F. n = 2 only.

   G. n = 2 or 3 only.

   H. n = 4 only.

   J. n = 2, 3, or 4.

39. The most energy will be required to remove an electron from shell:

   A. n = 3 in Si

   B. n = 3 in Cl

   C. n = 2 in C

   D. n = 2 in F

GO ON TO THE NEXT PAGE ⟶

40. Which of the following pairs of elements does not have the same value in Pauling units?

    F. Se and As
    G. N and Cl
    H. Ge and Si
    J. C and S

WRITING TEST

40 Minutes

Directions: This is a test of your writing skills. You will have forty (40) minutes to write an essay in English. Before you begin planning and writing your essay, read the writing prompt carefully to understand exactly what you are being asked to do. Your essay will be evaluated on the evidence it provides of your ability to do the following:

- Express judgments by evaluating the three perspectives given in the prompt, taking a position on an issue, and explaining the relationship among all four ideas
- Develop a position by using logical reasoning and by supporting your ideas
- Maintain a focus on the topic throughout the essay
- Organize ideas in a logical way
- Use language clearly and effectively according to the conventions of standard written English

You may use the unlined pages in this test booklet to plan your essay. These pages will not be scored. *You must write your essay in pencil on the lined pages in the answer folder.* Your writing on those lined pages will be scored. You may not need all the lined pages, but to ensure you have enough room to finish, do NOT skip lines. You may write corrections or additions neatly between the lines of your essay, but do NOT write in the margins of the lined pages. *Illegible essays cannot be scored, so you must write (or print) clearly.*

If you finish before time is called you may review your work. Lay your pencil down immediately when time is called.

GO ON TO THE NEXT PAGE

ACCESS TO TECHNOLOGY

To help ready students to become productive members of the workforce, schools concentrate on providing a strong foundation on which students can build their careers. Since job applicants who are proficient in word processing applications, email programs, and storage tools are more likely to be hired than applicants who do not have technology experience, it is to the benefit of students that schools offer technology instruction in high school. Given the importance of technology in today's society, should schools be responsible for providing ongoing access to computers for every student? Since many students will need to use computers in various capacities throughout their lifetimes, how well a school provides access to technology directly affects its student body.

Read and carefully consider these perspectives. Each discusses the importance of student access to technology.

Perspective One	Perspective Two	Perspective Three
Schools should be encouraged to incorporate technology objectives into homework assignments and class projects, but schools do not have an obligation to provide unlimited access to computers. Teachers can provide time during the school day for students to use on-site computer labs, which will allow students the tools they need to complete assignments that require computer technology.	Schools should be required to provide personal computers for students to use at least throughout their high school careers, if not during middle and elementary school as well. Unlimited access to a personal computer for every student will foster continual development of technological abilities, which is a highly valued skill set.	Schools and computer companies should work together to provide significant student discounts so that the majority of parents who have school-age children can afford to purchase at least one personal computer. Students who do not have their own computers can use their schools' computer labs or go to their local libraries to complete homework assignments that require computer technology.

ESSAY TASK

Write a unified, coherent essay in which you evaluate multiple perspectives regarding access to technology. In your essay, be sure to:

- analyze and evaluate the perspectives given

- state and develop your own perspective on the issue

- explain the relationship between your perspective and those given

Your perspective may be in full agreement with any of the others, in partial agreement, or wholly different. Whatever the case, support your ideas with logical reasoning and detailed, persuasive examples.

GO ON TO THE NEXT PAGE ⟹

PLANNING YOUR ESSAY

You may wish to consider the following as you think critically about the task:

Strengths and weaknesses of the three given perspectives

- What insights do they offer, and what do they fail to consider?

- Why might they be persuasive to others, or why might they fail to persuade?

Your own knowledge, experience, and values

- What is your perspective on this issue, and what are its strengths and weaknesses?

- How will you support your perspective in your essay?

_____

_____

_____

_____

_____

_____

_____

_____

_____

_____

_____

_____

_____

_____

_____

_____

_____

_____

GO ON TO THE NEXT PAGE

ACT®
Practice Test 3
For Courses Starting On or After 2/1/2016

PLEASE BE SURE TO RECORD THE FOLLOWING SCAN CODE ON YOUR ANSWER GRID. WITHOUT THIS INFORMATION, WE WILL NOT BE ABLE TO SCAN YOUR TEST OR PROVIDE YOU WITH YOUR TEST SCORES.

SCAN CODE: 8009

ENGLISH TEST

45 Minutes—75 Questions

Directions: In the following five passages, certain words and phrases are underlined and numbered. In the right-hand column are alternatives for each underlined portion. Select the one that best conveys the idea, creates the most grammatically correct sentence, or is most consistent with the style and tone of the passage. If you decide that the original version is best, select NO CHANGE. You may also find questions that ask about the entire passage or a section of the passage. These questions will correspond to small, numbered boxes in the text. For these questions, decide which choice best accomplishes the purpose set out in the question stem. After you've selected the best choice, fill in the corresponding oval on your Answer Grid. For some questions, you'll need to read the context in order to answer correctly. Be sure to read until you have enough information to determine the correct answer choice.

PASSAGE I

RELAXATION IN THE AGE OF OVERLOAD

It's hard to escape from information overload. Considering the stimuli vying for your attention. Your
1
computer signals when you have new email. Your cell phone alerts you that someone is calling or has sent you a text message. A video monitor at the grocery check-out counter offers unsolicited menu advice. A flashing billboard on the side of the road proclaims it's message as
2

1. **A.** NO CHANGE
    B. Consider
    C. A consideration of
    D. When considering

2. **F.** NO CHANGE
    G. there
    H. their
    J. its

you drive. Every organization to which you belong has a website that you're expected to read regularly to keep up
3
with the latest news; each one seems as worthy

3. **A.** NO CHANGE
    B. website that, you're expected to read regularly
    C. website, that you're expected to read, regularly
    D. website that you're, expected to read regularly,

GO ON TO THE NEXT PAGE ▶

of your attention <u>like</u> the others. Social networking sites
4

<u>were to offer</u> fun, but instead they distract you from
5
work that you need to do. If you're like most people, you

may find that each new source of information <u>exceeds</u>
6
your stress.

[1] Subsequently, a new class of professionals, the

relaxation guru, is now emerging. [2] Unsurprisingly,

while we as a society consume more information, we

also look for ways to recuperate from the overload.

[3] This group includes yoga teachers, massage thera-

pists, spiritual leaders, meditation instructors, psycholo-

gists, and life coaches. [4] All of these people try, in

various ways, to help us <u>to have gotten</u> more
7

balance in our lives. ⏺8⏺

<u>Psychologist's</u> tell us that the human brain needs
9
time to rest and recharge. Meditation instructors

encourage us to be aware of our breathing and

4. **F.** NO CHANGE
    G. for
    H. as
    J. with

5. **A.** NO CHANGE
    B. had offered
    C. can offer
    D. were offering

6. **F.** NO CHANGE
    G. adds to
    H. additionally
    J. surpasses

7. **A.** NO CHANGE
    B. get
    C. finally having gotten
    D. getting

8. For the sake of the logic and coherence of
    this paragraph, Sentence 2 should be placed:
    F. where it is now.
    G. before Sentence 1.
    H. before Sentence 4.
    J. after Sentence 4.

9. **A.** NO CHANGE
    B. Psychologists'
    C. Psychologists,
    D. Psychologists

<u>simply</u> notice what we feel. Spiritual leaders guide us to
10
become aware of a presence that is larger than ourselves.

Life coaches urge us to focus on what is really important

to <u>us, thus,</u> and let trivial matters go. Yoga teachers and
11

massage therapists help us relax our <u>bodies so that we can</u>
12
calm our minds.

All of these efforts sound good, but consequently raise

tension. With the <u>lively</u> awareness of stress management's
13
importance, relaxation can ironically become just one more

item on the to-do list. When a friend calls to ask you out

for breakfast on a Saturday morning, and you <u>are unable</u>
14
<u>to accept the invitation</u> because you have yoga class
14
before your scheduled massage, you may start to

wonder: When an appointment, even for a relaxing

activity, shows up on your calendar, can it truly

constitute relaxation?

10. Which of the following placements of the underlined portion would NOT be acceptable?
   F. where it is now.
   G. after the word *us*.
   H. after the word *of*.
   J. after the word *instructors*.

11. A. NO CHANGE
   B. us, for example,
   C. us, in contrast,
   D. us

12. F. NO CHANGE
   G. bodies, or we can
   H. bodies, and that is the way to
   J. bodies because it also needs to

13. Which choice most strongly suggests that the number of people concerned about stress management is increasing?
   A. NO CHANGE
   B. growing
   C. vivid
   D. reflective

14. F. NO CHANGE
   G. are forced not to go
   H. must decline
   J. have to refrain from going

GO ON TO THE NEXT PAGE

Question 15 asks about the preceding passage as a whole.

15. The writer is considering adding a subtitle to the title "Relaxation in the Age of Overload" that would emphasize the tension between finding time to relax and having an overscheduled calendar. Which of the following phrases would best accomplish that purpose?

   A. A New Prioritization for Many

   B. Suggestions for Achieving Balance

   C. A Matter of Health

   D. Is It Feasible?

PASSAGE II

MY PARENTS' COURTSHIP

My father wasn't particularly muscular, but he was strong, agile, and <u>an athlete.</u> He had a handsome face,
16

highlighted by <u>an aquiline nose, silver eyes; a thick</u>
                                    17
<u>shock of black hair</u> that he always wore combed straight
17

back in the style of the day. <u>When his face broke out</u>
                                           18
<u>into his wide, sparkling smile,</u> one couldn't help but like
           18
him. His demeanor and even temperament matched

his easy physical poise. He never spoke harshly and

16. F. NO CHANGE

   G. athletically

   H. athletic

   J. like an athlete

17. A. NO CHANGE

   B. an aquiline nose, silver eyes, and a thick shock of black hair

   C. an aquiline nose; silver eyes; a thick shock, of black hair

   D. an aquiline nose silver eyes, and a thick shock of black hair

18. F. NO CHANGE

   G. When his face broke out into his wide, sparkling smile;

   H. When his face broke out into his wide sparkling smile;

   J. When his face, broke out into his wide, sparkling, smile,

GO ON TO THE NEXT PAGE ▷

<u>meeting</u> everyone's gaze straight on with his warm eyes
19
and ever-present smile. There was nothing studied,

artificial, or pretentious about my dad; he just had a

natural grace that put people at ease. People chatting

with my father could never articulate why they left the

conversation feeling happier, <u>or even take conscious</u>
                                                      20
<u>notice of the new bounce in their step.</u> It was as though
                                   20
Dad's presence just made people feel lighter, as though

the weight of the world had been temporarily lifted off

their shoulders. <u>Dad just had a way of putting people at</u>
                                            21
<u>ease without them ever realizing it.</u>
                              21
    [1] Because of his gregarious and caring nature, my

father was given to excess when it came to bestowing

favors or gifts on any friend, acquaintance, or relation.

[2] My mother quickly became the beneficiary of his most

extravagant generosity. [3] As my father put it when he

described his first meeting with my mother, "I went nuts

as soon as I laid eyes on her." 22

19. **A.** NO CHANGE
    B. is meeting
    C. met
    D. had met

20. Assuming that all are true, which choice is the most logical and appropriate in context?
    F. NO CHANGE
    G. or remember where they were going before they ran into my father.
    H. or understand the economic crisis looming in the near future.
    J. or come to terms with the recently passed Prohibition laws.

21. **A.** NO CHANGE
    B. You couldn't put your finger on it, but something about him just put people at ease.
    C. Dad just had something that put people at ease, something almost magical.
    D. OMIT the underlined portion.

22. The author is considering adding the following sentence to the second paragraph:

    He acquired a particular reputation for lavishing gifts upon the girls whom he pursued, ranging from flowers to candy to the jeweled hair accessories worn by chic women in the 1920s.

Should it be added, and if so, where?
    F. Yes, after Sentence 3.
    G. Yes, after Sentence 2.
    H. Yes, after Sentence 1.
    J. No, it should NOT be added.

GO ON TO THE NEXT PAGE ⟹

My mother was a native of <u>the Midwest but, she</u>
                                            23
<u>had already experienced</u> the New York scene by the time
          23
my father entered her life. Unlike her previous suitors,

however, Dad <u>laid</u> out a banquet of all the city had to
                    24
offer. Not only did he take her to the theater, to baseball

games, and to nightclubs, <u>and</u> before each evening out,
                                    25
he had two dozen of the brightest and longest stemmed

red roses he could find delivered to her door.

   A night on the town meant evening clothes: my

father in a tuxedo and my mother in one of her chiffon

or beaded dresses, cut low down the back and the front

and held up by thin shoulder straps. Falling anywhere

from her knee to her ankle, the dresses hung loosely to

her body, except on the dance floor <u>when</u> my mother's
                                              26
movements would fan them into an arc around her.

23. **A.** NO CHANGE
    B. the Midwest, but she had already
        experienced
    C. the Midwest but; she had already
        experienced
    D. the Midwest: but she had already
        experienced

24. **F.** NO CHANGE
    G. lain
    H. would have lain
    J. will lay

25. **A.** NO CHANGE
    B. but also
    C. however
    D. additionally

26. **F.** NO CHANGE
    G. which
    H. where
    J. that

GO ON TO THE NEXT PAGE

<u>Years later I would find some of these exquisite dresses,</u>
27
<u>costumes from the Jazz Age, stored away in a steamer</u>
27
<u>trunk.</u>
27

All the extravagant outings aside, my mother and father truly came to love each other. Although at first reluctant to give up her independent lifestyle as a

self-sufficient shopgirl, <u>my father's repeated marriage</u>
28
<u>proposals eventually won my mother's heart.</u> In February
28
1927, on George Washington's birthday, my parents were married in a small ceremony at city hall. The wedding was attended by most of my mother's family,

some of my father's, and of course <u>their</u> close friends,
29
who, after the family members had retired, joined my parents in celebrating with a night of live jazz at the

Cotton Club. That night, <u>it was decided that they would</u>
30
<u>leave on their honeymoon</u> in two months—a plan that
30
was never fulfilled, for by then, my mother was already pregnant with me.

27. Given that all of the following are true, which provides the most specific information about dance outings in the era in which the author's parents were courting each other?

A. NO CHANGE

B. Even before the stock market crash, many women couldn't afford these dresses.

C. Some critics at the time called the flapper dresses "indecent," as they showed off so much skin.

D. The intoxicating whirl of colors, set to the vibrant jazz music, epitomized the Golden Age of the Roaring Twenties.

28. F. NO CHANGE

G. my father repeatedly proposed marriage to my mother and eventually won my mother's heart.

H. repeated marriage proposals from my father eventually won my mother's heart.

J. my mother eventually accepted one of my father's repeated marriage proposals.

29. A. NO CHANGE

B. his

C. my parents'

D. the family's

30. F. NO CHANGE

G. as it was decided by them, they would leave on their honeymoon

H. the decision having been reached, they would leave on their honeymoon

J. they decided to leave on their honeymoon

GO ON TO THE NEXT PAGE

PASSAGE III

COVERED BRIDGES

The American Northeast is <u>regions</u> of rivers, streams,
                              31

and creeks. <u>The newly imported European population</u>
                                    32
<u>settled along the beach when they first arrived.</u> Once the
                              32
settlers had moved inland, ferries and barges, at least at

first, <u>provided</u> adequate transportation across streams
        33
and rivers. As the population grew and trade increased,

<u>thus,</u> the need to transport larger numbers of people and
  34
heavier goods across waterways mandated another solu-

tion. Bridges were the obvious answer to connect these

divided communities. Coastal dwellers relied upon

inland farms for food, and inland dwellers returned to

31. **A.** NO CHANGE
    B. regional
    C. a region
    D. regionally

32. Assuming each choice is true, which one
    provides the most relevant information
    about the settlers' inward migration?

    F. NO CHANGE
    G. The newly imported European population
    was vulnerable to new diseases, and often
    settlements died out within a few years.
    H. The newly imported European population,
    needing land to farm and shelter from the
    harsh ocean weather, moved off the rocky
    beaches into the forested, arable interior
    realm.
    J. The newly imported European population,
    generally sea-faring folk, preferred to live
    on the beach, but generations born in the
    New World wanted to seek gold in the
    western region of the country.

33. **A.** NO CHANGE
    B. is provided
    C. providing
    D. do provide

34. **F.** NO CHANGE
    G. therefore,
    H. moreover,
    J. OMIT the underlined portion.

GO ON TO THE NEXT PAGE ⟩

the built-up coastal towns to make use of their schools,

houses of worship, and <u>shops</u>.
                         35

[1] The earliest bridges were simply logs stretched

across <u>supporting timbers, the span</u> of the bridge
                        36
was limited to the length of the supporting timber, or

stringer. [2] As the industry of bridge building evolved,

builders learned to create longer spans using trusses,

arches, and joined stringers. [3] <u>Like many structures</u>
                                                        37
<u>of the late 18th century, bridges were made almost</u>
                                                 37
<u>entirely of wood.</u> [4] These bridges exhibited advanced
                  37
engineering, but one problem still remained. [5]

<u>Exposed to the elements year round, New Englanders</u>
                        38
<u>found the joints of a wooden truss bridge would</u>
                        38
<u>deteriorate rapidly.</u> [6] The covered bridge was invented
                  38

in response <u>of</u> the need to protect the wood trusses and
            39
joints; covered wooden bridges last about three times

35. **A.** NO CHANGE
     B. to do their shopping
     C. for things such as supplies
     D. shopping

36. **F.** NO CHANGE
     G. supporting timbers the span
     H. supporting timbers; the span
     J. supporting timbers; however, the span

37. For the sake of logic and coherence of this paragraph, Sentence 3 should be placed:

     A. where it is now.
     B. before Sentence 5.
     C. before Sentence 2.
     D. before Sentence 1.

38. **F.** NO CHANGE
     G. Exposed to the elements year round, the joints of a wooden truss bridge would deteriorate rapidly, New Englanders found.
     H. With rapid deterioration, New Englanders found that the joints of a wooden truss bridge were exposed to the elements year round.
     J. Finding rapid deterioration, the joints of a wooden truss bridge in New England were exposed to the elements year round.

39. **A.** NO CHANGE
     B. to
     C. with
     D. for

GO ON TO THE NEXT PAGE ⟶

as long as those exposed to the elements. [7] Municipal

officials, <u>who</u> bore responsibility for town budgets,
    40

also <u>endorsed</u> covered bridges. [8] Most of them were
  41

paid from budget excess and knew that <u>as with any</u>
                                42
<u>well-made structure, better bridges,</u> meant reduced
                    42
maintenance costs.

      What <u>advances</u> the development of wooden covered
           43
bridges throughout the 18th and 19th centuries? It was

truly a combination of the plentiful old growth of the

northern forests, pressing need, and, as always, sheer

Yankee ingenuity. <u>The practice of building wooden</u>
                           44
<u>covered bridges spread quickly throughout the country,</u>
                      44
<u>and thousands were built during the 1800s.</u> In the
                44
northeastern United States, wooden covered bridge design

and construction reached its pinnacle, particularly in New

Hampshire, Vermont, and Maine. Nearby, Pennsylvania

40. **F.** NO CHANGE

    G. whom

    H. they who

    J. those whom

41. Three of these choices indicate that the officials had a liking for covered bridges. Which one does NOT do so?

    A. NO CHANGE

    B. rebuffed

    C. preferred

    D. supported

42. **F.** NO CHANGE

    G. as with any well-made structure better bridges;

    H. as with any well-made structure, better bridges

    J. as with any well-made structure; better bridges,

43. **A.** NO CHANGE

    B. advanced

    C. is advancing

    D. will advance

44. **F.** NO CHANGE

    G. Many states still build covered bridges to encourage tourism.

    H. Most wooden covered bridges ceased to be used for transit in the 20th century, when they could not bear the weight of more modern vehicles.

    J. OMIT the underlined portion.

GO ON TO THE NEXT PAGE ▷

boasted more covered bridges than any other state, and its extant bridges still bring in significant tourism revenue from visitors who have come to marvel at their functional, yet elegant, beauty. [45]

Question 45 asks about the preceding passage as a whole.

45. Provided all the choices are correct, which one, if inserted here, would best enhance the essay as well as maintain the tone of the paragraph?

   A. Covered bridges have also existed in Europe since medieval times; there were once hundreds of them in Switzerland, Austria, and Germany.

   B. In fact, because of their important role in the advancement of colonial life, many covered bridges that can no longer be used are now classified as historically preserved sites.

   C. Covered bridges can be dated back 2,000 years to a time when they were being built in China and even earlier in ancient Babylon.

   D. Many prominent farmers lived in the vicinity of covered bridges, and their descendants are often still living in those areas.

PASSAGE IV

VIOLET PALMER: THE JOURNEY TO NUMBER 12

Violet Palmer—professional basketball referee and one of the first women to officiate a National Basketball Association (NBA) game—started her journey to forging her name in <u>basketballs</u> history in a typical

46.

46. F. NO CHANGE
    G. basketball is
    H. basketballs'
    J. basketball's

way: she played the sport.
47

In her home state (a Compton, CA native) she
48
stayed to attend Cal Poly Pomona. As a player, Palmer,
48

whom was a three-year captain for her team, earned
49

recognition as a point guard and was a member of two
50
NCAA Division II women's championship basketball

teams.

Not only did Palmer study officiating as part of her

college major, but her late coach and mentor, Darlene

May, also worked as a basketball referee. "She was a big

influence in my becoming a referee," Palmer said. After

many years of refereeing at various levels, including

NBA pre-season and exhibition games, Palmer was

offered an opportunity to officiate the NCAA Division

I men's tournament in 1996. She accepted the offer, but

they were later retracted when NCAA members balked
51

47. **A.** NO CHANGE
    B. way of playing
    C. way; she played
    D. way she played

48. **F.** NO CHANGE
    G. In her home state to attend Cal Poly
       Pomona, she stayed (a Compton, CA
       native).
    H. She stayed in her home state (a Compton,
       CA native) to attend Cal Poly Pomona.
    J. A Compton, CA native, she stayed in her
       home state to attend Cal Poly Pomona.

49. **A.** NO CHANGE
    B. by being
    C. whom happened to be
    D. who was

50. **F.** NO CHANGE
    G. point guard and also being
    H. point guard, which she was
    J. point guard, where Palmer was

51. **A.** NO CHANGE
    B. they were taken from her
    C. was
    D. it was

at the idea of a female refereeing male players. She

<u>kept maintaining her single focus</u> on an officiating
52

career at the highest levels of basketball.

Palmer and Dee Kantner, another female referee,

were signed a year later by the <u>NBA. Becoming</u> the first
53

top-level female referees in any major U.S. professional

sport. The two referees further made sports history

when they officiated the NBA season opener between

the Vancouver Grizzlies and the Dallas Mavericks. 54

On April 25, 2006, Palmer <u>became another to add</u> her
55

name yet again to history as the first woman to officiate

an NBA playoff game. Her uniform number 12 flowed

up and down the court during the match between the

Indiana Pacers and New Jersey Nets. She <u>has officiated</u>
56

hundreds of NBA games, maintaining the typical referee

schedule of 10 to 11 games per month, or 55 to 70 games

per season.

---

52. **F.** NO CHANGE

G. would keep maintaining her simple focus

H. kept her maintenance of her focus

J. maintained her focus

53. **A.** NO CHANGE

B. NBA, becoming

C. NBA and becoming

D. NBA, by also becoming

54. At this point, the writer is considering adding the following true statement:

> Kantner was later released as a referee by the NBA. Would this be a relevant addition to make here?

F. Yes, because it supports the claim that Palmer is the only active female referee in the NBA.

G. Yes, because it gives information about another important professional female referee.

H. No, because it minimizes the accomplishments that Palmer has achieved in her professional career.

J. No, because it includes information that strays from the essay's focus on Palmer's career as a referee.

55. **A.** NO CHANGE

B. had become another addition with

C. was added again to

D. added

56. **F.** NO CHANGE

G. would have officiated

H. officiate

J. have officiated

GO ON TO THE NEXT PAGE

Being the only active female referee in the NBA is not without its challenges. Palmer, <u>celebrating</u> by many, has been a target of criticism by some. Her integrity has

57.
A. NO CHANGE
B. having been celebrated
C. who is celebrated
D. by celebrating

<u>so rare</u> been questioned, but her work as a game official

58.
F. NO CHANGE
G. rarely
H. rarer
J. more rare

has been criticized for <u>their</u> quality. However, Palmer maintains, "The only way to excel at refereeing in the NBA is to continually referee games. NBA training is

59.
A. NO CHANGE
B. it
C. this
D. its

the best, <u>and</u> until you step out on that floor with those players and 20,000 fans screaming at you night after night, you can't improve."

60.
F. NO CHANGE
G. but
H. nor
J. so

PASSAGE V

SONG OF THE CICADA

Midsummer in the Northeast is quickly identifiable by the humid weather and the sounds of cicadas <u>booming</u> through the day and night. The insects suddenly appear from their underground burrows as the temperature

61. Which choice would best help the reader visualize a repeated sound sustained over a long period of time?
A. NO CHANGE
B. beeping
C. droning
D. mixing

GO ON TO THE NEXT PAGE

grows hotter <u>every 2–17 years</u>. Continuing for about
                        62

two months, the choruses of these noisy critters are an

unmistakable sign of <u>the heat and the season</u>.
                              63
    Often called "locusts" colloquially, cicadas are

actually unrelated to true locusts. Instead, they are

large insects <u>that build</u> with prominent eyes set
                    64

<u>broadly</u> apart on the sides of their heads. Their short
      65
antennae protrude between or in front of their big eyes.

Cicadas use their well-veined, transparent wings to fly

and travel. Some humans find cicadas to be appropriate

pets as they are benign to humans and do not bite or

sting like some of their insect counterparts.

    <u>They are noted as the loudest sound-producing</u>
                              66
<u>insects on the planet.</u> Their name derives from the
      66

62. The best placement for the underlined portion would be:

   F. where it is now.

   G. at the beginning of this sentence (with appropriate capitalization and a comma after the word *years*).

   H. after the word *insects*.

   J. after the word *burrows*.

63. A. NO CHANGE

   B. the heat and, the season

   C. the heat, and the season

   D. the heat and the, season

64. F. NO CHANGE

   G. to build

   H. had been built

   J. built

65. A. NO CHANGE

   B. wide

   C. spaciously

   D. extensively

66. Given that all of the choices are true, which one would most effectively introduce the main subject of this paragraph?

   F. NO CHANGE

   G. Cicadas have larger versions of features common to most insects.

   H. There are many different ways to determine if an insect is a cicada, including watching the height of the cicadas' flight as they prefer to fly high to stay safe.

   J. While these many facts point to some of the discernable features of these creatures, it is their distinctive sound that makes cicadas most recognizable.

GO ON TO THE NEXT PAGE ⟶

<u>original</u> word in Latin *cicada*, meaning
67

"<u>buzzer;" a</u> comparison to a buzzer is quite accurate.
68

<u>Chiefly,</u> male cicadas create loud sounds using their
69
noisemakers called timbals, which are located at the

abdominal base. Contracting the internal timbal muscles

produces the cicada's clicking sound as the timbals

buckle <u>inwards. When</u> these muscles relax, the timbals
70
return to their original position producing another click.

The male cicada rapidly repeats this drumlike action to

create this sound that is amplified by the resonance of

their substantially hollow abdomen. 71 While

67. **A.** NO CHANGE
    B. ancient form of the
    C. originally
    D. OMIT the underlined portion.

68. **F.** NO CHANGE
    G. "buzzer." A
    H. "buzzer," so a
    J. "buzzer," a

69. **A.** NO CHANGE
    B. Moreover,
    C. Accordingly,
    D. Specifically,

70. Which of the following alternatives to the underlined portion would NOT be acceptable?
    F. inwards; when
    G. inwards. So when
    H. inwards, when
    J. inwards, and when

71. If the writer were to eliminate the words *rapidly* and *drumlike* from the preceding sentence, it would primarily lose:
    A. language that emphasizes the writer's depiction of cicadas as physically equipped to create their own style of music.
    B. details that contrast the idea that cicadas make their own sounds.
    C. a witty depiction of musical actions of the cicada.
    D. information that supports the idea that male cicadas are constructed differently from the female of their species.

GO ON TO THE NEXT PAGE ⟶

humans whom hear these noises may think cicadas all
72
sound the same, each species has its own distinct song.

Male cicadas use their sounds to lure mates to come
73
toward them, but their melodies also attract predators,
73
including large raptors like the Swainson's Hawk and
the Mississippi Kite. These birds eat cicadas at every
opportunity they get. Most cicadas use their strong
wings to fly away, but their unique songs still attract
74
these predators and fill the ears of Northeast residents
74

during their seasonal visits. [75]

72. **F.** NO CHANGE
 G. humans, whom
 H. humans who
 J. humans, which

73. **A.** NO CHANGE
 B. to draw and attract mates during an appealing process
 C. to encourage mates to keep coming toward them
 D. to lure mates

74. **F.** NO CHANGE
 G. will attract predators
 H. to attract these predators
 J. are attracting these predators

75. The writer is concerned that the final statement is not appropriate for this essay and, therefore, is considering deleting the last sentence. Should the writer make this deletion?
 A. Yes, because the statement has a much less formal tone than the rest of the passage.
 B. Yes, because the statement has nothing to do with the rest of the passage.
 C. No, because the statement summarizes key details in the passage and the concluding paragraph.
 D. No, because the statement supports the claim that humans are aware of cicadas.

MATHEMATICS TEST

60 Minutes—60 Questions

Directions: Solve each of the following problems, select the correct answer, and then fill in the corresponding space on your answer sheet.

Don't linger over problems that are too time-consuming. Do as many as you can, then come back to the others in the time you have remaining.

The use of a calculator is permitted on this test. Though you are allowed to use your calculator to solve any questions you choose, some of the questions may be most easily answered without the use of a calculator.

Note: Unless otherwise noted, all of the following should be assumed.

1. Illustrative figures are *not* necessarily drawn to scale.

2. All geometric figures lie in a plane.

3. The term *line* indicates a straight line.

4. The term *average* indicates arithmetic mean.

1. If a and b are positive integers such that the greatest common factor of a^4b and a^2b^3 is 75, which of the following is a possible value for a?

    A. 75

    B. 25

    C. 9

    D. 5

    E. 3

2. A long-distance phone company offers a rate plan that charges $0.10 per minute for up to 200 minutes per month, and $0.15 for each minute over 200 minutes. If you talk for 250 minutes in one month, how much will you be charged?

    F. $20.00

    G. $25.00

    H. $27.50

    J. $30.00

    K. $37.50

3. What is the solution set of $3x - 11 \geq 22$?

    A. $x \geq -11$

    B. $x < -3$

    C. $x \geq 0$

    D. $x \geq 3$

    E. $x \geq 11$

4. How many integers between 1 and 50 are divisible by 4 ?

    F. 11

    G. 12

    H. 13

    J. 14

    K. 15

GO ON TO THE NEXT PAGE

5. The school band has a collection of 300 pieces of music. Of these, 10% are movie theme songs. Out of the rest of the pieces of music, 80 of the pieces are marches. How many of the band's pieces of music are neither marches nor movie theme songs?

    A. 190

    B. 198

    C. 210

    D. 220

    E. 270

6. At a certain time of day, Carrie casts a 380-centimeter-long shadow, and Wade casts a 400-centimeter-long shadow (assume that Carrie and Wade are standing vertically on level ground). If Wade is 180-centimeters tall, how many centimeters tall is Carrie?

    F. 160

    G. 171

    H. 180

    J. 189

    K. 200

7. $-6 + |4 - 8| = ?$

    A. −18

    B. −10

    C. −2

    D. 2

    E. 6

8. Square *ABCD* is shown below, with one side measuring 6 centimeters. What is the area of triangle *BCD*, in square centimeters?

    F. 3

    G. 6

    H. 12

    J. 18

    K. 36

9. Edwin is playing a game in which he must move his game piece clockwise around a circular game board. After his last turn, he has gone $\frac{1}{2}$ of the way around the board. What is the measure of the central angle formed by Edwin's game piece from the starting point to the point where his piece is now?

    A. 0°

    B. 90°

    C. 180°

    D. 270°

    E. 340°

GO ON TO THE NEXT PAGE

10. Which expression can be used to find the perimeter, in units, of an equilateral triangle that has a side length of 12 units?

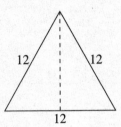

   F. 12^2

   G. 12 • 12 • 12

   H. 12 + 12 + 12

   J. $\dfrac{1}{2}(6\sqrt{3})(12)$

   K. $6\sqrt{3}(12)$

11. A piece of letter-sized paper is $8\dfrac{1}{2}$ inches wide and 11 inches long. Suppose you want to cut strips of paper that are $\dfrac{5}{8}$ inch wide and 11 inches long. What is the maximum number of strips of paper you could make from 1 piece of letter-sized paper?

   A. 5

   B. 6

   C. 12

   D. 13

   E. 14

12. Which of these is equivalent to $(4x - 1)(x + 5)$?

   F. $4x^2 + 8x$

   G. $4x^2 - 10x - 5$

   H. $4x^2 + 15x + 5$

   J. $4x^2 + 19x - 5$

   K. $4x^2 + 19x + 5$

13. Look at the coordinate plane below.

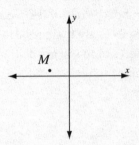

   If a and b are positive integers, which could be the coordinates of point M?

   A. $(0,-b)$

   B. $(a,-b)$

   C. $(-a,0)$

   D. $(-a,-b)$

   E. $(-a,b)$

14. A scientist had a container of liquid nitrogen that was at a temperature of –330°F. If the temperature of the room was 72°F, how much must the temperature of the liquid nitrogen change to become the room's temperature? (Note: "+" indicates a rise in temperature, and "–" indicates a drop in temperature.)

   F. –330°F

   G. –258°F

   H. +72°F

   J. +402°F

   K. +474°F

15. Which of these is equivalent to $b^5 \cdot b^7$?

   A. b^{-2}

   B. b^2

   C. b^{12}

   D. b^{35}

   E. b^{57}

GO ON TO THE NEXT PAGE

16. The volume of a cylinder is given by the formula $V = \pi r^2 h$, where V is the volume, r is the radius, and h is the height. Which expression can be used to find the radius, in centimeters, of a cylinder with a volume of 240 cm³ and a height of 9 cm?

F. $\dfrac{9\pi}{240}$

G. $\dfrac{240}{9\pi}$

H. $\sqrt{\dfrac{240}{9\pi}}$

J. $\sqrt{\dfrac{240\pi}{9}}$

K. $\sqrt{\dfrac{9\pi}{240}}$

17. In the figure below, $AD \parallel CE$. What is $\angle CBD$?

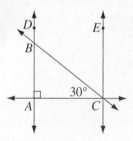

A. 30°

B. 60°

C. 90°

D. 120°

E. 150°

18. Four numbers are in a sequence with 8 as its first term and 36 as its last term. The first 3 numbers are in an arithmetic sequence with a common difference of –7. The last 3 numbers are in a geometric sequence. What is the common ratio of the last 3 terms of the sequence?

F. –10

G. –6

H. 0

J. 10

K. 32

19. Neal has the thermostat in his house set to 70°F. When the temperature in his house is below 70°F, the heat will turn on. Which of these shows the temperatures, T, in degrees Fahrenheit at which Neal's heat will be running?

A. $T = 70$

B. $T \geq 70$

C. $T > 70$

D. $T \leq 70$

E. $T < 70$

20. The size of a rectangular video screen is usually measured by its diagonal. If a portable DVD player has a screen that measures 7 inches, and the width of the screen is 6 inches, what is the approximate height of the screen, in inches?

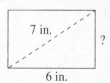

F. 3.6

G. 5.0

H. 5.1

J. 6.5

K. 6.6

GO ON TO THE NEXT PAGE

21. If w, x, y, and z are all positive real numbers and $w^{-1} > x^{-1} > y^{-1} > z^{-1}$, which of the numbers has the least value?

    A. w

    B. x

    C. y

    D. z

    E. Cannot be determined from the given information

22. If $2(t - 4) = 3t + 2$, then $t = ?$

    F. -10

    G. -6

    H. $-\dfrac{6}{5}$

    J. $\dfrac{6}{5}$

    K. 2

23. What is the solution of the system of equations below?

    $$-x + y = 3$$
    $$-3x + y = -5$$

    A. $(-8, -5)$

    B. $(-4, -1)$

    C. $(3, -5)$

    D. $(4, 7)$

    E. $(8, 11)$

24. If a and b are positive real numbers, which of the following is NOT equivalent to $(-a)b$?

    F. $(-a)(-b)$

    G. $-ab$

    H. $\dfrac{-a}{\frac{1}{b}}$

    J. $a(-b)$

    K. $(-\dfrac{a}{2})(2b)$

25. In the figure below, all of the small triangles are the same size. What percent of the entire figure is shaded?

    A. 8%

    B. 24%

    C. $33\dfrac{1}{3}$ %

    D. 50%

    E. $66\dfrac{2}{3}$ %

26. A scientist has 100 grams of a radioactive substance that has a half-life of 25 days. The table below shows the number of grams of the substance remaining certain numbers of days.

Number of days	0	28	56	84	112	x
Number of grams remaining	100	50	25	12.5	6.25	28

    Which expression best represents the number of grams of the substance remaining after x days?

    F. $28 \cdot \left(\dfrac{1}{2}\right)^{x}$

    G. $28 \cdot 2^{x/100}$

    H. $100 \cdot 2^{x/28}$

    J. $100 \cdot \left(\dfrac{1}{2}\right)^{x/28}$

    K. $100\left(\dfrac{1}{2}\right)^{x}$

27. Morris is offered two different jobs as a sales-person. At company A, he will earn a base salary of $300 per week, plus a commission of $20 per sale. At Company B, he does not have a base salary, but will earn $35 per sale. If s is positive and represents the number of total sales, for what values of s will Morris earn more at Company A than Company B?

A. $s > 20$

B. $s \geq 20$

C. $s \leq 20$

D. $s < 20$

E. $s \geq 0$

28. Which of these is an equation of the line that crosses through (–3,4) and (3,6)?

F. $x + 3y = 15$

G. $-x + 3y = 15$

H. $\frac{1}{3}x - y = 5$

J. $3x + y = 5$

K. $-3x + y = 5$

29. What is the value of $x + y$ in the figure below?

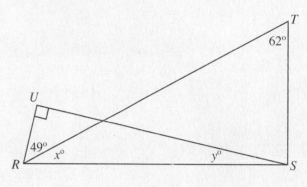

A. 77°

B. 62°

C. 41°

D. 28°

E. 13°

30. What is the area of circle C, in square feet, if the circumference is 16π?

F. 4π

G. 8π

H. 16π

J. 32π

K. 64π

31. A farmer wants to enclose a plot of land with a certain amount of fencing. The plot is in the shape of a right triangle, with a base that is 7 yards longer than the height. If the area of the plot is 60 square yards, how many yards of fencing does the farmer need to completely enclose the plot of land?

A. 34

B. 40

C. 46

D. 80

E. 96

GO ON TO THE NEXT PAGE

32. In a right triangle, if $\sin A = \dfrac{8}{17}$ and $\cos A = \dfrac{15}{17}$, what is $\tan A$?

    F. $\dfrac{8}{15}$

    G. $\dfrac{15}{8}$

    H. $\dfrac{17}{8}$

    J. $\dfrac{17}{15}$

    K. $\dfrac{23}{17}$

33. In the graph below, what is the distance between point A and point B, in coordinate units?

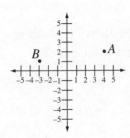

    A. $\sqrt{2}$
    B. $\sqrt{8}$
    C. $\sqrt{50}$
    D. 7
    E. 8

34. What is the slope of the line through the points $(-10,0)$ and $(0,-6)$?

    F. $-\dfrac{5}{3}$

    G. $-\dfrac{3}{5}$

    H. $\dfrac{3}{5}$

    J. $\dfrac{5}{3}$

    K. 0

35. If $f(x) = 16x^2 - 20x$, what is the value of $f(3)$?

    A. -12
    B. 36
    C. 84
    D. 144
    E. 372

36. Which of these shows that y varies inversely as x and directly as the square of z?

    F. $y = \dfrac{kx^2}{z}$

    G. $y = \dfrac{kz^2}{x}$

    H. $y = \dfrac{kx}{z^2}$

    J. $y = kxz^2$

    K. $y = kx^2z$

37. Which of these is NOT a factor of $x^6 - 81x^2$?

    A. $x + 9$
    B. $x^2 + 9$
    C. x^2
    D. $x - 3$
    E. $x + 3$

GO ON TO THE NEXT PAGE

38. In the right triangle below, what is cos C ?

F. $\dfrac{7}{25}$

G. $\dfrac{7}{24}$

H. $\dfrac{24}{25}$

J. $\dfrac{24}{7}$

K. $\dfrac{25}{7}$

39. The figure on the coordinate plane is a rectangle. What coordinate pair corresponds to point B ?

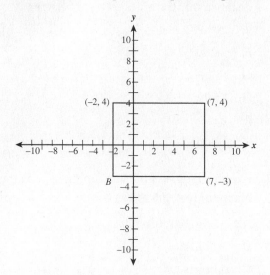

A. $(-2,-3)$

B. $(-2,4)$

C. $(2,-3)$

D. $(-3,4)$

E. $(3,-2)$

40. In the figure below, $LM = LP$. Which statement must be true?

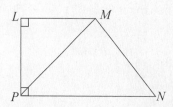

F. $LM = MP$

G. $PN < LM$

H. $MN = PN$

J. $LP < MP$

K. $MN > LP$

41. A cooking class has 20 spaces available for each daily session. Data showed that 19 people attended the first session, 17 people attended the second session, and 15 people attended each of the remaining sessions. If the average number of attendees was exactly 16 per class session, how many total sessions of the cooking class were there?

A. 3

B. 4

C. 6

D. 11

E. Cannot be determined from the given information

42. The equation of a circle is $(x - 2)^2 + (y + 1)^2 = 14$. What are the coordinates of the circle's center, and what is the length of the circle's radius?

F. Center: $(-1,2)$; Radius: $\sqrt{14}$

G. Center: $(-1,2)$; Radius: 7

H. Center: $(2,-1)$; Radius: $\sqrt{14}$

J. Center: $(2,-1)$; Radius: 7

K. Center: $(-2,1)$; Radius: 14

GO ON TO THE NEXT PAGE

43. The point $(-3,-2)$ is the midpoint of the line segment in the standard (x,y) coordinate plane joining the point $(1,9)$ and (m,n). Which of the following is (m,n)?

   A. $(-7,-13)$

   B. $(-1,7)$

   C. $(-2,5.5)$

   D. $(2,5.5)$

   E. $(5,20)$

44. Which equation represents the line that is parallel to $y = 4x + 7$ and passes through $(-5,1)$?

   F. $y = x + 20$

   G. $y = -5x - 19$

   H. $y = 4x + 19$

   J. $y = -4x + 20$

   K. $y = 4x + 21$

45. Margaret made a stage prop that is the shape of a right, triangular prism. The prop has a width of 6 feet, a height of 2 feet, and a length of 6 feet. What is the volume, in cubic feet, of the right triangular prism?

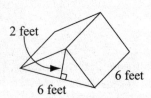

   A. 14

   B. 36

   C. 45

   D. 72

   E. 144

Use the following information to answer questions 46–49.

A hiker planned to hike a small mountain during the course of a day. The hiker began at 7 AM at an altitude of 4,000 feet. When the hiker is climbing the mountain, she climbs at a constant speed for an hour. She finished her hike back at 4,000 feet at 1 PM. The hiker's altitude, in feet, is shown in the graph below.

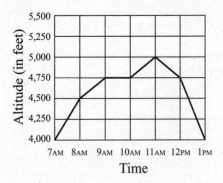

46. What is the closest, in feet, to the total vertical distance that the hiker traveled between 8:00 AM and 1:00 PM?

   F. 250

   G. 1,000

   H. 1,500

   J. 1,750

   K. 2,000

47. For how long, in hours and minutes, was the hiker above 4,500 feet?

   A. 1 hour 20 minutes

   B. 3 hours

   C. 4 hours

   D. 4 hours 20 minutes

   E. 5 hours

GO ON TO THE NEXT PAGE

48. Which graph best represents the absolute value of velocity that the hiker travels, in vertical feet per hour?

(Note: Ignore acceleration and deceleration at the beginning and end of each one-hour interval.)

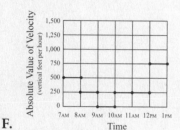

F.

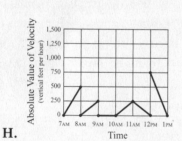

G.

H.

J.

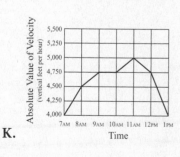

K.

49. Which description best describes the hiker's altitude from 9 AM to 12 PM?

A. The hiker stayed at the same altitude, then ascended the mountain.

B. The hiker ascended the mountain, then descended the mountain at a faster rate.

C. The hiker descended the mountain at one rate, then descended the mountain at a faster rate.

D. The hiker ascended the mountain, then stayed at the same altitude, then descended the mountain.

E. The hiker stayed at the same altitude, then ascended and descended the mountain at the same rate.

50. Quadrilateral *LMNO* has vertices *L*(1,4), *M*(4,4), *N*(4,2), and *O*(1,2) in the (*x*,*y*) coordinate plane shown below. The rectangle is translated such that the image of each point *P*(*x*,*y*) is the point *P*′(*x*′,*y*′), and *x*′ = *x* + 2 and *y*′ = *y* − 3. In which quadrant(s) do the vertices of quadrilateral *L*′*M*′*N*′*O*′ lie?

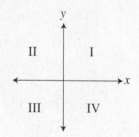

Quadrant of the
(*x*,*y*) Coordinate Plane

F. Quadrant I only

G. Quadrant IV only

H. Quadrants I and II only

J. Quadrants I and IV only

K. Quadrants I, II, III, and IV

GO ON TO THE NEXT PAGE ▷

51. Ginny wants to prove that $\triangle QRS \cong \triangle STQ$, using the Angle-Side-Angle (ASA) congruence postulate. She knows that $\angle SQR \cong \angle QST$. Which of the following congruences, if established, is sufficient to prove the triangles are congruent?

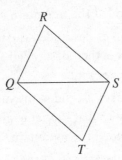

A. $\angle SQR \cong \angle RQS$

B. $\angle SQR \cong \angle RSQ$

C. $\angle SQR \cong \angle TQS$

D. $\angle RSQ \cong \angle QST$

E. $\angle RSQ \cong \angle TQS$

52. In the right triangle below, what is the value of x?

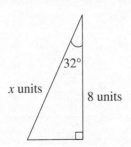

F. $8\sin 32°$

G. $8\cos 32°$

H. $8\tan 32°$

J. $\dfrac{8}{\sin 32°}$

K. $\dfrac{8}{\cos 32°}$

53. The radius of a circle is increased so that the radius of the resulting circle is double that of the original circle. How many times larger is the area of the resulting circle than that of the original circle?

A. 0.5

B. 1

C. 2

D. π

E. 4

54. A scientist was studying a meadow and the birds that lived in the meadow. He kept a count of the birds that appeared in the meadow by tagging them so that the individual birds could be distinguished from one another. There are only three types of birds that live in the meadow: buntings, larks, and sparrows. He found that the ratio of buntings to total birds in the meadow was 35:176, while the ratio of larks to total birds was 5:11. If the scientist randomly chooses one individual bird that he had previously counted, which type of bird is he most likely to choose?

F. Bunting

G. Lark

H. Sparrow

J. All bird types are equally likely

K. Cannot be determined from the given information

55. Assume m and n are nonzero real numbers such that $|m| = m$ and $|n| = -n$. Which of the following *must* be negative?

A. $-n^m$

B. $-mn$

C. m^n

D. $-n - m$

E. $n - m$

56. If $x^2 + 4x - 9 = 0$, which of the following is a possible value of x? Remember the quadratic formula:

$$x = \frac{-b \pm \sqrt{b^2 - 4ac}}{2a}$$

F. -7

G. $-2 - \sqrt{52}$

H. $-2 \pm \dfrac{\sqrt{52}}{2}$

J. $2 \pm \dfrac{\sqrt{52}}{2}$

K. 7

57. What is $\cos \dfrac{5\pi}{12}$ given that $\dfrac{5\pi}{12} = \dfrac{2\pi}{3} - \dfrac{\pi}{4}$ and that $\cos(x - y) = (\cos x)(\cos y) + (\sin x)(\sin y)$?

(Note: You may use the following table of values.)

θ	$\sin \theta$	$\cos \theta$
$\dfrac{\pi}{4}$	$\dfrac{\sqrt{2}}{2}$	$\dfrac{\sqrt{2}}{2}$
$\dfrac{2\pi}{3}$	$\dfrac{\sqrt{3}}{2}$	$-\dfrac{1}{2}$
$\dfrac{5\pi}{6}$	$\dfrac{1}{2}$	$-\dfrac{\sqrt{3}}{2}$

A. $-\dfrac{\sqrt{3}}{4}$

B. $-\dfrac{\sqrt{3}}{2}$

C. $\dfrac{2 - \sqrt{3}}{4}$

D. $\dfrac{-1 - \sqrt{2}}{2}$

E. $\dfrac{\sqrt{6} - \sqrt{2}}{4}$

58. The lengths of the legs of the right triangle below are $10 \sin \theta$ and $10 \cos \theta$ respectively. If $0° \leq \theta \leq 90°$, what is the length of the hypotenuse of the triangle?

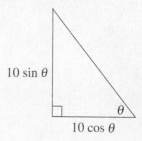

F. 1

G. $\sqrt{10}$

H. 5

J. 10

K. 100

59. If r, s, and t represent nonzero values such that $r = \dfrac{s}{t}$, which expression must be equivalent to rs?

A. $\dfrac{s}{t}$

B. $\dfrac{r}{t^2}$

C. st

D. $\dfrac{s^2}{t}$

E. $\dfrac{1}{t}$

60. When $-1 \leq a \leq 1$ and $-4 \leq b \leq 3$, what is the greatest possible value of the expression $a \times b$?

F. 4

G. 3

H. 2

J. -3

K. -12

IF YOU FINISH BEFORE TIME IS CALLED, YOU MAY CHECK YOUR WORK ON THIS SECTION ONLY. DO NOT TURN TO ANY OTHER SECTION IN THE TEST.   **STOP**

READING TEST

35 Minutes—40 Questions

Directions: There are four passages in this test. Each passage is followed by several questions. After reading a passage, choose the best answer to each question and fill in the corresponding oval on your Answer Grid. You may refer to the passages as often as necessary.

PASSAGE I

PROSE FICTION

The following passage is adapted from the novel Sons and Lovers *by D.H. Lawrence, (© 1913).*

The Bottoms consisted of six blocks of miners' dwellings, two rows of three, like the dots on a blank-six domino, and twelve houses in a block.
Line This double row of dwellings sat at the foot of the
(5) rather sharp slope from Bestwood, and looked out, from the attic windows at least, on the slow climb of the valley towards Selby.

The houses themselves were substantial and very decent. One could walk all round, seeing
(10) little front gardens with auriculas and saxifrage in the shadow of the bottom block, sweet-williams and pinks in the sunny top block; seeing neat front windows, little porches, little privet hedges, and dormer windows for the attics. But that was
(15) outside; that was the view on to the uninhabited parlors of all the colliers' wives. The dwelling-room, the kitchen, was at the back of the house, facing inward between the blocks, looking at a scrubby back garden, and then at the ash-pits. And between
(20) the rows, between the long lines of ash-pits, went the alley, where the children played and the women gossiped and the men smoked. So, the actual conditions of living in the Bottoms, that was so well built and that looked so nice, were quite unsavory
(25) because people must live in the kitchen, and the kitchens opened on to that nasty alley of ash-pits.

Mrs. Morel was not anxious to move into the Bottoms, which was already twelve years old and on the downward path, when she descended to it
(30) from Bestwood. But it was the best she could do. Moreover, she had an end house in one of the top blocks, and thus had only one neighbor; on the other side an extra strip of garden. And, having an end house, she enjoyed a kind of aristocracy among
(35) the other women of the "between" houses, because her rent was five shillings and sixpence instead of five shillings a week. But this superiority in station was not much consolation to Mrs. Morel.

She was thirty-one years old, and had been
(40) married eight years. A rather small woman, of delicate mould but resolute bearing, she shrank a little from the first contact with the Bottoms women. She came down in July, and in September expected her third baby.

(45) Her husband was a miner. They had only been in their new home three weeks when the wakes, or fair, began. Morel, she knew, was sure to make a holiday of it. He went off early on the Monday morning, the day of the fair. The two children were
(50) highly excited. William, a boy of seven, fled off immediately after breakfast, to prowl round the wakes ground, leaving Annie, who was only five, to whine all morning to go also. Mrs. Morel did her work. She scarcely knew her neighbors yet, and
(55) knew no one with whom to trust the little girl.

William appeared at half-past twelve. He was a very active lad, fair-haired, freckled, with a touch of the Dane or Norwegian about him.

"Can I have my dinner, mother?" he cried,
(60) rushing in with his cap on. "'Cause it begins at half-past one, the man says so."

"You can have your dinner as soon as it's done," replied the mother.

"Isn't it done?" he cried, his blue eyes staring at
(65) her in indignation. "Then I'm goin' be-out it."

"You'll do nothing of the sort. It will be done in five minutes. It is only half-past twelve."

GO ON TO THE NEXT PAGE ⟩

"They'll be beginnin'," the boy half cried, half shouted.

(70)   "You won't die if they do," said the mother. "Besides, it's only half-past twelve, so you've a full hour."

The lad began hastily to lay the table. They were eating batter-pudding and jam, when the boy

(75) jumped off his chair and stood perfectly stiff. Some distance away could be heard the first small braying of a merry-go-round, and the tooting of a horn. His face quivered as he looked at his mother.

1. Which of the following best summarizes the narrator's description of homes in the Bottoms?

   A. Entirely decent for mining families
   B. Minimally furnished
   C. Completely forlorn
   D. Deceptively handsome

2. The usage of the phrase "a kind of aristocracy" in line 34 most nearly suggests that:

   F. Mrs. Morel belonged to a higher social class than the other wives of the Bottoms.
   G. having one neighbor was considered a privilege among the women of the Bottoms.
   H. Mrs. Morel regards herself as superior to her neighbors in the Bottoms.
   J. none of her neighbors can afford the extra expense for an end house in the Bottoms.

3. The narrator suggests that Mrs. Morel's attitude toward her new life in the Bottoms is probably:

   A. despairing.
   B. disgruntled.
   C. indifferent.
   D. elated.

4. Which of the following best summarizes the purpose of the fourth paragraph?

   F. to illustrate the emotional strength of a heroic woman
   G. to elicit sympathy from the reader about a tragic occurrence
   H. to inform the reader about the background of a central character
   J. to criticize a character for her poor decision making

5. The author includes the line "Morel, she knew, was sure to make a holiday of it," in order to:

   A. condemn Mr. Morel as an irresponsible spouse.
   B. emphasize the allure of the "Wakes" fair.
   C. explain the absence of Mrs. Morel's husband.
   D. illustrate the perks of working as a miner.

6. The fifth paragraph suggests that Mrs. Morel:

   F. is inconvenienced by the Wakes.
   G. is not interested in the fair.
   H. is angry with her children's behavior.
   J. does not intend to go to the fair.

7. The discussion of William's actions in the last paragraph seems to suggest that:

   A. he does not want to eat the food Mrs. Morel has prepared.
   B. he is willing to miss the beginning of the fair.
   C. he is habitually an ill-mannered child.
   D. he is impatient to finish his meal so that he may go to the fair.

GO ON TO THE NEXT PAGE ▷

8. The phrase "on the downward path" in line 29 seems to suggest:

   F. only the poorest miners would live in the Bottoms.

   G. the houses were built on an angle from the valley.

   H. the mining company was unwilling to pay for repairs.

   J. houses in the Bottoms were beginning to deteriorate.

9. The comparison between rents in lines 36–37 most nearly suggests that:

   A. the convenience of an end house is not worth the extra expense.

   B. six pence was a lot of money to the Morel family.

   C. privacy was a valuable commodity in the Bottoms community.

   D. Mr. Morel did not earn enough to pay the family's rent.

10. The phrase "But that was the outside" in lines 14–15 most closely agrees in meaning with:

    F. The Bottoms homes were specifically designed to hide their unglamorous interiors.

    G. The living areas of homes in the Bottoms angered most of their tenants.

    H. The Mining Company did not care about the opinions of its employees.

    J. A viewer's first impression of the homes in the Bottoms would not necessarily be correct.

PASSAGE II

SOCIAL STUDIES

The following passage is adapted from "Free Culture" by Lawrence Lessig, as found on wikisource.org.

Since the inception of laws regulating creative property, there has been a war against "piracy." The precise contours of this concept are hard to sketch,

Line but the animating injustice is easy to capture. As
(5) Lord Mansfield wrote in a case that extended the reach of English copyright law to include sheet music, "A person may use the copy by playing it, but he has no right to rob the author of the profit, by multiplying copies and disposing of them for his
(10) own use."

Today we are in the middle of another "war" against "piracy." The Internet has provoked this war. The Internet makes possible the efficient spread of content. Peer-to-peer (p2p) file sharing
(15) is among the most efficient of the efficient technologies the Internet enables. Using distributed intelligence, p2p systems facilitate the easy spread of content in a way unimagined a generation ago.

This efficiency does not respect the traditional
(20) lines of copyright. The network doesn't discriminate between the sharing of copyrighted and uncopyrighted content. Thus has there been a vast amount of sharing of copyrighted content. That sharing in turn has excited the war, as
(25) copyright owners fear the sharing will "rob the author of the profit."

The warriors have turned to the courts, to the legislatures, and increasingly to technology to defend their "property" against this "piracy."
(30) A generation of Americans, the warriors warn, is being raised to believe that "property" should be "free." Forget tattoos, never mind body piercing—our kids are becoming thieves!

There's no doubt that "piracy" is wrong, and
(35) that pirates should be punished. But before we summon the executioners, we should put this notion of "piracy" in some context. For as the concept is increasingly used, at its core is an extraordinary idea that is almost certainly wrong.
(40) The idea goes something like this: Creative work

GO ON TO THE NEXT PAGE →

has value; whenever I use, or take, or build upon the creative work of others, I am taking from them something of value. Whenever I take something of value from someone else, I should have their
(45) permission.

This view runs deep within the current debates. It is what NYU law professor Rochelle Dreyfuss criticizes as the "if value, then right" theory of creative property—if there is value, then someone
(50) must have a right to that value. It is the perspective that led a composers' rights organization, ASCAP, to sue the Girl Scouts for failing to pay for the songs that girls sang around Girl Scout campfires. There was "value" (the songs) so there must have
(55) been a "right"—even against the Girl Scouts.

This idea is certainly a possible understanding of how creative property should work. It might well be a possible design for a system of law protecting creative property. But the "if value,
(60) then right" theory of creative property has never been America's theory of creative property. It has never taken hold within our law. Instead, in our tradition, intellectual property is an instrument. It sets the groundwork for a richly creative society
(65) but remains subservient to the value of creativity. The current debate has this turned around. We have become so concerned with protecting the instrument that we are losing sight of the value.

The source of this confusion is a distinction that
(70) the law no longer takes care to draw: the distinction between republishing someone's work, on the one hand, and building upon or transforming that work on the other. Copyright law at its birth had only publishing as its concern; copyright law today
(75) regulates both.

Before the technologies of the Internet, this conflation didn't matter all that much. The technologies of publishing were expensive; that meant the vast majority of publishing was
(80) commercial. Commercial entities could bear the burden of the law—even the burden of the byzantine complexity that copyright law has become. It was just one more expense of doing business. But with the birth of the Internet,
(85) this natural limit to the reach of the law has disappeared. The law controls not just the creativity

of commercial creators, but effectively that of anyone. Although that expansion would not matter much if copyright law regulated only "copying,"
(90) when the law regulates as broadly and obscurely as it does, the extension matters a lot.

The burden of this law now vastly outweighs any original benefit—certainly as it affects noncommercial creativity, and increasingly as
(95) it affects commercial creativity as well. Thus the law's role is less and less to support creativity, and more and more to protect certain industries against competition. Just at the time digital technology could unleash an extraordinary range
(100) of commercial and noncommercial creativity, the law burdens this creativity with insanely complex and vague rules and with the threat of obscenely severe penalties. We may be seeing, as Richard Florida writes, the "rise of the creative class."
(105) Unfortunately, we are also seeing an extraordinary rise of regulation of this creative class.

11. The main point of the last paragraph is that copyright law:

   A. hinders creativity.

   B. encourages competition.

   C. has less and less of an impact.

   D. has never been useful.

12. According to the passage, the difference between copyright law as it was originally created and as it is today is largely the result of:

   F. decreased commercial interest in the publishing industry.

   G. an increase in piracy of copyrighted material.

   H. the technological capabilities provided by the Internet.

   J. the rise of the creative class.

GO ON TO THE NEXT PAGE

13. As it is used in line 77, the word *conflation* most nearly means:

    A. regulation.

    B. conception.

    C. combination.

    D. theft.

14. The author suggests that the "if value, then right" theory of creative property (line 48) is inappropriate because it:

    F. does not accurately reflect how the law has historically treated creative property.

    G. is based upon legal concepts that are too vague to enforce.

    H. can never govern both commercial interests and creative interests.

    J. has been unable to provide a clear definition of piracy.

15. The author appears to feel that the case of the Girl Scouts being sued by ASCAP is an example of:

    A. the ease with which younger generations tend to commit piracy.

    B. noncommercial creativity being produced without technology.

    C. flaws in the popular conception of creative work.

    D. intellectual property being used as an instrument.

16. The author states that the Internet and file sharing technologies:

    I. must be regulated by copyright laws.

    II. allow increased production of noncommercial creative property.

    III. have led to an increase in sharing of copyrighted materials.

    F. II only

    G. I and III only

    H. II and III only

    J. I, II, and III

17. When the author uses the term "warriors" in Paragraph 4 (lines 27–33), he is referring to:

    A. the generation in danger of becoming thieves.

    B. the law professors and legislators who attempt to define piracy.

    C. those people who believe that piracy is acceptable.

    D. those people who seek legal protection from piracy.

18. The author appears to feel that digital technology's potential to increase noncommercial creativity:

    F. should not be hindered by unnecessary regulation.

    G. is an inevitable consequence of deficient regulation of the Internet.

    H. will lead to more cases of piracy.

    J. will lead to increased competition among producers of creative property.

GO ON TO THE NEXT PAGE

19. The author's comment that "this natural limit to the reach of the law has disappeared" (lines 85–86) refers to the effect of:

   A. the emergence of piracy as a legitimate concern to copyright holders.

   B. copyright laws becoming too complex to be understood.

   C. misguided attempts to define a correct theory of creative property.

   D. technologies that have allowed creative property to be produced inexpensively.

20. The author indicates that the fight against piracy began after:

   F. the establishment of laws dealing with creative property.

   G. the birth of the Internet.

   H. the development of the concept of creative property.

   J. courts established a distinction between creative and commercial property.

PASSAGE III

HUMANITIES

What is the best approach to curriculum and classroom pedagogy for United States public school classrooms? Psychologists, public officials, reformers, and educators have been struggling to answer this question for over a century. The pair of passages that follows represents two opposing opinions on the question.

Passage A

Recent efforts on the part of some reformers to influence education policy in the public and academic arena have created the danger of a devolution that would do away with a hundred
(5) years of progress in educational methodology. Some proponents of the so-called "instructivist" movement would see our educational institutions return to the days of the factory schools of the nineteenth century, when teachers taught an
(10) inflexible, programmed curriculum to students who learned to regurgitate it by rote, abstracted from any connection with real-world applications or usability and under constant threat of swift punishment for any deviation or intellectual
(15) digression. History clearly demonstrates that such educational arrangements not only fail to foster the divergent and creative thinking vital to success in today's world, but they do not even accomplish the goals they purport to—as the
(20) decades of widespread illiteracy and ignorance that accompanied the practice of such methods can attest. In contrast, the educational approach most pervasive in schools today, known typically as "constructivism," delivers students from the
(25) oppression of the factory school model and into the student-centered environment of communal, hands-on, complex learning.

The constructivist approach to education uses principles of cognitive psychology, particularly the
(30) work of Piaget and Erikson, to understand how students learn and then to design curricula that address those learning patterns. In one famous example, education researcher J. Bruner led students to an understanding of prime numbers
(35) by having them sort beans into different sized groups. Through this sorting exercise, students discovered for themselves the essential principles of multiplication and division. For example, the discovery that some quantities of beans cannot be
(40) sorted without some left over beans leads to an understanding of prime numbers. Researchers tell us that students who come to discover knowledge for themselves in this way— who "construct" knowledge in this pattern—are better able to
(45) comprehend, retain, and transfer that knowledge to new contexts. Theorists emphasize that students subjected to rote memorization of prime numbers and multiplication tables do not incorporate as deep an understanding as students who are led to
(50) discover such principles for themselves.

In contrast to the rigidly hierarchic, authoritarian classrooms of the past, the constructivist classroom is collaborative. Facts and principles are always placed in the context

GO ON TO THE NEXT PAGE →

(55) of real-world problems or complex projects, and never abstracted from a life situation to which they are applicable. Learning becomes a social negotiation, highly cooperative, with each student encouraged to contribute. The teacher acts only as (60) a guide and facilitator who creates and maintains the appropriate learning environment. The course of a lesson is subject to all the errors, false starts, and stalls of student-driven experimentation, but learning acquired this way is ultimately broader (65) and more useful than sets of abstracted facts. The class is capable of transcending the limits of the curriculum and the expectations of educators alike.

Passage B

Most people, if they saw it for themselves, would be horrified by the style of "education" (70) that goes on in classrooms across the country today. Gone are the straight rows, the orderly progress of instruction, the traditional skills and intensive practice that makes for true mastery of school subjects. Instead, observers would see (75) a mishmash of students in circles and groups fumbling around with ill-defined "projects," striving to figure out something that they're not instructed in by teachers who aren't even allowed to correct them or tell them when they're wrong. (80) Training and practice in discrete skills is discarded. Assessment as a motivation is de-emphasized in favor of "facilitating" learning that is "incidental" or "intuitive" to the prescribed activities.

The philosophy that drives this style of (85) education is a hodgepodge of unsubstantiated theory called "constructivism." This approach, which has taken hold of many classrooms all over the country, flies in the face of common sense. Do constructivists really mean to suggest that (90) knowledge cannot be learned by instruction, or that principles and skills cannot be broken into smaller segments and abstracted from their contexts for ease of learning? Do they really intend to propose that objective assessment of student (95) learning is impossible or undesirable? A growing body of evidence, and a few well-publicized fiascos, suggest that constructivists are strolling down the primrose path. Some emerging studies have failed

to show any significant increase in the effectiveness (100) of constructivist methods compared with direct instructional approaches. Moreover, some critics have started to question whether constructivist ideas are founded on a strong and supportable body of empirical research, or whether the whole (105) approach has been patched together from scraps of cognitive psychology with liberal amounts of speculation.

Consider, for example, one of the common ways in which a constructivist classroom causes (110) students to waste time. If a pupil needs practice in one specific task that is part of a larger task, that student might be required to repeat mastered skills unnecessarily, in order to get the opportunity to try out the skill that needs practice. For example, (115) a student who is a skilled writer but needs work on thesis sentences might have to spend weeks working through an extended project of research and writing in order to get the single opportunity to practice writing a thesis sentence. On the other (120) hand, in a traditional classroom, the learner would receive practice, instruction, and correction in this one problem area until it was mastered. This is just one of a multitude of instances where constructivism fails to efficiently accomplish what (125) it purports to do: to actually teach.

No one is advocating a reversion to the days of pointless memorization, drill for its own sake, and draconian discipline. But the unconscionable waste of time, resources and student potential that (130) constructivism supports in the name of progressive education does today's students a grave disservice.

Questions 21–23 ask about Passage A.

---

21. The main goal of Passage A is to:

   A. identify and summarize a set of fallacies.

   B. argue for the superiority of a particular approach.

   C. dispute the significance of recent research.

   D. describe the history of a controversial issue.

GO ON TO THE NEXT PAGE ⟶

22. The author of Passage A asserts that endeavoring to "understand how students learn" (lines 30–31) would most likely:

   F. bring about more debate and discussion about the best path for education.

   G. lead to the development of many radically different educational philosophies.

   H. affect the way that studies on student learning are carried out.

   J. result in improved education and teaching approaches.

23. The work of J. Bruner (lines 32–41) supports the author's main idea that:

   A. teachers can use simple learning aids to help them instruct students in principles of advanced mathematics.

   B. the understanding of prime numbers is vital to the subsequent learning of multiplication and division.

   C. schools should return to traditional models of direct teacher instruction.

   D. students are capable of discovering complex concepts on their own through experimentation.

Questions 24–26 ask about Passage B.

24. Lines 81–83 mainly highlight which negative aspect of the constructivist classroom?

   F. Students aren't taught practical skills.

   G. Using grades to reward or punish student performance is discouraged.

   H. The classroom is chaotic and disorganized.

   J. Only students who show high levels of achievement are rewarded.

25. The author of Passage B believes that the "student" and the "pupil" in line 110 are similar to each other in that they:

   A. are forced by a constructivist classroom to repeat skills they have already mastered.

   B. exhibit strong writing skills but have trouble with transitions and conclusions.

   C. show a high level of skill at working in collaborative and cooperative environments.

   D. receive instruction in discrete skills until they can demonstrate mastery of those skills.

26. The statement in lines 98–101 of Passage B ("Some emerging…approaches") mainly functions to:

   F. introduce evidence to support a point.

   G. make a transition to a new subject.

   H. expand on a theory.

   J. contrast two opposing arguments.

Questions 27–30 ask about both passages.

27. The author of Passage B would most likely respond to the description of the teacher's role in lines 59–61 of Passage A with the argument that:

   A. teachers need to provide hands-on, collaborative environments that encourage student discovery.

   B. research demonstrates that teachers must give direct instruction if students are to master skills.

   C. students will not learn as accurately or efficiently without a teacher's coaching and correction.

   D. students will tend to waste time, effort, and resources unless teachers strictly discipline and constantly drill them.

GO ON TO THE NEXT PAGE

28. The educational approach that produces the type of classroom described in lines 71–83 of Passage B is the same type of educational approach endorsed by:

    F. Piaget and Erikson in line 30.
    G. J. Bruner in line 33.
    H. "some critics" in line 101.
    J. "No one" in line 126.

29. It can be inferred that the authors would disagree with each other most strongly on which of the following issues?

    A. Whether students learn best by rote memorization
    B. Whether constructivist approaches create more false starts and student errors than direct instruction
    C. Whether research results from cognitive psychology should be used in determining educational approaches
    D. Whether discrete skills should be abstracted from real-world situations

30. Which of the following best summarizes the attitudes of the two authors toward educational methodologies?

    F. Passage A endorses theoretical, speculative approaches, while Passage B endorses research-based educational approaches.
    G. Passage A argues for tolerant, permissive classroom environments, while Passage B argues for strict, disciplinarian classrooms.
    H. Passage A suggests that writing is learned through projects and collaboration, while Passage B suggests that writing is best taught as a set of abstracted skills.
    J. Passage A makes a case for collaborative, discovery-based curricula, while Passage B makes a case for traditional direct instruction.

PASSAGE IV

NATURAL SCIENCE

This passage is adapted from the article "Fight the Bite! Avoid Mosquito Bites to Avoid Infection" published by the American Centers for Disease Control (© 2009).

In epidemiology, a vector is a disease-carrying agent—anything from a door handle to a cup of water. One of the most effective, and dangerous,
Line transmitters of blood-borne infections is the
(5) mosquito. Unlike most vectors, which rely on a chance encounter to transmit germs, mosquitoes deliberately fly from host to host collecting blood and inadvertently mixing small quantities of blood. For this reason, mosquitoes are one of the most
(10) pernicious pests that humans face.

For centuries, the cause of yellow fever was unknown, but Cuban doctor Carlos Finlay speculated that it was spread by mosquitoes. His theory was confirmed in 1900 by U.S. Army
(15) physician Walter Reed, which initiated mosquito eradication measures that ultimately saved the Panama Canal project.

There are at least 3,500 known species of mosquitoes in temperate and tropical climates
(20) all over the world. The mosquito life cycle begins when the female lays eggs in standing water. After a brief incubation period, the eggs hatch and release swimming larvae that feed on algae and bacteria. The larvae enter cocoons during the short pupal
(25) stage, after which they metamorphose into adult mosquitoes. Both male and female mosquitoes derive their primary nourishment from simple sugars, which provide the energy needed for flight. Though mosquitoes can also feed on scraps of human food,
(30) the primary source of sugar comes from plant nectar.

Mosquitoes are active at dawn or dusk, when their fragile bodies are least exposed to temperature extremes. Only female mosquitoes consume blood because plant nectar does not provide the protein
(35) necessary for egglaying. After mating, females seek prey from which to draw blood necessary for reproduction. In their search for blood, female mosquitoes will either wait in tall grass until an animal passes by or track their prey by following

GO ON TO THE NEXT PAGE ⇒

(40) the carbon dioxide emissions from mammalian respiration and perspiration. Mosquitoes follow the carbon dioxide trail to its source, similar to a shark following a blood trail in water.

When they find the source of carbon dioxide, (45) mosquitoes stab their prey with a long needlelike proboscis. Their saliva contains a natural anticoagulant, so that blood will continue to flow freely into their mouths. Most people do not feel the actual bite of a mosquito but suffer from the (50) itch afterward as the immune system reacts to leftover saliva.

It appears that some people are more attractive to mosquitoes than others. Although the exact combination of attributes is unknown, people with (55) higher body temperatures or people who breathe heavily, sweat profusely, or wear strong scents are more likely to be bitten by mosquitoes than others. There is a lucrative industry producing repellent sprays, or at least ones that mask human scent.

(60) Today doctors recognize the mosquito as the single worst disease vector in existence— responsible for millions of deaths historically and thousands more fatalities each year. Mosquitoes are known to pass yellow fever, dengue fever, (65) and malaria. Fortunately, research has revealed numerous methods by which these pests can be controlled. Some ways to hinder mosquito breeding are to drain stagnant water and to not allow large puddles to remain near places of human (70) habitation. Window screens and mosquito nets are also effective preventative measures. People should be careful opening doors and windows because mosquitoes are known to wait near openings that emit human scent. Finally, the survival of mosquito (75) predators such as spiders, frogs, and dragonflies is a useful deterrent against mosquito breeding, as is the deployment of sonic bug repellants and electric bug zappers.

31. According to the first paragraph, mosquitoes:

  A. effectively transmit germs between organisms.

  B. deliberately infect animals with lethal germs.

  C. are surpassed by other objects as disease vectors.

  D. cannot be prevented by scientists from spreading disease.

32. According to the passage, why are other disease vectors less effective at passing germs than mosquitoes?

  F. Other vectors are not alive and cannot support living germs.

  G. Other vectors fail to rely on chance in the transmission of disease.

  H. Other vectors are specifically targeted by scientists for eradication.

  J. Other vectors are not intentionally guided between potential hosts.

33. The passage states that each of the following was responsible for hindering progress on the Panama Canal EXCEPT:

  A. disease vectors.

  B. mosquito-borne illness.

  C. yellow fever.

  D. the work of Walter Reed.

34. Which of the following is the current sequence of the mosquito life cycle?

  F. larvae consume algae, eggs hatch, adults emerge from pupae, females drink blood

  G. eggs hatch, larvae consume algae, adults emerge from pupae, females drink blood

  H. females drink blood, adults emerge from pupae, eggs hatch, larvae consume algae

  J. larvae consume algae, adults emerge from pupae, eggs hatch, females drink blood

GO ON TO THE NEXT PAGE

35. According to the passage, why do male mosquitoes not consume blood?

A. Blood contains insufficient nutrition for male mosquitoes.

B. Males gain all the energy they need from sugar.

C. Males are not required for mosquito reproduction.

D. Plant nectar contains the protein necessary for males to survive.

36. How does the author characterize the habits of mosquitoes in Paragraph 4 (lines 31–43)?

F. Mosquitoes are superior to sharks in tracking prey.

G. Male mosquitoes seek out prey using a carbon dioxide trail.

H. Mosquitoes fly erratically in strong wind conditions.

J. Mosquitoes are especially active under certain conditions.

37. The author most likely includes the reference to a shark in lines 41–43 to:

A. present an example to help the reader visualize mosquito behavior.

B. offer a comparison to the effectiveness of mosquito tracking techniques.

C. highlight the hazards presented by the feeding of female mosquitoes.

D. cite an organism that is unaffected by mosquito feeding habits.

38. In the final paragraph, each of the following is mentioned as a mosquito prevention measure EXCEPT:

F. using caution when entering and exiting dwellings.

G. covering windows and doors to prevent mosquitoes from entering dwellings.

H. elimination free-flowing water sources near human habitation.

J. releasing organisms that feed on mosquitoes.

39. According to the passage, which of the following may attract mosquitoes?

A. High blood pressure

B. Mild cosmetic scents

C. Elevated body temperature

D. Shallow breathing

40. The information from the passage most clearly supports which of the following statements?

F. Numerous diseases can only be transmitted between organisms through the intercession of mosquitoes.

G. Malaria is the most significant threat to public health that health care providers currently face.

H. Elimination of mosquitoes would probably result in fewer deaths from a number of blood-borne infections.

J. Doctors are not currently doing everything within their power to control the spread of disease by mosquitoes.

SCIENCE TEST

35 Minutes—40 Questions

Directions: There are several passages in this test. Each passage is followed by several questions. After reading a passage, choose the best answer to each question and fill in the corresponding oval on your Answer Grid. You may refer to the passages as often as necessary. You are NOT permitted to use a calculator on this test.

PASSAGE I

Metabolism is the process by which organisms produce energy. Metabolism occurs in a number of *metabolic pathways*, each of which is critical to the organism's processing of energy. The *Krebs cycle* is one of the central cycles in the overall metabolic process. The Krebs cycle enables an organism to process proteins, carbohydrates, and fats. Even while at rest, an organism will undergo metabolism.

STUDY 1

When an organism is at rest, the measurement of its ability to metabolize is called the *Basal Metabolic Rate* (BMR). Numerous factors affect an organism's BMR. Three different subjects—a human, a bear, and a bear in hibernation—were studied at various ages. Their BMRs were evaluated relative to the average peak metabolic rate of each species. The results are shown in Table 1.

Table 1

Age (years)	BMR (% of peak)		
	Human	Bear	Bear (hibernation)
1	0	0	0
7	75	80	30
14	85	100	30
21	100	80	30
28	86	40	30
35	72	0	0

STUDY 2

The normal weight of a male of average build who is 1.8 m tall is approximately 73 kg. Scientists continued studying the human BMR of male individuals, aged 25, who were approximately 1.8 m tall and who had varying weights. The results are shown in Table 2.

Table 2

Weight (kg)	BMR (% of peak)
62	90
63	92
65	93
67	94
69	96
71	98
73	100

GO ON TO THE NEXT PAGE

STUDY 3

Study 2 was repeated, but 100 25-year-old males weighing 73 kg were studied at different internal body temperatures. The results are shown in Table 3.

Table 3

Internal body temperature (°C)	BMR (% of peak)
35.0	72
35.5	78
36.0	85
36.5	93
37.0	100
37.5	108
38.0	115
38.5	122
39.0	129

1. In Study 2, if researchers had collected data for a 68 kg individual, the measured BMR as a percent of a normal peak would most likely have been:

   A. 93%.
   B. 94%.
   C. 95%.
   D. 96%.

2. A researcher hypothesized that a 25-year-old male with an above-average weight would have a BMR that is greater than 100%. Do the results of Study 2 support this hypothesis?

   F. Yes, because as weight increases, BMR increases.
   G. Yes, because as weight increases, BMR decreases.
   H. No, because as weight increases, BMR increases.
   J. No, because as weight increases, BMR decreases.

3. How did Studies 1 and 2 differ? In Study 1:

   A. 3 different subjects were studied; in Study 2, only 1 subject was studied.
   B. 3 different subjects were studied; in Study 2, only 2 subjects were studied.
   C. only 1 subject was studied; in Study 2, 3 different subjects were studied.
   D. only 1 subject was studied; in Study 2, 2 different subjects were studied.

4. Which of the following statements about bears is supported by Study 1? As a bear's age increases from 1 to 35 years, the bear's BMR:

   F. increases only.
   G. decreases only.
   H. increases, then decreases.
   J. decreases, then increases.

5. Suppose researchers studied the metabolism of a 25-year-old human male who has an internal temperature of 37°C. If this person experienced significant weight loss, his BMR would consequently:

   A. decrease, because lower weights correspond to lower BMRs.
   B. decrease, because lower weights correspond to higher BMRs.
   C. increase, because lower weights correspond to lower BMRs.
   D. increase, because lower weights correspond to higher BMRs.

6. Which of the following is a plausible model for why BMR was seen to increase or decrease throughout Studies 1–3? Variations in BMR are caused by a subject's:

   F. corresponding need for energy.
   G. participation in the Krebs cycle.
   H. selection of different metabolic pathways.
   J. typical longevity.

GO ON TO THE NEXT PAGE ⇒

7. If several of the subjects in Study 3 wanted to gain mass, what is the optimal internal body temperature to do so?

   A. Less than 35°C

   B. 36.5°C

   C. 37°C

   D. Greater than 37.5°C

PASSAGE II

Human blood types have been extensively studied for their compatibility and genetic characteristics. The blood types A, B, AB, and O are the *phenotypes,* or apparent characteristics that emerge from the *genotypes* present in an individual's chromosomes. Table 1 shows the compatibility of different blood types for the purposes of transfusion.

Table 1

Blood type	RhD type	Compatible with transfusion of:			
		A–	A+	B–	B+
AB	+	Yes	Yes	Yes	Yes
AB	–	Yes	No	Yes	No
B	+	No	No	Yes	Yes
B	–	No	No	Yes	No

GO ON TO THE NEXT PAGE

Table 2 shows the most frequently inherited blood types over two generations of offspring. The parental genotypes are presented in terms of their *alleles*, the pairings of genes in the chromosomes of an individual.

Table 2

Group	Parental genotypes				Frequent offspring phenotype
	Male, Generation 1	Female, Generation 1	Male, Generation 2	Female, Generation 2	
1	AO	AO	AO	AO	A
2	AO	AO	AA	OO	A
3	AO	AO	OO	BO	O
4	AO	AA	AO	BO	AB, A, B, and O
5	AO	AA	AO	BB	AB and B
6	AO	AA	AA	OO	A
7	AO	BB	AB	OO	A and B
8	AO	BB	AB	BB	AB and B
9	AO	BB	BO	OO	O
10	BO	BO	BO	BO	B
11	BO	BO	BB	AA	AB
12	BO	BO	OO	AO	O
13	BO	BB	BO	AO	AB, A, B, and O
14	BO	BB	BO	AA	AB and A
15	BO	BB	BB	OO	B
16	BO	AA	AB	OO	A and B
17	BO	AA	AB	AO	A
18	BO	AA	AO	OO	O

8. According to Table 1, an RhD positive blood type of a particular phenotype will be compatible with:

   F. all blood types.
   G. no blood types.
   H. all blood types of its phenotype.
   J. all negative blood types.

9. According to Table 2, the generations in which of the following groups had the greatest frequency of type A alleles?

   A. Group 1
   B. Group 6
   C. Group 10
   D. Group 16

10. A patient with blood type B+ is in need of a transfusion. Based on Table 1, which of the following blood types would be suitable for the patient to receive?

    F. Blood type A+ only
    G. Blood types A+ and A–
    H. Blood type B+ only
    J. Blood types B+ and B–

GO ON TO THE NEXT PAGE

11. If the parents of an individual both had BO genotypes, which of the following would most likely be the phenotype of that individual?

    A. A
    B. AB
    C. B
    D. O

12. Table 2 does NOT include any lineage with which of the following pairings of genotypes?

    F. First-generation AO with AO; second-generation AA with BB.
    G. First-generation AO with AO; second-generation AA with OO.
    H. First-generation BO with BO; second-generation AA with BB.
    J. First-generation BO with BO; second-generation OO with AO.

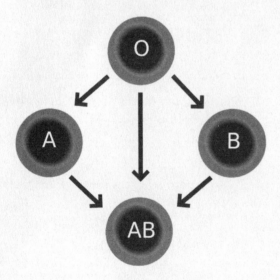

Figure 1

13. Another way to explain blood type is with a pictorial (Figure 1). Based on this figure, what blood type would be known as the universal receiver?

    A. A
    B. B
    C. O
    D. AB

PASSAGE III

Earth's magnetic field has two distinct poles, labeled North and South. Certain materials, such as iron and steel, are sensitive to Earth's magnetic field. The origin and behavior of the magnetic field is modeled by *dynamo theory*, which links the magnetic field with the geologic activity of Earth's molten core.

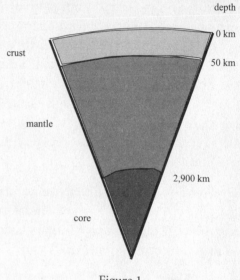

Figure 1

Evidence has been found of complete reversals in the polarity of the magnetic field, called *geomagnetic reversals*. Concentrated deposits of rock with reversed magnetic properties have been found on the ocean floor. The magnetic anomalies observed suggest that Earth undergoes a geomagnetic reversal sporadically over time spans of thousands of years (the last geomagnetic reversal occurred approximately 780,000 years ago). Two scientists discuss the possible causes of geomagnetic reversal.

SCIENTIST 1

Dynamo theory suggests that a constantly moving fluid can help maintain a magnetic field. Earth's core is made of molten nickel and iron. The constant motion of this portion of the core creates eddy currents, which in turn help to create Earth's magnetic

GO ON TO THE NEXT PAGE

field. The motions of the molten core can often be chaotic, and in turn disturb the magnetic field. It is this necessary by-product of dynamo theory which causes spontaneous geomagnetic reversal.

SCIENTIST 2

Earth's molten core is responsible for the creation, maintenance, and shifts of the magnetic field. The motions of the core, in accordance with dynamo theory, create a magnetic field from eddy currents. The motions of tectonic plates and other seismic events can have a powerful effect on Earth's core. Such events can disrupt the motion of the core to such an extent that the magnetic field effectively turns off. When the regular motions of the core resume, the resulting magnetic field will either resume as it was, or emerge as a reversal of its previous state.

14. Dynamo theory can be applied to other planets that have molten cores. Based on this information, which of the following planetary bodies would the theory most likely NOT apply to?

   F. Neptune

   G. Mars

   H. Venus

   J. Mercury

15. Which of the following pairs of statements best accounts for Earth's geomagnetic reversal according to the viewpoints of the 2 scientists?

	Scientist 1	Scientist 2
A.	Magnetic field resets after seismic disturbance	Natural consequence of the dynamo effect
B.	Seismic disturbance caused by magnetic field	Natural consequence of the dynamo effect
C.	Natural consequence of the dynamo effect	Magnetic field resets after seismic disturbance
D.	Natural consequence of the dynamo effect	Seismic disturbance caused by magnetic field

16. According to the passage, seismic activity which affects Earth's molten core resonates to depths of:

   F. 50 km.

   G. 700 km.

   H. 1,500 km.

   J. 2,900 km.

17. Which of the following statements is most consistent with the theories expressed in Scientist 1's viewpoint?

   A. The motion of molten nickel and iron creates a magnetic field.

   B. The motion of molten nickel and iron counteracts magnetic fields already in existence.

   C. The melting of nickel and iron creates a magnetic field.

   D. Nickel and iron are found only in Earth's core.

18. Which of the following hypotheses would both scientists agree upon?

   F. The dynamo theory accounts for shifts in Earth's magnetic field.

   G. Eddy currents create seismic disturbances.

   H. Seismic disturbances cause geomagnetic reversal.

   J. The dynamo theory is relevant only every few thousand years.

19. According to the passage, which of the following is a reliable indicator of Earth's magnetic field?

   A. Molten nickel and iron

   B. Deposits of magnetized rock

   C. Seismic activity

   D. Shifts in solar magnetism

GO ON TO THE NEXT PAGE

20. If it were discovered that Earth's magnetic field is directly altered by the Sun's magnetic field, how would this affect the viewpoints of each scientist?

   F. It would strengthen the viewpoint of Scientist 1 only.

   G. It would weaken the viewpoint of Scientist 2 only.

   H. It would strengthen the viewpoints of both scientists.

   J. It would weaken the viewpoints of both scientists.

21. In a computer simulation, the effect of seismic activity on the motion of Earth's molten core was studied. Which of the following findings would be consistent with Scientist 2's viewpoint? The seismic activity would:

   A. be caused by motion of the molten core.

   B. cause significant disturbance in the molten core.

   C. have no effect on the motion of the molten core.

   D. cause eddy currents in the molten core.

PASSAGE IV

Faraday's law relates changes in magnetic fields to electric voltage. Any instance of change in magnetic field (*magnetic flux*) will create a charge, or *electromotive force* (emf). This relationship is commonly called *electromagnetic induction*.

Students conducted 3 experiments to study electromagnetic induction.

EXPERIMENT 1

A magnet was passed through a coiled wire at varying speeds as shown in Figure 1. The various speeds created a corresponding magnetic flux (in webers).

A voltmeter was used to measure the resulting emf (in volts). The results are shown in Table 1.

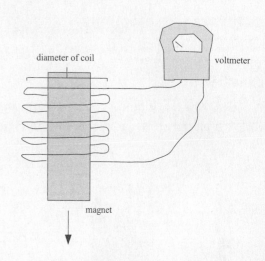

Figure 1

Table 1

Trial	Diameter of coil (cm)	Magnetic flux (w)	emf (volts)
1	2	0.3	0.22
2	2	0.5	0.41
3	2	0.7	0.63
4	4	0.5	0.12

EXPERIMENT 2

A coiled wire was rotated at various velocities within a constant magnetic field, creating magnetic flux, as shown in Figure 2. Again, a voltmeter was used to measure the resulting emf. The results are shown in Table 2.

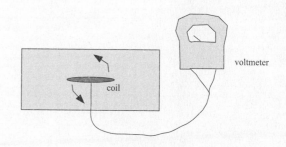

Figure 2

GO ON TO THE NEXT PAGE

Table 2

Trial	Magnetic flux (w)	emf (volts)
5	0.2	0.2
6	0.4	0.4
7	0.6	0.6

EXPERIMENT 3

A coiled wire was mounted on a pole and a metal ring was placed on the pole, as shown in Figure 3.

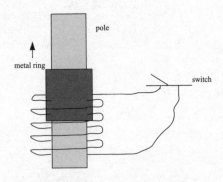

Figure 3

A current was sent through the wire, and the metal ring floated up the pole. The students used the same amount of current in each trial, but used wires with different amounts of coils. The height that the metal ring reached on the pole was recorded for each trial. The results are shown in Table 3.

Table 3

Trial	Number of coils	Height (cm)
8	50	1.1
9	100	1.5
10	150	2.1

22. Based on Table 3, it can be concluded that the magnetic field generated by the wires in Experiment 3:

   F. did not change based on the number of coils in the wire.

   G. increased based on the number of coils in the wire.

   H. decreased based on the number of coils in the wire.

   J. decreased based on the amount of current passing through the wire.

23. In Experiment 2, if the wire were slowed down to a rotational velocity of 0 m/s, in which trial would there be current passing through the wire?

   A. Trial 5

   B. Trial 6

   C. Trial 7

   D. None of the trials

24. If the number of coils in a wire is 1, a magnetic flux of 1 w will produce an emf of 1 volt. In which of the following trials was the number of coils not equal to 1?

   F. Trial 4

   G. Trial 5

   H. Trial 6

   J. Trial 7

GO ON TO THE NEXT PAGE

25. Based on the results of Experiment 1, the relationship between magnetic flux and induced emf is best represented by which of the following graphs?

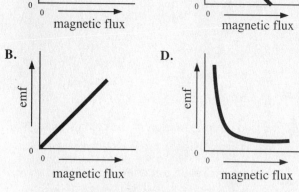

A.   **C.**

B.   **D.**

26. In Experiment 1, students used coils of two different diameters, rather than only one, in order to study the relationship between:

F. number of coils and area.

G. number of coils and emf.

H. area and emf.

J. magnetic field and emf.

27. In Trial 9, if the current being passed through the wire had doubled, which of the following would most likely have been the recorded height of the metal ring?

A. 0.7 cm

B. 1.1 cm

C. 1.5 cm

D. 2.9 cm

28. If the students conducting Experiment 1 decided to repeat trials 1–3 with the 4 cm coil, what would the expected relationship between emf and magnetic flux be?

F. Magnetic flux would increase as emf decreases.

G. Magnetic flux would decrease as emf increases.

H. Magnetic flux would increase as emf increases.

J. Magnetic flux would decrease as emf decreases.

PASSAGE V

An acid is defined as any substance that can donate a hydrogen ion in a solution, while a base is defined as any substance that can accept a hydrogen ion. Acids and bases are measured by the pH scale, as indicated in Table 1.

Table 1 shows how pH level corresponds to hydrogen ion concentration, indicated by [H^+].

Table 1

[H^+]	pH level
1×10^0	0
1×10^{-1}	1
1×10^{-2}	2
1×10^{-3}	3
1×10^{-4}	4
1×10^{-5}	5
1×10^{-6}	6
1×10^{-7}	7
1×10^{-8}	8
1×10^{-9}	9
1×10^{-10}	10
1×10^{-11}	11
1×10^{-12}	12
1×10^{-13}	13
1×10^{-14}	14

GO ON TO THE NEXT PAGE

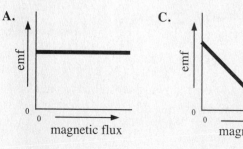

Table 2 shows categorizations of acids and bases according to pH level. Strong acids and bases can be dangerous to handle.

Table 2

Categorization	pH level
strong acid	0–4
weak acid	4–6
neutral substance	7
weak base	8–10
strong base	11–14

Table 3 names several strong acids and bases.

Table 3

Strong bases	Strong acids
sodium hydroxide	nitric acid
calcium hydroxide	sulfuric acid
barium hydroxide	hydrobromic acid

Table 4 lists the hydrogen ion concentration [H$^+$] in several common substances.

Table 4

Substance	[H$^+$]
ammonia	1×10^{-11}
baking soda	1×10^{-9}
lemon juice	1×10^{-2}
milk	1×10^{-6}
vinegar	1×10^{-3}
water	1×10^{-7}

29. An unknown substance is tested in order to determine if it is an acid or a base. The hydrogen ion concentration is found to be 1×10^{-11}. This substance would be considered a:

   A. strong acid.

   B. weak acid.

   C. strong base.

   D. weak base.

30. Based on Table 4, which of the following substances has the greatest hydrogen ion concentration?

   F. Ammonia

   G. Lemon juice

   H. Milk

   J. Vinegar

31. Which of the following substances would be classified as a strong acid?

   A. Milk

   B. Vinegar

   C. Baking soda

   D. Ammonia

32. Based on information in the passage, which of the following is the most accurate statement?

   F. As hydrogen ion concentration increases, a substance becomes more dangerous.

   G. A substance with a pH close to 0 is considered safe.

   H. The difference in hydrogen ion concentration is greater between a strong acid and a strong base than between a weak acid and a weak base.

   J. The difference in hydrogen ion concentration is greater between a weak base and a strong base than between a weak acid and a strong acid.

33. Which of the following substances has the highest pH level?

   A. Baking soda

   B. Nitric acid

   C. Barium hydroxide

   D. Vinegar

GO ON TO THE NEXT PAGE

34. The hydrogen ion concentration [H⁺] of a substance is inversely proportional to the substance's hydroxide ion concentration [OH⁻]. For example, a substance with a pH of 2 has a pOH of 12, and a substance with a pH of 11 has a pOH of 3. Based on this information, which of the following substances has the highest pOH?

F. Sulfuric acid

G. Calcium hydroxide

H. Water

J. Ammonia

PASSAGE VI

A group of 10 students proposed a hypothesis that the presence of carbonation (or froth) in various bottled liquids would affect *balance time* (the time it took a bottle to reach equilibrium from being initially off-balance). Figure 1 shows the bottle held by 2 fixed points on a hinged incline. As the hinge closes and the angle of inclination approaches zero, the liquid in the bottle achieves optimal balance time when it no longer moves within the bottle.

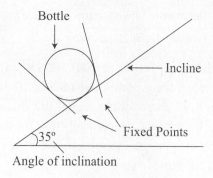

Figure 1

Each student tested the hypothesis in different trials and recorded average balance times. The initial angle of inclination is 35° for all 3 experiments. Identical 2-L glass bottles were used in all 3 experiments.

EXPERIMENT 1

The students added 1 L of clear fruit juice, which is uncarbonated, to an empty bottle. After sealing it, they placed it between the fixed points and closed the hinge. The balance time was then recorded. Next, they added 1 L of the same juice to the second empty bottle, sealed and shook it, and found that balance time. They repeated these 2 procedures with 2 additional liquids: carbonated seltzer that contained a lot of froth, and root beer that had been frozen and was recently thawed to 4°C (thereby flat tasting). The results of these experiments are shown in the table below.

Table 1

	Balance Time (in seconds)		
Trial	Liquid	Before Shaking	After Shaking
1	Clear Fruit Juice	20.01	20.01
2	Carbonated Seltzer	21.35	22.97
3	Root Beer	20.01	22.48

EXPERIMENT 2

The students added 1 L of the root beer to an empty bottle. After sealing and shaking the bottle, they set it aside for 10 minutes. At that time they found the bottle's balance time before and immediately after shaking it (Trial 4). They set it aside again for an additional 90 minutes and found the balance time before and immediately after shaking it (Trial 5). The results can be seen in the table below.

Table 2

	Balance Time (in seconds)	
Trial	Before Shaking	After Shaking
4	20.83	22.67
5	20.01	22.45

GO ON TO THE NEXT PAGE ⟶

EXPERIMENT 3

The students added 1 L of root beer to an empty bottle and 1 L of carbonated seltzer to the second empty bottle. They then sealed both bottles. When they balanced each bottle on the incline, bubbles did not form. After shaking both bottles and seeing froth form, the students set them aside for observation. At 10 minutes into the experiment, fewer bubbles were visible in the bottle with carbonated seltzer. At 90 minutes into the experiment, there were no bubbles remaining in either bottle.

35. Which of the following conclusions is most strongly supported by the results of Experiment 3? When shaken, root beer:

    A. had a higher level of carbonation than seltzer.

    B. has a lesser amount of carbonation than seltzer.

    C. had a greater quantity of liquid than seltzer.

    D. balanced at twice the speed as seltzer

36. When comparing trials 1 through 5 in Experiments 1 and 2, in which two trials, after shaking, are the balance times the most similar?

    F. Trials 1 and 5

    G. Trials 1 and 3

    H. Trials 2 and 4

    J. Trials 3 and 5

37. In Experiment 2, shaking the bottle of root beer resulted in:

    A. decreasing the number of bubbles in the beverage immediately.

    B. increasing the balance time of the bottle of root beer.

    C. decreasing the balance time of the bottle of root beer.

    D. increasing the mass of the bottle of root beer.

38. According to the results of these three experiments, is it likely that bubbles were present immediately before the bottle was shaken in Trial 4?

    F. Based on Experiment 1, it is likely the bubbles were present before being shaken.

    G. Based on Experiment 1, it is unlikely the bubbles were present before being shaken.

    H. Based on Experiment 3, it is likely the bubbles were present before being shaken.

    J. Based on Experiment 3, it is unlikely the bubbles were present before being shaken.

39. Suppose a sixth trial existed in which the same bottle of root beer was set aside for an additional 90 minutes after the fifth trial was completed. Based on the results of Experiment 2, what would the balance time most likely be if the students do not shake the bottle?

    A. Less than 20.83 seconds

    B. Between 20.83 seconds and 22.45 seconds

    C. Between 22.46 seconds and 22.67 seconds

    D. Greater than 22.67 seconds

40. Based on the results of trials 3–5 and Experiment 3, if the students had added 1 L of root beer to an empty bottle, sealed and shook it, how long would it most likely take for the bubbles to become too few to affect the bottle's balance time?

    F. 0 minutes

    G. Between 1 minute and 9 minutes

    H. Between 10 minutes and 90 minutes

    J. More than 90 minutes

IF YOU FINISH BEFORE TIME IS CALLED, YOU MAY CHECK YOUR WORK ON THIS SECTION ONLY. DO NOT TURN TO ANY OTHER SECTION IN THE TEST. **STOP**

WRITING TEST

40 Minutes

Directions: This is a test of your writing skills. You will have forty (40) minutes to write an essay in English. Before you begin planning and writing your essay, read the writing prompt carefully to understand exactly what you are being asked to do. Your essay will be evaluated on the evidence it provides of your ability to do the following:

- Express judgments by evaluating the three perspectives given in the prompt, taking a position on an issue, and explaining the relationship among all four ideas
- Develop a position by using logical reasoning and by supporting your ideas
- Maintain a focus on the topic throughout the essay
- Organize ideas in a logical way
- Use language clearly and effectively according to the conventions of standard written English

You may use the unlined pages in this test booklet to plan your essay. These pages will not be scored. ***You must write your essay in pencil on the lined pages in the answer folder.*** Your writing on those lined pages will be scored. You may not need all the lined pages, but to ensure you have enough room to finish, do NOT skip lines. You may write corrections or additions neatly between the lines of your essay, but do NOT write in the margins of the lined pages. ***Illegible essays cannot be scored, so you must write (or print) clearly.***

If you finish before time is called you may review your work. Lay your pencil down immediately when time is called.

DO NOT OPEN THIS BOOKLET UNTIL TOLD TO DO SO.

GO ON TO THE NEXT PAGE

GOVERNMENT FUNDING FOR THE ARTS

The arts play an important role in the educational, economic, and civic life of our society. Student engagement in arts programs has been shown to correlate with improved outcomes in math and literacy. A vibrant arts sector provides jobs and stimulates business activity, leading to increased tax revenue. Arts and culture create a shared sense of community and a higher quality of life. In pursuit of these and other benefits, state, local, and national governments regularly provide public funding in support of the arts. To what extent is it appropriate to use taxpayer resources to promote arts and culture in a community? Given the fiscal budget constraints faced by many governments, a careful analysis of the impact of public funding for the arts is essential to drive informed policy decisions.

Read and carefully consider these perspectives. Each suggests a particular way of thinking about government funding for the arts.

Perspective One	Perspective Two	Perspective Three
Governments should recognize the direct and indirect benefits of the arts. A vibrant arts life creates a competitive edge in attracting tourists and encouraging people to move to the community. Public funding should be allocated to the arts to protect these benefits to society.	While the arts play a positive role in society, government funds should be spent on more pressing priorities. Core civic functions, such as crime prevention and infrastructure improvement, should not compete with arts initiatives for increasingly limited public funding. The arts are more appropriately supported by private funding sources.	Government funding for the arts threatens the artistic integrity of the artwork itself. Artists as individuals should have the freedom to create without considering the goals of government policy makers.

ESSAY TASK

Write a unified, coherent essay in which you evaluate multiple perspectives regarding government funding for the arts. In your essay, be sure to:

- analyze and evaluate the perspectives given
- state and develop your own perspective on the issue
- explain the relationship between your perspective and those given

Your perspective may be in full agreement with any of the others, in partial agreement, or wholly different. Whatever the case, support your ideas with logical reasoning and detailed, persuasive examples.

GO ON TO THE NEXT PAGE ⇒

PLANNING YOUR ESSAY

You may wish to consider the following as you think critically about the task:

Strengths and weaknesses of the three given perspectives

- What insights do they offer, and what do they fail to consider?
- Why might they be persuasive to others, or why might they fail to persuade?

Your own knowledge, experience, and values

- What is your perspective on this issue, and what are its strengths and weaknesses?
- How will you support your perspective in your essay?

_____

_____

_____

_____

_____

_____

_____

_____

_____

_____

_____

_____

_____

_____

_____

_____

_____

_____

GO ON TO THE NEXT PAGE

TEST PREP AND ADMISSIONS

ACT®

Practice Test 4

For Courses Starting On or After 2/1/2016

PLEASE BE SURE TO RECORD THE FOLLOWING SCAN CODE ON YOUR ANSWER GRID. WITHOUT THIS INFORMATION, WE WILL NOT BE ABLE TO SCAN YOUR TEST OR PROVIDE YOU WITH YOUR TEST SCORES.

SCAN CODE: 8010

ENGLISH TEST

45 Minutes—75 Questions

Directions: In the following five passages, certain words and phrases are underlined and numbered. In the right-hand column are alternatives for each underlined portion. Select the one that best conveys the idea, creates the most grammatically correct sentence, or is most consistent with the style and tone of the passage. If you decide that the original version is best, select NO CHANGE. You may also find questions that ask about the entire passage or a section of the passage. These questions will correspond to small, numbered boxes in the text. For these questions, decide which choice best accomplishes the purpose set out in the question stem. After you've selected the best choice, fill in the corresponding oval on your Answer Grid. For some questions, you'll need to read the context in order to answer correctly. Be sure to read until you have enough information to determine the correct answer choice.

PASSAGE I

VISUAL LEARNING

Traditional educational theories stressed lecture-based methods in which students learned by listening to an instructor, but contemporary studies have noted that students learn best when they see, hear, and experience. Based on these studies, current educational theories emphasize auditory, visual, and experiential learning. Such theories <u>are not groundbreaking</u>. For example,
1
medical education has stressed this model for decades. Young doctors in their residency training often repeat the mantra, "see it, do it, teach it." Interestingly, much of the development in the <u>area of</u> visual and experiential
2
learning fields has come from the business world. Many businesses, from corporate management to consulting, utilize presentations. Traditionally, business presentations had included slides filled with dense text that merely repeated the presenter's words. Though these

1. **A.** NO CHANGE
   B. were not groundbreaking
   C. had been groundbreaking
   D. in groundbreaking

2. **F.** NO CHANGE
   G. subject of
   H. topic of
   J. OMIT the underlined portion.

GO ON TO THE NEXT PAGE

slides did provide a visual aspect, <u>the slides</u> were difficult
                                           3
to read, which detracted from their effectiveness.

[1] Over the past decade, <u>technological advances</u>
                                                    4
<u>have created</u> additional presentation options, business
  4
leaders have teamed with public speaking experts to

continue to refine the visual presentation style.

[2] <u>A very important development revealed</u> that less
                                             5
cluttered visual aids work better than denser ones.

[3] This development led to the understanding that

text repeating a presenter's script did not <u>enhance or</u>
                                                        6
<u>improve</u> student or audience learning. [4] Studies showed
  6
that visual aids should not simply present a speaker's

words, but instead <u>demonstrate or add to them</u> in some
                                                7
way. [5] These studies emphasized the efficacy of visual

representations of the presenter's dialogue in the form

of graphs, charts, art, or pictures. [8]

---

3. **A.** NO CHANGE
   B. the slides'
   C. the slide's
   D. they

4. **F.** NO CHANGE
   G. technological advances were creating
   H. as technological advances have created
   J. that technological advances have created

5. **A.** NO CHANGE
   B. On the other hand, a very important development revealed
   C. A very important development similarly revealed
   D. In contrast, a very important development revealed

6. **F.** NO CHANGE
   G. lead to an improvement in
   H. better enhance or improve
   J. improve

7. **A.** NO CHANGE
   B. they can be demonstrated or added to
   C. demonstrating or adding to them
   D. demonstrate adding for them

8. After reviewing the essay, the writer is considering inserting the following true statement in this paragraph:

   > Audio aids, though infrequently used, can also help audiences focus on a presentation.

   Should this sentence be added to this paragraph, and if so, what is the most logical placement for it?

   F. Yes, after Sentence 2.
   G. Yes, after Sentence 4.
   H. Yes, after Sentence 5.
   J. No, the sentence should NOT be added.

GO ON TO THE NEXT PAGE →

Several studies <u>in listeners have been published in</u>
                                9
<u>respected journals, that reveal that aesthetically</u>
                              9
<u>appealing presentations improve comprehension.</u>
                         9

<u>It has been determined by researchers that a learning aid</u>
                                10
<u>can be created from any pleasing image, even one that</u>
                                10
<u>is irrelevant.</u> Using this model, many presenters have
        10
begun projecting nature scenes or famous paintings to

accompany

<u>presentations. Audience</u> members report not being
              11
distracted by the irrelevant images. In fact, most audience

members find the pleasing images helpful in creating a

positive environment which, in turn, helps <u>him or her</u>
                                                      12
focus on the presentation.

[1] <u>Even more recently, of late,</u> cognitive
                     13
psychologists have noted that students and audience

---

9. A. NO CHANGE

   B. revealing that aesthetically appealing
   presentations improve comprehension
   in listeners have been published in
   respected journals.

   C. in listeners that reveal that aesthetically appealing presentations improve
   comprehension in respected journals
   have been published.

   D. have been published in respected
   journals by revealing in listeners that
   aesthetically appealing presentations
   improve comprehension.

10. F. NO CHANGE

   G. Researchers have determined that any
   pleasing image, even an irrelevant one,
   can serve as a learning aid.

   H. As researchers have determined, that
   any pleasing image, even an irrelevant
   one, can serve as a learning aid.

   J. A pleasing image, even an irrelevant
   one, researchers have determined it can
   serve as a learning aid.

11. A. NO CHANGE

   B. presentations, audience

   C. presentations, and that audience

   D. presentations and that audience

12. F. NO CHANGE

   G. one

   H. you

   J. them

13. A. NO CHANGE

   B. Not so long ago, in recent times,

   C. Lately, in addition,

   D. Recently,

GO ON TO THE NEXT PAGE

members <u>use multiple senses to take in information.</u>
                                                    14
[2] In fact, many experts believe that a teacher's or

presenter's body language is the most important factor

in student or audience reaction. [3] Therefore, many

education and public speaking experts <u>are interested in</u>
                                                         15
<u>investigating other factors in student and audience</u>
                                15
<u>reaction.</u> [4] While these developments have not
    15
coalesced to form one paradigm for public speaking

and presenting, they have underscored many of the

new theories in the field of communication. [5] These

developments continue to influence trends in the

academic world.

PASSAGE II

THE GIFT OF WATER

[1]

I visited Bangalore, India, on a student exchange

program while I was in college. It was my first time

traveling out of the <u>country I</u> was very excited to see
                              16
a new place and meet new people. I had no idea how

much I would learn from the experience and how

thankful I would be for the gift of water.

14. Given that all of the following are true, which choice would provide the most effective and logical link between Sentences 1 and 2?

  F. NO CHANGE
  G. learn not only from images, but also from body language.
  H. pay more attention to visual images that incorporate color or suggest movement.
  J. recall more information when they are asked by the presenter or speaker to take notes or write questions.

15. At this point, the writer would like to show how education and public speaking experts have been influenced by the theory about the importance of body language. Given that all of the following are true, which choice best achieves the writer's purpose?

  A. NO CHANGE
  B. now teach presenters to make purposeful movements and focused gestures.
  C. have adjusted the focus of their public speaking workshops for teachers and business professionals.
  D. question how the size of an audience affects the power of a presenter's body language.

16. F. NO CHANGE
  G. country, I
  H. country; I
  J. country. And I

[2]

I <u>was met by my host family</u> at the airport and we
                    17
we all piled into their little car to go to their house.

As we drove along hot, bumpy dirt roads, <u>very dusty</u>
                                              18
<u>and drylandscape I noticed</u>. I expected to see lush green
      18
trees and rolling hills of tea leaves, one of the

<u>country</u> main exports.
   19

<u>Instead,</u> I saw bare branches in the middle of summer,
   20
dirt as far as the eye could see, and animals that looked

very weak and thin. <u>My host family passionately</u>
                              21
<u>explained</u> that the country had been suffering from a
   21
drought. Water was scarce; that night I learned from

experience.

17. **A.** NO CHANGE
    B. My host family was met by me
    C. My host family and me met
    D. My host family met me

18. **F.** NO CHANGE
    G. noticing very dusty and dry landscape.
    H. I noticed the landscape was very dusty and dry.
    J. landscape I noticed was very dusty and dry.

19. **A.** NO CHANGE
    B. country's
    C. countries
    D. countries'

20. **F.** NO CHANGE
    G. While
    H. Since
    J. Instead of

21. Which of the choices would NOT be acceptable here?
    A. Passionately, my host family explained
    B. My host family explained passionately
    C. My host family passionate explained
    D. My host family explained with passion

GO ON TO THE NEXT PAGE

[3]

When we arrived at their house, my host family served a delicious traditional meal. They had prepared *poori* and vegetable stew. 22 After a wonderful dinner,

22. In order to emphasize the hospitality of the host family, the writer intends to add to the preceding sentence the following phrase:

> to welcome me

The phrase would effectively serve the above-stated purpose if added after the word:

F. family.

G. served.

H. prepared.

J. meal.

it was time to get ready for bed <u>after we ate</u>. I went into
23

23. **A.** NO CHANGE

B. after eating

C. right after we ate

D. OMIT the underlined portion.

the bathroom <u>I was hoping</u> for a hot shower, but there
24
was only a water faucet close to the ground and a hole in

24. **F.** NO CHANGE

G. hoping

H. for I had hoped

J. I was hopeful

the floor. I wondered what I was supposed to do. 25

25. Which of the following sentences, if added at the beginning of Paragraph 4, would most effectively introduce the new subject of the paragraph?

A. I asked my host sister if the shower was outside.

B. I decided to call it a night and go to bed.

C. It is very humorous to try showering without a shower.

D. My host sister and I talked late into the night.

GO ON TO THE NEXT PAGE

[4]

She laughed and told me that you fill a bucket with water to bathe and then empty the water down the drain in the floor. I laughed too and went back into the bathroom to turn on the faucet. [26] I thought the water would warm up after running for a minute, but

instead it <u>stopped entirely running</u>. I spent the next
                        27
fifteen minutes trying to figure out how to make the most of my bucket of water. First, I brushed my teeth and washed my face. Then, I contemplated how I would wash my hair, and decided that dunking my head into a bucket of cold water would have to wait.

[5]

[1] During my visit to <u>India, as I</u> discovered how
                            28

26. The writer wants to add a sentence here that would further support the predicament in which she finds herself. Given that all of the following statements are true, which would most effectively accomplish this?

F. To my dismay, the water was cold as ice.

G. Fortunately, it was a warm summer night.

H. I was glad I had a thick, warm towel with me.

J. Then, I went to the kitchen.

27. A. NO CHANGE

B. ran entirely without stopping.

C. running entirely stopped.

D. stopped running entirely.

28. F. NO CHANGE

G. there I

H. India, when I

J. India, I

GO ON TO THE NEXT PAGE ▷

precious water is and how resourceful people are. [29]

[2] I became very aware of how much water people freely consumed each day without a second thought.

[3] When I think of my family in India, I remember that every drop of water counts. [4] After I returned to the United States, I no longer took long showers or left the

water running while I brushed my teeth. [30]

29. Which of the following sentences, if added at this point, would most directly support the idea that people in India are resourceful with water?

   A. When it is very hot, people often carpool to the beach to take a swim in the ocean.

   B. The same water that was used to boil an egg was then used to wash the dishes.

   C. Instead of drinking tap water, many people drink sodas.

   D. They buy a lot of bottled water when the store has bottles in supply.

30. For the sake of unity and coherence in Paragraph 5, Sentence 4 should be placed:

   F. where it is now.

   G. after Sentence 1.

   H. after Sentence 2.

   J. at the end of Paragraph 4.

PASSAGE III

LOS ANGELES FREEWAYS

I recently traveled to Los Angeles to visit my cousin and to finally see California. As the pilot informed us that we had crossed over the Nevada-California border, I began gazing out of the window. We descended into Los Angeles, and my attention was drawn to the rugged terrain of forested mountains and brush-filled hillsides. I realized that the city roads hugged and straddled the topography. As I would soon find out, this is a significant and major source of traffic congestion.
   31
Upon arriving at my cousin's home, I shared my plan to scour the city armed with a handful of tourist

31. A. NO CHANGE

   B. major source

   C. significant contributor to the problem

   D. primary root cause

maps <u>that I had picked up at the airport.</u> However, my
32

cousin <u>replied only with a puzzled gaze,</u> when I asked
33

about public transportation. <u>Indeed,</u> Los Angeles
34
residents, like almost all Californians, drive their own

cars. Being a New Yorker, I had very little driving

experience, even though I possessed a driver's license.

    <u>Instead of using public transportation, I rented a</u>
35
<u>car for my stay in Los Angeles.</u> The avenues, which are
35
laid out in a square grid, are often eight lanes wide.

32. Given that all of the following are true, which choice would provide the most specific information about tourist destinations in and around Los Angeles?

  F. NO CHANGE

  G. that provided me with several ideas for day trips in the city.

  H. of local attractions, from beaches to ski resorts to stars' homes.

  J. outlining the most popular places visited by both tourists and native Angelinos.

33. **A.** NO CHANGE

  B. replies only with a puzzled gaze,

  C. replies only with a puzzled gaze

  D. replied only with a puzzled gaze

34. **F.** NO CHANGE

  G. However,

  H. Apparently,

  J. Furthermore,

35. Given that all of the statements below are true, which choice most effectively introduces this paragraph?

  A. NO CHANGE

  B. At first, I felt comfortable driving through the streets of Los Angeles.

  C. I found myself becoming excited about the opportunity to drive in a new city.

  D. Initially, the thought of driving was intimidating.

However, in most places, <u>it isn't</u> numbered as in
36
New York, so finding your way around isn't as easy as it

can be for a tourist in the Big Apple.

Eventually, when I hit the hills, I began to feel <u>far</u>
37
<u>less surer</u> about my ability to navigate the city. The flat
37
maps I was using had no way of representing all of the

hills and mountains cutting the city into pieces.

There was no way around the hills and mountains,

unless, of course, I felt like driving miles and hours out

of my way. When I wanted to see the Hollywood sign,

I had to climb a perilously winding, one-lane, two-

way artery reminiscent of the scenery in 1970s Italian

movies. In order to see the Rose Bowl, I had to drive

congested freeways that tunneled through mountain

passes—where changing lanes was all but impossible—

<u>and rose</u> to hang off hillsides. To see television shows
38

36. **F.** NO CHANGE
    G. they aren't
    H. they weren't
    J. it wasn't

37. **A.** NO CHANGE
    B. far less sure
    C. less surer
    D. less surest

38. **F.** NO CHANGE
    G. so rose
    H. and rise
    J. and

GO ON TO THE NEXT PAGE

taped in Burbank, I drove a Grand Prix-like road up and

over the hills. [39]

During peak hours, the city's road system clogs

with <u>commuters: its like</u> an obstructed plumbing pipe.
      40
I experienced the frustrations that this city's residents

must feel on their journeys to and from work, a

frustration that I do not feel at home in New York City.

<u>Traffic is less frustrating in New York.</u> New York
              41
roadways are congested, but subways deliver their riders

on time regardless of street traffic. <u>On the other hand,</u> a
                                          42
New Yorker can always walk. However, as I sat in traffic

39. The writer is considering inserting the following true statement:

> Of course, it is also challenging to navigate the Times Square area in New York City to get to a Broadway show.

Should this sentence be inserted here?

A. Yes, because it informs the reader that other metropolitan areas are also challenging to navigate.

B. Yes, because New York City is compared to Los Angeles at other points in the essay.

C. No, because it is not related to the topic of the paragraph and does not follow the structure of the sentences in the paragraph.

D. No, because the writer is comfortable finding his way around New York City.

40. **F.** NO CHANGE

G. commuters, its like

H. commuters, it's like

J. commuters; it's like

41. **A.** NO CHANGE

B. New York traffic delays typically do not irritate me in this way.

C. Because of the efficient subway system, New York traffic is less of an irritant to commuters.

D. OMIT the underlined portion.

42. **F.** NO CHANGE

G. Conversely,

H. Besides,

J. Likewise,

GO ON TO THE NEXT PAGE ▷

on the freeway, I <u>from my vantage point saw, high atop</u>
<u>the Foothills,</u> the sun setting into the Pacific Ocean,
43

less than thirty miles away. In my rearview mirror lay

<u>beautiful, snowcapped, mountains contrasting with the</u>
<u>palm trees</u>
44

near the side of the road. 45

43. **A.** NO CHANGE

B. saw, from my vantage point high atop
the Foothills,

C. saw, high atop the Foothills, from my
vantage point,

D. saw atop the Foothills, high from my
vantage point

44. **F.** NO CHANGE

G. beautiful snowcapped, mountains
contrasting with the palm trees

H. beautiful snowcapped mountains
contrasting with the palm trees,

J. beautiful snowcapped mountains
contrasting with the palm trees

45. Inserted at this point, which of the following
sentences would make the best conclusion
for the paragraph while maintaining the
focus of the essay?

A. My cousin is truly fortunate to live in a
place with such natural beauty.

B. At last I had learned how to navigate
the area with the maps I had picked up
at the airport.

C. Sometimes, perhaps, traffic congestion
can actually be a good thing.

D. At long last, the traffic began to slowly
move again.

PASSAGE IV

JUST PLANT A TREE

As Dr. Wangari Muta Maathai explains it, <u>the Green Belt Movement started at</u> a simple question: Why not
₄₆
plant trees? In the mid-1970s, women in her Kenyan

community were complaining of not having enough

firewood and water. <u>Why did Maathai decide to lead?</u>
₄₇

<u>In Kenya, in the villages, she organized women to</u>
₄₈
<u>plant trees.</u> Their efforts serve as a means of both
₄₈
environmental restoration and community building.

<u>The women thought it was important to come together</u>
₄₉
<u>as a community and to help the environment at</u>
₄₉
<u>the same time.</u> Maathai, and the many women who
₄₉
participate through the Green Belt Movement, empower

each other by planting trees as a way of addressing the

immediate and long-term needs of their families. As of

2009, Maathai's Green Belt Movement has planted more

than thirty-five million trees.

46. F. NO CHANGE
G. the Green Belt Movement started from
H. the Green Belt Movement start from
J. the Green Belt Movement starts at

47. A. NO CHANGE
B. How did Maathai respond?
C. Where did Maathai start?
D. What did Maathai want to do?

48. F. NO CHANGE
G. In the villages of Kenya, she organized women to plant trees.
H. She organized women to plant trees in the villages of Kenya.
J. She, in the villages of Kenya, organized women to plant trees.

49. A. NO CHANGE
B. They found ways to make a difference in the community and for the environment.
C. Helping their community and the environment were priority for these women.
D. OMIT the underlined portion.

GO ON TO THE NEXT PAGE ▷

[50] She was born in the Nyeri District of Kenya in 1940. After completing her high-school education in her home country, Maathai traveled to the United States to complete her

Bachelor's degree in biology and <u>to earn</u> her Master's
                                  51
degree in biological sciences. In 1971, her continuing

studies in Germany and Kenya <u>leaded</u> her to earn a
                                52
Ph.D. in Veterinary Medicine from the University of Nairobi. She went on to hold several positions at the

University of <u>Nairobi while</u> eventually becoming the
                 53
first woman to head a department at the university.

50. Assuming that all are true, which of the following sentences, if added here, would most effectively introduce this paragraph?

F. Maathai's journey to becoming an influential leader started early in her East African home.

G. Maathai has gained the respect of many people in East Africa and around the world.

H. Before founding the Green Belt Movement, Maathai traveled all over the world.

J. Kenya, the place of Maathai's birth, is situated in East Africa.

51. A. NO CHANGE
    B. earning
    C. earn for
    D. earned

52. F. NO CHANGE
    G. led
    H. leads
    J. OMIT the underlined portion.

53. A. NO CHANGE
    B. Nairobi while also
    C. Nairobi, and
    D. Nairobi,

GO ON TO THE NEXT PAGE

<u>In addition to her many educational and leadership</u>
54
<u>achievements, Maathai has repeatedly demonstrated</u>
54
<u>her dedication to improving conditions for the Kenyan</u>
54
<u>people.</u>
54

54. F. NO CHANGE

G. Maathai has repeatedly demonstrated her dedication to improving conditions, in addition to her many educational and leadership achievements, for the Kenyan people.

H. Her achievements in education and leadership, for the Kenyan people, have repeatedly demonstrated Maathai's dedication to improving conditions.

J. The Kenyan people, who have benefited from her achievements in education and leadership, have repeatedly demonstrated Maathai's dedication to improving conditions.

She has served <u>in a wide range of positions and</u>
55
<u>initiatives that go from</u> being an elected member of
55
parliament to chairing the National Council of Women
of Kenya.

55. A. NO CHANGE

B. for a wide range of positions and initiatives

C. in a wide range of positions and initiatives, from

D. in different ways through varying positions and initiatives to include

The year 2004 marked another achievement when

<u>her was</u> rewarded by the international community.
56

56. F. NO CHANGE

G. Maathai was

H. were for Maathai

J. her were

She <u>was honored</u> with a Nobel Peace Prize, the first
57
African American woman to receive this award, for

57. A. NO CHANGE

B. honor

C. honoring

D. were honored

<u>her really good actions of</u> community organization
58

58. F. NO CHANGE

G. her way of doing things of

H. her unique actions of

J. OMIT the underlined portion.

GO ON TO THE NEXT PAGE

and environmental activism. 59 The Norwegian Nobel Committee cited Maathai's contribution to "sustainable development, democracy and peace," acknowledging the

peaceful impact of her work. 60

59. The writer is considering adding the following sentence:

> The Nobel Peace Prize, considered by many to be one of the highest possible honors, is awarded to an individual or institution that successfully fosters the most fraternity between people or nations.

Would this sentence be an appropriate addition to this essay, and why?

A. Yes, because it shows why Maathai deserved to win the Nobel Peace Prize.

B. Yes, because it explains why the Nobel Peace Prize is an internationally important award.

C. No, because it includes details that detract from the focus of this paragraph.

D. No, because it doesn't provide enough information about the significance of the award.

Question 60 asks about the preceding passage as a whole.

60. Suppose the writer wanted to submit this essay to a newsletter about the role of women in African policy making. Would this essay successfully fulfill the newsletter's purpose?

F. No, because the essay centers on the life of an African woman who led through nongovernmental agencies.

G. No, because the essay indicates that African women are not part of the policy-making process.

H. Yes, because the essay details how Maathai's actions have affected the policies in her African country and beyond.

J. Yes, because the essay reflects how Maathai's story is similar to other African woman policy-makers.

GO ON TO THE NEXT PAGE ➡

PASSAGE V

MY SECOND TRIP

It was my second visit to the black sands of Punalu'u Beach when I realized just how special this place is. From my first trip to Punalu'u, all I remembered was the <u>sand. Because of</u> its uniqueness.
61
Most beaches around the world have brown or white sand. There are even pink-sand beaches in tropical destinations, like the Bahamas. These more common sands are composed of finely divided rocks, like silica and <u>limestone. But,</u> at this famous beach in Hawaii, the
62
sand is created by lava flowing into the ocean.

Once the lava hits the ocean, it explodes and cools, turning into the granules that line this Big Island coast. My heart still <u>sores</u> as I think of the sand that felt like
63
ink-stained sugar as it massaged my feet.

64 Of course, I again

61. **A.** NO CHANGE
   B. sand, because
   C. sand: because
   D. sand because,

62. **F.** NO CHANGE
   G. limestone but
   H. limestone: but
   J. limestone, but

63. **A.** NO CHANGE
   B. soar
   C. sore
   D. soars

64. Which of the following would best introduce the information in this paragraph?
   F. As the years pass, the Punalu'u Beach continues to grow in splendor.
   G. The second time I arrived at Punalu'u Beach was when I began to take in the whole experience.
   H. There are many fascinating parts to this historic Hawaiian beach.
   J. When I think about my visits to Punalu'u Beach, images of the sand and the trees keep coming to mind.

GO ON TO THE NEXT PAGE

would marvel at the beautiful black sand and
 65
picturesque coconut palms leaning toward the distant

horizon. But, during this trip, I went into the swimming

area. They was accurate in describing the waters as
 66

rocky and tricky to navigate. My feets' tempo increased
 67
as I carefully made my way into the depths of the brisk

water. It was beneath, and not above, the water's surface
 68

where I discovered even more of the beach's beauty.
 69
  There is a large amount of underground fresh water

at the beach. This water is quite cold and looks

like swirls of gasoline mixed with water. From one
 70
perspective area legend, early Hawaiians would dive
 70
underwater with jugs to get fresh water during times

of drought. It was also underwater that I discovered

65. **A.** NO CHANGE
    B. marvel
    C. marveled
    D. would be

66. **F.** NO CHANGE
    G. We
    H. My guidebook
    J. The lifeguards

67. **A.** NO CHANGE
    B. feet's tempo
    C. feets tempo
    D. feets' tempo's

68. **F.** NO CHANGE
    G. beneath the view from
    H. beneath the top of
    J. beneath

69. Which of the choices would be most consistent with the essay and best suggest the reason for going into the rocky water of this beach?
    A. NO CHANGE
    B. content
    C. sand
    D. life forms

70. **F.** NO CHANGE
    G. Because of an
    H. According to an
    J. While it is stated in

GO ON TO THE NEXT PAGE

a Green Sea turtle on <u>coarse</u> to the shoreline. This
                      71
majestic reptile peacefully swam past my left side using

71. **A.** NO CHANGE
    B. coarser
    C. course
    D. coursing

the least amount of effort possible. <u>Still I</u> knew not to
                                      72
touch the turtle as they are endangered and susceptible

to bacteria from humans. While I watched this rare

72. **F.** NO CHANGE
    G. Because I
    H. Nevertheless, I
    J. I

creature, I could see why <u>many calls</u> Punalu'u Beach one
                          73
of the best beaches in the world.

73. **A.** NO CHANGE
    B. many call
    C. many themselves call
    D. many calling

When I returned to land, I took another look at the

sand, the source of my initial fascination with Punalu'u.

<u>I want</u> to take a handful of it home with me, a small
  74
reminder of this natural wonder and a way to prove my

trip to my friends back home in Illinois. Since many

signs around the beach informed me that it was illegal

to take any of the sand, I instead took home many

pictures and <u>memories: as</u> my souvenirs.
              75

74. **F.** NO CHANGE
    G. Before, I wanted
    H. Having wanted
    J. I wanted

75. **A.** NO CHANGE
    B. memories; as my
    C. memories as my
    D. memories. As my

IF YOU FINISH BEFORE TIME IS CALLED, YOU MAY CHECK YOUR WORK ON THIS SECTION ONLY. DO NOT TURN TO ANY OTHER SECTION IN THE TEST. **STOP**

MATHEMATICS TEST

60 Minutes—60 Questions

Directions: Solve each of the following problems, select the correct answer, and then fill in the corresponding space on your answer sheet.

Don't linger over problems that are too time-consuming. Do as many as you can, then come back to the others in the time you have remaining.

The use of a calculator is permitted on this test. Though you are allowed to use your calculator to solve any questions you choose, some of the questions may be most easily answered without the use of a calculator.

Note: Unless otherwise noted, all of the following should be assumed.

1. Illustrative figures are *not* necessarily drawn to scale.
2. All geometric figures lie in a plane.
3. The term *line* indicates a straight line.
4. The term *average* indicates arithmetic mean.

1. In the United States, the lowest city can be found at 186 feet below sea level. The elevation of the highest city is 10,152 feet above sea level. By how many feet do the elevations of these cities differ?

   A.   67 feet
   B.   186 feet
   C.   9,966 feet
   D. 10,152 feet
   E. 10,338 feet

2. If Town A has a population of 450, how many people are leaving if 30% of Town A's population are moving away?

   F.   15
   G.   30
   H. 135
   J. 200
   K. 315

3. In order to determine some information about local gas prices, Sally must find the average cost of gasoline per gallon in her neighborhood. She visits 4 gas stations near her house and finds that the price per gallon at each store is $2.15, $2.05, $2.15, and $1.97, respectively. Among these 4 stations, what is the average price of gasoline per gallon?

   A. $2.06
   B. $2.07
   C. $2.08
   D. $2.09
   E. $2.10

GO ON TO THE NEXT PAGE

4. In the figure below, *ABCD* is a trapezoid, *BC* is parallel to *AD*, ∠*ABC* = ∠*BCD*, and *AB* = *CD*. The measure of ∠*CDE* is as marked. What is the measure of ∠*BAD*?

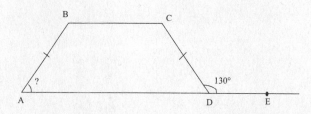

   F. 130°

   G. 80°

   H. 75°

   J. 50°

   K. 25°

5. Polygon *ABCD* is a square, and the circle centered at point *C* has a radius of 4. If points *B*, *D*, and *E* lie on the circumference of the circle, what is the area of square *ABCD*?

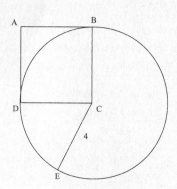

   A. 16

   B. 20

   C. 16π

   D. 36

   E. 36π

6. The amount of paint used to paint a wall is directly proportional to the surface area of that wall. If a house with 900 square feet of wall space will require 2.25 gallons of paint, how much paint will be needed to paint a house with 852 square feet of wall space?

   F. 1.45 gallons

   G. 1.77 gallons

   H. 2.05 gallons

   J. 2.13 gallons

   K. 2.45 gallons

7. In the figure below, $\overline{AC}$ is parallel to $\overline{DF}$. $\overline{PQ}$ intersects $\overline{AC}$ at point *B* and intersects $\overline{DF}$ at point *E*. Which of the following must be true?

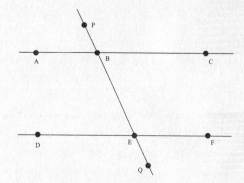

   A. ∠*PBA* + ∠*DEQ* = 180°

   B. ∠*PBA* + ∠*BED* = 90°

   C. ∠*PBA* = ∠*DEQ*

   D. ∠*PBA* = 90°

   E. ∠*DEQ* = 90°

8. If $7x - 24 = 8x - 39$, then $x = ?$

   F. −63

   G. −15

   H. $-\dfrac{63}{8}$

   J. $\dfrac{63}{8}$

   K. 15

GO ON TO THE NEXT PAGE ▷

9. Which of the following is always equal to
   $2c(3 + c) - 7(c - 2)$?

   A. $c - 6$

   B. $c + 4$

   C. $2c^2 - c + 14$

   D. $2c^2 - c - 14$

   E. $2c^3 - 14$

10. One ticket is drawn from a bag containing
    5 pink, 4 yellow, and 3 green tickets. What is the
    probability that the ticket drawn is NOT yellow?

    F. $\dfrac{5}{6}$

    G. $\dfrac{1}{3}$

    H. $\dfrac{2}{3}$

    J. $\dfrac{2}{15}$

    K. $\dfrac{1}{9}$

11. Scientists are modeling population trends, and
    have noticed that when a certain population
    changes, the change is based on a linear
    function. When $t = 21$, the population is 3.
    When $t = 35$, the population is 5. Which of
    the following describes the population, in
    terms of t?

    A. $\dfrac{t}{7}$

    B. $t - 18$

    C. $t - 30$

    D. $3t - 60$

    E. $3t - 100$

12. In the figure below, the ratio of the area of
    polygon $BCDEFG$ to the area of square $ABCD$
    is 3:1. What is the ratio of the area of square
    $AEFG$ to the area of square $ABCD$?

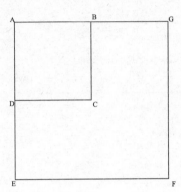

    F. 4:1

    G. 2:1

    H. 1:3

    J. 1:4

    K. Cannot be determined from the infor-
       mation given

13. A film that is 3 hours 40 minutes long must
    be cut into two equal parts. What will be the
    duration of each part?

    A. 1 hour 10 minutes

    B. 1 hour 30 minutes

    C. 1 hour 50 minutes

    D. 1 hour 55 minutes

    E. 2 hours 20 minutes

GO ON TO THE NEXT PAGE

14. Which of the following statements describes the total of the first n terms of the sequence below?

$$1, 3, 5, 7, 9, \ldots$$

F. The total is always equal to 25 regardless of n.

G. The total is always $2n$.

H. The total is always $3n$.

J. The total is always equal to n^2.

K. There is no consistent pattern for the total.

15. In the circle shown below, the length of chord $\overline{AB}$ is 24 and the length of $\overline{OC}$ is 5. What is the radius of the circle with center O?

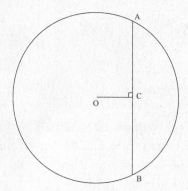

A. 12

B. 13

C. 15

D. $13\sqrt{2}$

E. $15\sqrt{2}$

16. What is the value of the expression $a^4 + a^3 - 4a + 6$ for $a = -3$?

F. -27

G. 54

H. 60

J. 66

K. 72

17. What is the fifth term in the following geometric sequence: $-108, 36, -12, 4, \ldots$?

A. $-\dfrac{35}{6}$

B. $-\dfrac{8}{3}$

C. $-\dfrac{4}{3}$

D. 0

E. 1

18. On a map, $\dfrac{1}{2}$ inch represents an actual distance of 5 miles. What is the actual area, in square miles, of a rectangular region that is $4\dfrac{1}{3}$ inches by 5 inches on the map?

F. $53\dfrac{2}{3}$

G. $107\dfrac{1}{3}$

H. $541\dfrac{2}{3}$

J. $2166\dfrac{2}{3}$

K. $4377\dfrac{2}{3}$

19. If $x \geq 0$ and $y < 0$, which of the following MUST be true?

A. $xy > 0$

B. $xy < 0$

C. $xy = 0$

D. $xy \geq 0$

E. $xy \leq 0$

GO ON TO THE NEXT PAGE

20. If $\dfrac{1}{45} = y - \dfrac{4}{5}$, then $y = ?$

   F. -36

   G. $-\dfrac{1}{9}$

   H. $\dfrac{1}{9}$

   J. $\dfrac{17}{45}$

   K. $\dfrac{37}{45}$

21. If the equation of a line is $4x - 7y = 14$, what is the slope of the line?

   A. -7

   B. $-\dfrac{4}{7}$

   C. $\dfrac{4}{7}$

   D. $\dfrac{7}{4}$

   E. 7

22. Which of the following expressions represents the area, in square meters, of a square that has a side length of $(5t - 2)$ meters?

   F. $25t^2 - 20t + 4$

   G. $25t^2 - 10t - 4$

   H. $10t^2 - 20t + 4$

   J. $25t^2 + 4$

   K. $10t^2 - 4$

23. Which of the following pairs of binomials are factors of $x^2 - 6x - 16$?

   A. $(x - 6)$ and $(x - 10)$

   B. $(x - 2)$ and $(x + 8)$

   C. $(x + 2)$ and $(x - 8)$

   D. $(x + 6)$ and $(x - 10)$

   E. $(x + 8)$ and $(x - 8)$

24. In the expression $(2)^{\frac{1}{r}}$, r represents a positive integer. As r increases without bound, the value of $(2)^{\frac{1}{r}}$:

   F. gets closer and closer to 0.

   G. gets closer and closer to 1.

   H. gets closer and closer to 2.

   J. remains constant.

   K. increases without bound.

25. Some parts of Antarctica frequently reach temperatures as low as $-60°C$. Using the formula $F = \dfrac{9}{5}C + 32$, what is this temperature, in degrees Fahrenheit?

   A. $-28°F$

   B. $-76°F$

   C. $-108°F$

   D. $-140°F$

   E. $-180°F$

26. The legs of an isosceles triangle are 1 more than 3 times its base. If the base of the triangle is x and the perimeter of the triangle is 30 units, what is the value of x?

   F. 3

   G. 4

   H. $\dfrac{32}{7}$

   J. 5

   K. $\dfrac{16}{3}$

27. For what values of x does $f(x) = 2x^2 + 7x - 4 = 0$?

   A. $x = -1$, $x = -\dfrac{5}{2}$

   B. $x = -\dfrac{1}{2}$, $x = -4$

   C. $x = -\dfrac{1}{2}$, $x = 4$

   D. $x = \dfrac{1}{2}$, $x = -4$

   E. $x = 1$, $x = \dfrac{5}{2}$

GO ON TO THE NEXT PAGE

28. Brooks scored an average of 30 points per game on his basketball team. The numbers of points he scored in each game are shown below.

Game	1	2	3	4	5	6
Points	28	31	20	42	32	?

How many points did Brooks score in Game 6?

F. 24

G. 27

H. 30

J. 31

K. 33

29. If a, b, and c are positive integers, then $c^{\frac{1}{a}} \cdot c^{\frac{1}{b}} = ?$

A. $c^{\frac{1}{ab}}$

B. $2c^{\frac{1}{ab}}$

C. $c^{\frac{1}{a+b}}$

D. $c^{\frac{a+b}{ab}}$

E. $c^{\frac{2}{a+b}}$

30. What is the circumference, in meters, of a circle with a radius equal to 6 meters?

F. 3π

G. 6π

H. 9π

J. 12π

K. 36π

31. To qualify for a particular scholarship, a student must receive an A in both calculus and physics classes. Based on past performances, 30% of the applicants receive an A in calculus and 60% of those who received an A in calculus also receive an A in physics. Based on these results, how many applicants in a random group of 200 students would you expect to get a scholarship?

A. 18

B. 36

C. 60

D. 120

E. 180

32. If $\cos B = \dfrac{12}{13}$, then which of the following could be $\sin B$?

F. $\dfrac{5}{13}$

G. $\dfrac{5}{12}$

H. $\dfrac{12}{15}$

J. $\dfrac{13}{12}$

K. 13

33. If y is any number other than -3 and 2, then $-\dfrac{(2-y)(y+3)}{(y+3)(y-2)} = ?$

A. -6

B. -1

C. 0

D. 1

E. 6

GO ON TO THE NEXT PAGE ▷

34. $\sqrt{48} + \sqrt{27} = ?$

   F. $\sqrt{75}$

   G. $7\sqrt{3}$

   H. $12\sqrt{3}$

   J. $3\sqrt{16} + 3\sqrt{9}$

   K. $25\sqrt{3}$

35. $\triangle LMN$ is similar to $\triangle RST$. LM is 4 inches long, MN is 10 inches long, and LN is 12 inches long. If the shortest side of $\triangle RST$ is 6 inches long, what is the perimeter, in inches, of $\triangle RST$?

   A. 26

   B. 32

   C. 39

   D. 42

   E. 50

36. Side QR of square $QRTS$ has a midpoint P, as shown below. If QR is 4 inches long, what is the area, in square inches, of the shaded region?

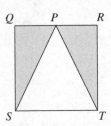

   F. 2

   G. 4

   H. 8

   J. 12

   K. 16

37. In the figure below, DE is the diameter of the circle, F is a point on the circle, and $\overline{EF} \cong \overline{FD}$. What is the degree measure of $\angle DEF$?

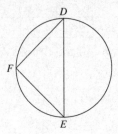

   A. 30°

   B. 45°

   C. 60°

   D. 90°

   E. Cannot be determined from the given information

38. In the standard (x,y) coordinate plane, what are the coordinates of the midpoint of a line segment with endpoints $(1,-5)$ and $(2,7)$?

   F. $\left(\dfrac{1}{2},1\right)$

   G. $(1,2)$

   H. $(1,13)$

   J. $\left(\dfrac{3}{2},-2\right)$

   K. $\left(\dfrac{3}{2},1\right)$

39. In a crew race, Ashwin rowed 0.8 miles in 5 minutes and 20 seconds. How many miles per hour did he row?

   A. 4

   B. 5

   C. 7

   D. 9

   E. 10

GO ON TO THE NEXT PAGE

40. For the 2 functions $f(x)$ and $g(x)$, tables of values are shown below. What is the value of $f(g(1))$?

x	$f(x)$
-2	8
-1	6
0	4
1	2

x	$g(x)$
-1	-4
1	0
2	2
4	6

F. 0

G. 1

H. 2

J. 4

K. 6

41. For positive real numbers x, y, and z, which of the following expressions is equivalent to $x^{\frac{2}{3}} y^{\frac{1}{4}} z^{\frac{5}{2}}$?

A. $\sqrt[3]{x^2 y z^5}$

B. $\sqrt[4]{x^2 y z^5}$

C. $\sqrt[6]{x^2 y z^5}$

D. $\sqrt[6]{x^4 y^2 z^{10}}$

E. $\sqrt[12]{x^8 y^3 z^{30}}$

42. The formula for the area of a triangle is $A = \frac{1}{2}bh$, where b is the length of the base and h is the length of the triangle's height. Which of the following is an expression for h?

F. $\dfrac{2A}{b}$

G. $\dfrac{A}{2b}$

H. $\dfrac{Ab}{2}$

J. $\dfrac{A-b}{2}$

K. $2Ab$

43. The line graphed below shows the predicted amount of ice sold at a certain store. Which of the following is the closest estimate of this store's predicted rate of ice cream sales, in gallons per day?

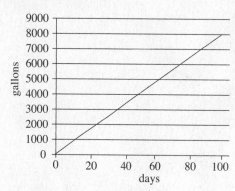

A. 60

B. 72

C. 80

D. 88

E. 100

GO ON TO THE NEXT PAGE

44. The graph of $y = ax^2 + bx + c$ is in the standard (x,y) coordinate plane is shown below.

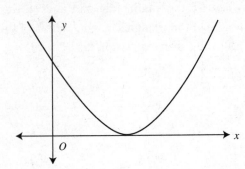

When $y = 0$, which of the following best describes the solution set for x?

F. 2 real solutions

G. 1 double real solution only

H. 1 real and 1 imaginary solution

J. 1 double imaginary solution only

K. 2 imaginary solutions

45. If $|x| = -2x + 1$, then $x = ?$

A. −1

B. $-\dfrac{1}{3}$

C. 0

D. $\dfrac{1}{3}$

E. 1

46. What fraction lies exactly halfway between $\dfrac{4}{5}$ and $\dfrac{5}{6}$?

F. $\dfrac{5}{7}$

G. $\dfrac{9}{10}$

H. $\dfrac{13}{15}$

J. $\dfrac{23}{30}$

K. $\dfrac{49}{60}$

47. Maria keeps a record of the amount of money in her piggy bank. She takes $1.25 out of the piggy bank to buy a candy bar. When figuring the new amount of money in the piggy bank, she accidentally adds $1.25 to the total rather than subtracting it. Assuming she had the recorded the correct amount of money prior to this error, the total amount of money she has recorded is:

A. $2.50 less than it should be.

B. $1.25 less than it should be.

C. the correct amount.

D. $1.25 more than it should be.

E. $2.50 more than it should be.

48. Five books are to be placed on a bookshelf. If all 5 books are placed on the shelf in order, from left to right, in how many different ways can the books be placed?

F. 5

G. 14

H. 60

J. 120

K. 720

49. In the standard (x,y) coordinate plane, what is the distance between the points $(-2,3)$ and $(1,-1)$?

A. 3

B. 4

C. 5

D. 6

E. 7

GO ON TO THE NEXT PAGE

50. A formula for the volume, V, of a right circular cylinder is $V = \pi r^2 h$, where r is the radius and h is the height. The cylindrical swimming pool shown below is filled completely with water and has a radius of 6 feet and a depth of 4 feet.

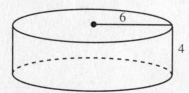

If 1 cubic foot of water weighs approximately 62.4 pounds, then the weight, in pounds, of the water in the swimming pool is:

F. less than 20,000.

G. between 20,000 and 25,000.

H. between 25,000 and 30,000.

J. between 30,000 and 35,000.

K. more than 35,000.

51. What are the values of θ, between 0° and 360°, when $\sin \theta = \dfrac{\sqrt{3}}{2}$?

A. 30° and 120° only

B. 60° and 120° only

C. 45° and 135° only

D. 60° and 150° only

E. 60° only

52. Which of the following is an equation of a circle with its center at $(-2,1)$ and tangent to the y-axis in the standard (x,y) coordinate plane?

F. $(x + 2)^2 + (y - 1)^2 = 1$

G. $(x - 2)^2 + (y + 1)^2 = 1$

H. $(x - 2)^2 + (y - 1)^2 = 2$

J. $(x + 2)^2 + (y - 1)^2 = 4$

K. $(x - 2)^2 + (y + 1)^2 = 4$

53. Which of the following best represents the graph of $y \geq ax + b$ for some negative a and negative b?

A.

B.

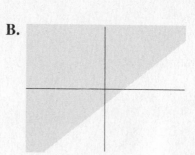

C.

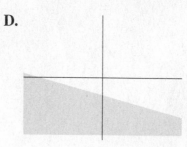

D.

E.

GO ON TO THE NEXT PAGE

54. One of the graphs below is that of $y = \cos(n\theta)$ for θ between 0 and 6.28 radians, where n is a constant. Which graph?

F.

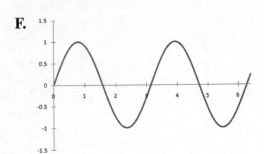

G.

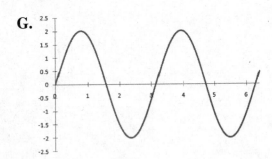

H.

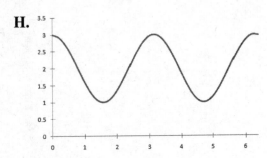

J.

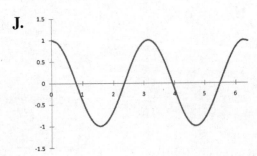

K.

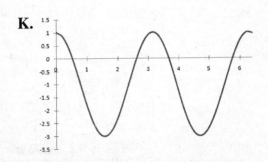

55. In the figure below, M, N, and O are the midpoints of the sides $\overline{DE}$, $\overline{EF}$, and $\overline{DF}$, respectively. If the measure of $\angle EDF$ is 20°, and the measure of $\angle DFE$ is 80°, what is the measure of $\angle OMN$?

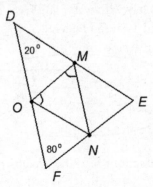

A. 20°

B. 40°

C. 70°

D. 80°

E. 90°

56. A formula for the volume (V) of the rectangular solid shown below is $V = lwh$, where l represents length, w represents width, and h represents height. By halving each of the dimensions (l, w, and h), the volume will be multiplied by what factor?

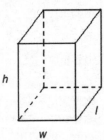

F. $\dfrac{1}{2}$

G. $\dfrac{1}{4}$

H. $\dfrac{1}{6}$

J. $\dfrac{1}{8}$

K. $\dfrac{1}{12}$

GO ON TO THE NEXT PAGE

57. If $\sin x = \dfrac{1}{2}$ and $\tan x = \dfrac{1}{\sqrt{3}}$, then $\csc x = ?$

   A. -2

   B. $-\sqrt{3}$

   C. $\dfrac{2}{\sqrt{3}}$

   D. $\sqrt{3}$

   E. 2

58. In a rhombus, all 4 sides are the same length. Rhombus *LMNO* below has vertices at $L\,(0,0)$ and $N\,(5,5)$. What is the slope of diagonal *MO*?

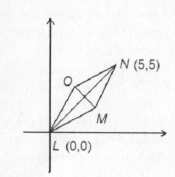

   F. -1

   G. $-\dfrac{1}{2}$

   H. $-\dfrac{1}{5}$

   J. $\dfrac{1}{5}$

   K. 1

59. Charles earned a score of 76 on a recent 50-question multiple-choice exam. The scoring for the exam was such that each correct answer earned +5 points, each incorrect answer earned –1 point, and each unanswered question received 0 points. What is the maximum number of questions Charles could have answered correctly?

   A. 15

   B. 18

   C. 21

   D. 23

   E. 25

60. In the standard (x,y) coordinate plane, the graphs of the 3 equations $y - x = 2$, $y + 2x = 5$, and $y = -2$ form the boundary of a triangle. What is the area of this triangle, expressed in square coordinate units?

   F. 12.75

   G. 15

   H. 18.75

   J. 37.5

   K. 75

IF YOU FINISH BEFORE TIME IS CALLED, YOU MAY CHECK YOUR WORK ON THIS SECTION ONLY. DO NOT TURN TO ANY OTHER SECTION IN THE TEST.   **STOP**

READING TEST

35 Minutes—40 Questions

Directions: There are four passages in this test. Each passage is followed by several questions. After reading a passage, choose the best answer to each question and fill in the corresponding oval on your Answer Grid. You may refer to the passages as often as necessary.

PASSAGE I

PROSE FICTION

This passage is excerpted from the novel Jane Eyre, *by Charlotte Bronte (©1897).*

His manner was polite; his accent, in speaking, struck me as being somewhat unusual,—not precisely foreign, but still not altogether English: his
Line age might be about Mr. Rochester's,—between thirty
(5) and forty; his complexion was singularly sallow: otherwise he was a fine-looking man, at first sight especially. On closer examination, you detected something in his face that displeased, or rather that failed to please. His features were regular, but too
(10) relaxed: his eye was large, but the life looking out of it was a tame, vacant life—at least so I thought.

The sound of the bell dispersed the party. It was not till after dinner that I saw him again: he then seemed quite at his ease. But I liked his
(15) physiognomy even less than before: it struck me as being at the same time unsettled and inanimate. His eye wandered, and had no meaning in its wandering: this gave him an odd look, such as I never remembered to have seen. For a handsome
(20) and not an unamiable-looking man, he repelled me exceedingly: there was no power in that smooth-skinned face of a full oval shape: no firmness in that aquiline nose and small cherry mouth; there was no thought on the low, even forehead; no com-
(25) mand in that blank, brown eye.

As I sat in my usual nook, and looked at him with the light on the mantelpiece beaming full over him—for he occupied an arm-chair drawn close to the fire, and kept shrinking still nearer, as if he were
(30) cold—I compared him with Mr. Rochester. I think (with deference be it spoken) the contrast could

not be much greater between a sleek gander and a fierce falcon: between a meek sheep and the rough-coated keen-eyed dog, its guardian.

(35) He had spoken of Mr. Rochester as an old friend. A curious friendship theirs must have been: a pointed illustration, indeed, of the old adage that "extremes meet."

Two or three of the gentlemen sat near him, and
(40) I caught at times scraps of their conversation across the room. At first I could not make much sense of what I heard; for the discourse of Louisa Eshton and Mary Ingram, who sat nearer to me, confused the fragmentary sentences that reached me at
(45) intervals. These last were discussing the stranger; they both called him "a beautiful man." Louisa said he was "a love of a creature," and she "adored him;" and Mary instanced his "pretty little mouth, and nice nose," as her ideal of the charming.

(50) "And what a sweet-tempered forehead he has!" cried Louisa,—"so smooth—none of those frowning irregularities I dislike so much; and such a placid eye and smile!"

And then, to my great relief, Mr. Henry Lynn
(55) summoned them to the other side of the room, to settle some point about the deferred excursion to Hay Common.

I was now able to concentrate my attention on the group by the fire, and I presently gathered
(60) that the new-comer was called Mr. Mason; then I learned that he was but just arrived in England, and that he came from some hot country: which was the reason, doubtless, his face was so sallow, and that he sat so near the hearth, and wore a suit
(65) out in the house. Presently the words Jamaica,

GO ON TO THE NEXT PAGE ⟶

Kingston, Spanish Town, indicated the West Indies as his residence; and it was with no little surprise I gathered, ere long, that he had there first seen and become acquainted with Mr. Rochester. He spoke (70) of his friend's dislike of the burning heats, the hurricanes, and rainy seasons of that region. I knew Mr. Rochester had been a traveler: Mrs. Fairfax had said so; but I thought the continent of Europe had bounded his wanderings; till now I had never heard (75) a hint given of visits to more distant shores.

1. The first paragraph suggests that the narrator finds Mr. Mason's appearance:

   A. handsome.
   B. thrilling.
   C. unsettling.
   D. ordinary.

2. It is reasonable to infer from the passage that the narrator's response to Mr. Mason:

   I. is shared by other women.
   II. is due to an unexplainable attraction to the stranger.
   III. is based on appearance only.

   F. I only
   G. III only
   H. I and II only
   J. II and III only

3. The passage most strongly supports the inference that the narrator considers Mr. Mason:

   A. polite.
   B. unattractive.
   C. unassertive.
   D. shallow.

4. The statement "A curious friendship theirs must have been: a pointed illustration, indeed, of the old adage that 'extremes meet'" (lines 36–38) functions in the passage to support the narrator's view that:

   F. Mr. Mason and Mr. Rochester are rivals.
   G. Mr. Rochester met Mr. Mason under extreme circumstances.
   H. Mr. Mason and Mr. Rochester have much in common.
   J. Mr. Mason is nothing like Mr. Rochester.

5. The phrase "a tame, vacant life" (line 11) most strongly suggests that Mr. Mason is:

   A. empty-headed.
   B. trustworthy.
   C. submissive.
   D. fearless.

6. The narrator can most accurately be characterized as:

   F. unconcerned.
   G. curt.
   H. introspective.
   J. sad.

7. The narrator discovers the reason for Mr. Mason's sickly complexion by:

   A. comparing Mr. Mason to Mr. Rochester.
   B. observing Mr. Mason first-hand.
   C. overhearing Mary and Louisa.
   D. eavesdropping on Mr. Mason's conversation.

GO ON TO THE NEXT PAGE

8. The main point of the last paragraph is that:

   F. Mr. Mason arrived from the West Indies.

   G. Mr. Rochester once lived in the West Indies.

   H. Mr. Rochester was once a traveler.

   J. Mr. Mason and Mr. Rochester met each other in the West Indies.

9. Which of the following does NOT describe one of the narrator's descriptions of Mr. Mason?

   A. He has smooth skin.

   B. He has commanding eyes.

   C. He is polite.

   D. He is amiable-looking.

10. As it is used in line 31, the word *deference* most nearly means:

   F. delay.

   G. uncertainty.

   H. respect.

   J. contempt.

PASSAGE II

SOCIAL SCIENCE

The traditional empires of Japan and China had to decide how much they wanted to reform as a new industrial world emerged in the 19th century. They both tried to change with the times, but with varying degrees of success. In both cases, conservative forces came to resist the attempts at reforms.

PASSAGE A

Japan took radical steps in its response to the challenges of reform and reaction, and emerged from this period as a world power. Even as it con-
Line tinued to selectively isolate itself from the rest of
(5) world, it was changing from a feudal to a commercial economy.

Outside forces played a role in the evolution. The Japanese knew of China's humiliation at the hands of the British in the mid-1800s, thus becom-
(10) ing acquainted with the influence of the Western, and more industrialized powers. After the California Gold Rush of 1849, the United States became more interested in Pacific commerce, sending a mission to conclude a trade agreement with Japan. It arrived
(15) in Edo (Tokyo) Bay in 1853 with a modern fleet of armed steamships. For the Japanese, who had restricted their trade from much of the world for over two centuries, this was an awe-inspiring sight. The Americans were told to leave, but this caused
(20) tense polemics between the shogun (military leader appointed by, but separate from, the Emperor) and the samurai (military) classes.

Two clans in the south—Satsuma and Choshu—supported a new policy to "revere the emperor
(25) and repel the barbarians." In essence, this meant the overthrow of the shogun and restoration of the Kyoto emperor's power, and a veiled critique of the shogun in Edo, whom they perceived as unable to ward off the Western "barbarians" as opprobrious.

(30) A younger generation of reform-minded samurai from domains distant from Edo made bold plans to undermine the bakufu, the military dictatorship of the shogun. These "men of spirit" banded together to overthrow the shogun and promote
(35) Japanese modernization. They armed themselves with guns from the West, and civil war broke out in 1866. When the rebels showed the superiority of their Western firepower, the momentum began to shift in their favor.

(40) By 1868, the overthrow of the Tokugawa regime was complete when the victorious reformers pronounced that they had restored the emperor to his throne. They titled him Meiji, or Enlightened One, reflecting their belief that Meiji was a beacon of
(45) national revitalization. The nation rallied around the 16-year-old emperor, and plans were made to move the imperial "presence" to the renamed capital of Tokyo. This great transition in Japanese history has been called both a revolution and a

GO ON TO THE NEXT PAGE

(50) restoration. Historians debate about which term to use because the Japanese did not overthrow the old order and replace it with something new; rather, they reached into their past and used an older model to transform their nation.

(55)   In the Meiji period, the rapidity of the industrialization and modernization of Japan proved a marvel to the observing world. Within the first generation of that period, Japan had built a modern infrastructure and military, defeated the Chinese and Russians in
(60) war, and begun building an empire in the Pacific that European powers had to recognize as both legitimate and potentially formidable. This was a clear sign that industrialization was achievable by non-Europeans and that impending power shifts were forthcoming.

PASSAGE B

(65)   The Chinese had to deal with issues of reform and reaction in the 1800s. During the Qing dynasty, it is estimated that the Chinese population quadrupled to 420,000,000. This increase placed great strains on the nation, and famines became
(70) increasingly common. A series of wars and rebellions that followed further weakened the dynasty.

   Aggressive British traders began to import opium from India into China, and a customs dispute in Guangzhou led to the first Opium War
(75) in 1839. This resulted in two humiliating defeats for China and a series of unequal treaties that gave Britain and other European nations commercial entry into China.

   Uprisings such as the Taiping Rebellion placed
(80) further stress on China. An obscure scholar named Hong Xiuquan, who believed he was the brother of Jesus Christ, founded an offshoot of Christianity. A social reform movement grew from this movement in the 1850s, which the government began
(85) to suppress. Hong established the Taiping Tianguo (Heavenly Kingdom), and his followers created an army that, within two years of fighting, controlled a large territory in central China. Internal disputes within the Taipings finally helped the Qing dynasty
(90) defeat them, but the 10-year death toll is estimated in the millions, making it the bloodiest civil war in human history.

   The government attempted reforms in an effort to change with the times. With government-
(95) sponsored grants in the 1860s and 1870s, local leaders built modern shipyards, railroads, and weapon industries, and created academies for the study of science. It was an ambitious effort, but one that brought only minimal change, since it experi-
(100) enced resistance from the imperial bureaucracy.

   The last major reform effort was known as the Hundred Days of Reform. The emperor Guangzu instituted a program to change China into a constitutional monarchy, guarantee civil liberties,
(105) and encourage foreign influence. These proposed changes were strongly resisted by the imperial household. Particularly upset was the empress dowager Cixi, who cancelled the reforms and imprisoned the emperor. With that, China's chance
(110) for a reformed society ended.

   Amidst all of these rebellions and attempts at reform, a revolutionary movement was slowly emerging in China. It was composed of young men and women who had traveled outside Asia and seen
(115) the new liberalism and modernization of the West, and who hoped to import it to China. Cells were organized in Guangzhou and overseas in Tokyo and Honolulu, where plots to overthrow the Qing were made.

   Under the leadership of Sun Yixian (Sun Yat-
(120) sen), many unsuccessful uprisings were mounted, but it wasn't until 1911 that the Qing were forced to abdicate. With the dynasty in considerable chaos, the modern Republic of China was proclaimed. Sun dreamed of a progressive and democratic
(125) China based on his Three Principles of the People, but his dream would be shattered by a civil war and the subsequent rise of Communist China in the mid-20th century.

GO ON TO THE NEXT PAGE ⟶

11. Which phrase in the passage best describes those who wanted to undermine the bakufu?

    A. "Two clans in the south—Satsuma and Choshu—supported a new policy to 'revere the emperor and repel the barbarians.'" (lines 23–25)

    B. "Outside forces played a role in the evolution." (line 7)

    C. "They titled him Meiji, or Enlightened One, reflecting their belief that Meiji was a beacon of national revitalization." (lines 63–65)

    D. "Men of spirit" (line 33)

12. The "tense polemics" (line 20) described in the second paragraph suggest that:

    F. the shogun and the samurai classes were able to reach an agreement.

    G. the shogun and the samurai classes both expressed dissatisfaction at the arrival of American steamships.

    H. the heated dispute caused considerable civil unrest.

    J. the Americans agreed to compromise with the Japanese.

13. According to the author, the debate questioning if the Meiji government was the result of a revolution or a restoration centers on whether:

    A. future power shifts were to be expected.

    B. it took the form of a brand new, or an older model of government.

    C. Japan could be an industrial power.

    D. the civil war was justified.

14. The author refers to the Taiping Rebellion to:

    F. describe the last major reform effort.

    G. support the Imperial government.

    H. highlight the role of Christianity in China.

    J. provide an example of attempts at reform.

15. In the context of the passage, the word "strains" (line 69) most nearly means:

    A. inherited qualities.

    B. groups of people with shared ancestry.

    C. very small amounts.

    D. widespread distress.

16. In the context of the passage, the word "cells" (line 116) most nearly means:

    F. groups of rebels.

    G. parts of the body.

    H. confinement rooms in jails.

    J. foreign organizations.

17. Both passages include:

    A. evidence of improved governments as a result of rebellions.

    B. foreign influences that had an extensive effect on domestic governments.

    C. reforms that resulted in democratic governments.

    D. beneficial modernization.

18. In Passage B the author states that the revolutionary movement in China was composed of "young men and women" (lines 113–114). Which statement in Passage A refers to a similar group in Japan?

 F. "The nation rallied around the 16-year-old emperor, and plans were made to move the imperial 'presence' to the renamed capital of Tokyo."

 G. "The last major reform effort was known as the Hundred Days of Reform."

 H. "A younger generation of reform-minded samurai from domains distant from Edo made bold plans to undermine the bakufu . . . "

 J. "Two clans in the south—Satsuma and Choshu—supported a new policy to 'revere the emperor and repel the barbarians.'"

19. Given the focus of each passage, it is likely that both authors are:

 A. sociologists.

 B. experts on Japan.

 C. public policy developers.

 D. historians.

20. Unrest in both China and Japan was partially the result of:

 F. foreign trade.

 G. revolution in China.

 H. Opium war.

 J. Meiji restoration.

PASSAGE III

HUMANITIES

This passage is adapted from the book The Art of Interior Decoration, *by Grace Wood and Emily Burbank (©1917). This excerpt is from Chapter IV: The Story of Textiles.*

The first silk looms were set up in the royal palaces of the Roman kings in the year 533 A.D. The raw material was originally brought from the East,
Line but in the sixth century two Greek monks, while in
(5) China, studied the method of rearing silk worms and obtaining the silk. Upon their departure, they concealed the eggs of silk worms in their staves. They are credited with introducing silk manufacturing into Greece and hence into Western Europe.
(10) After that Greece, Persia and Asia Minor made this material, and Byzantium was famed for its silks.

Metals (gold, silver and copper) were flattened out and cut into narrow strips for winding around cotton twists. These were the gold and silver
(15) threads used in weaving. The Moors and Spaniards used strips of gilded parchment, instead of metals, to weave with the silk.

We know that England was weaving silk in the thirteenth century, and velvets seem to have also
(20) been used at a very early date. The introduction of silk and velvet into different countries had an immediate and much-needed influence on civilization. It is hard to believe, but in the thirteenth century when Edward I married Eleanor of Castile,
(25) the highest nobles of England slept on the straw-covered floors of baronial halls, and jeered at the Spanish courtiers who hung the walls and stretched the floors of Edward's castle with silks in preparation for his Spanish bride.

(30) The progress of art and culture always came from the East and moved slowly. As far back as the thirteenth century, James I of England owned no stockings, and had to borrow a pair in order to receive the English ambassador. In the eleventh
(35) century, Italy manufactured her own silks, and into them were woven precious stones, corals, seed

GO ON TO THE NEXT PAGE ⟶

pearls and colored glass beads, which were made
in Greece and Venice, as well as gold and silver
spangles.

(40)   Interior decoration and design were even
discussed in religious books, like the Bible: "I have
woven my bed with cords, I have covered it with
painted tapestry brought from Egypt."[1] There were
painted tapestries made in Western Europe at a
(45) very early date, and collectors eagerly sought them.
In the fourteenth century, these painted tapestries
were referred to as "Stained Cloth."

         Embroidery as an art, as we have already seen,
antedates silk weaving. The youngest of the three
(50) arts is tapestry. The oldest embroidery stitches are
the feather stitch and the cross-stitch. The feather
stitch, so called because every stitch took one direction, the stitches over-lapping, like the feathers of a
bird; the cross-stitch or "cushion" style got its name
(55) because it was used on church cushions, made for
kneeling when at prayer. Hand-woven tapestries
are called "comb-wrought" because the instrument
used in weaving was comb-like. "Cut-work" is
embroidery that is cut out and appliquéd, or sewed
(60) on another material.

         Carpets, which were used in Western Europe
in the Middle Ages, were seldom seen. The
Kensington Museum owns two specimens, both
of them Spanish, one from the fourteenth and one
(65) from the fifteenth century.

         In speaking of Gothic art we called attention to
the fostering of art by the Church during the Dark
Ages. This continued, and we find that in Henry
VIII's time those who visited monasteries and
(70) afterward wrote accounts of them call attention to
the fact that each monk was occupied either with
painting, carving, modelling, embroidering or writing. They worked primarily for the Church, decorating it for the glory of God, but the homes of the
(75) rich and powerful laity, even so early as the reign of
Henry III (1216–1272), boasted some very beautiful interior decorations, tapestries, painted ceilings
and stained glass, as well as carved panelling.

[1]Book of Proverbs, Chapter vii, Verse 16

21. In line 67, the word *fostering* most nearly
means:

A. opposing.

B. destroying.

C. promoting.

D. creating.

22. The author's remarks in lines 23–29 most
strongly indicate:

F. English nobility were not mannerly
toward the Spanish courtiers.

G. English nobility were infatuated with
the Spanish silks.

H. English nobility refused to accept the
silks from the Spanish courtiers.

J. English nobility were unimpressed with
the Spanish silks.

23. The passage suggests that two Greek monks
are accredited with introducing silk manufac-
ture into the West because:

A. they brought the raw material from
China.

B. they developed a unique manufacturing
process.

C. they transported the production
material and know-how from China.

D. they traveled to Persia and Asia Minor
with their silk production.

GO ON TO THE NEXT PAGE

24. It may be reasonably inferred from the seventh paragraph (lines 61–65) that:

    F. historians have some knowledge of carpets used in Spain during the Middle Ages.

    G. the Kensington Museum owns the only two surviving carpets from Western Europe constructed during the Middle Ages.

    H. surviving carpets from Western Europe in the Middle Ages are of no value.

    J. Spain produced more carpets during the Middle Ages than any other area of Western Europe.

25. The author of the passage states that as early as the 13th century, artwork appeared in:

    A. baronial halls.

    B. museums.

    C. books.

    D. homes of wealthy citizens.

26. It may be reasonably inferred from the passage that the author considers the introduction of silk and velvet into different countries (lines 20–29):

    F. a constructive influence on Western European culture.

    G. a significant boon to the economies.

    H. an insignificant contribution to Western European culture.

    J. a reflection of the Church's influence in Western Europe.

27. It may be reasonably inferred that the author's main purpose in writing this passage is to describe:

    A. the significance of textiles in the art and cultural history of early Western Europe.

    B. the foundation of Western European silk production.

    C. the significance of Western European artifacts to collectors.

    D. the slow progression of art and culture from the East to the West.

28. In the second paragraph (lines 12–17), the author most strongly suggests that Western Europeans considered metals:

    F. unsightly.

    G. good luck.

    H. aesthetic.

    J. malleable.

29. The significance of the Biblical quote (lines 41–43) is that:

    A. Egyptians taught Western Europeans the craft of tapestry painting.

    B. Western Europeans drew artistic inspiration from the Bible.

    C. collectors eagerly seek the tapestries mentioned in the Biblical passage.

    D. painted tapestry is an ancient art form.

30. The passage indicates that colored glass beads were woven into the silks manufactured in:

    F. Greece.

    G. Italy.

    H. Spain.

    J. England.

GO ON TO THE NEXT PAGE

PASSAGE IV

NATURAL SCIENCE

This passage is adapted from the article "Disappearing Polar Bears and Permafrost: Is a Global Warming Tipping Point Embedded in the Ice? (©2007, Hearing Before the Subcommittee on Investigations and Oversight Committee on Science and Technology in the United States House of Representatives.)

One of the unique features of the Arctic and Subarctic regions is the extensive presence of cold soils and permafrost. Permafrost is soil and
Line ground material that remain frozen for more than
(5) two years. Permafrost forms when mean annual temperatures are below freezing, generally in the range of 0 to –2°C. Differences in soil texture, water content, and site characteristics can allow permafrost to form at annual temperatures equal to
(10) freezing, or require annual temperatures well below freezing. Permafrost everywhere disappears at a great enough depth where heat from the geothermal gradient overcomes cold surface temperatures. Permafrost (the frozen material itself) occurs at
(15) a range of temperatures from near 0°C to ten or more degrees below. As a result, the coldest regions make up a continuous permafrost zone across the landscape.

Slightly warmer cold regions are within the dis-
(20) continuous permafrost zone, where occurrence of the frozen state is influenced by local factors. Areas with only isolated or sporadic masses of permafrost make up a third zone. Permafrost can be ice-rich, in which case thawing melts the frozen water content
(25) and causes ground subsidence, or it can be dry, leading to little potential for surface change between the frozen or thawed condition. Temperature trends in permafrost are increasing clearly across nearly all the Arctic and Subarctic. Permafrost temperatures
(30) are in exceptionally close agreement with predictive models of mean annual air temperature, snow depth and duration, and soil composition. Reliable permafrost temperature measurements generally date back only to about 1970, although predictive models
(35) can be used to look back and forth in time with confidence. Observations of permafrost thawing

at its southernmost limits in the U.S., Canada, and central Asia are widespread.

Surface-disturbing activities, such as road and
(40) building construction, as well as natural events such as wildfire, can tip the thermal equilibrium toward thawing in warmer permafrost regions, and have for some time. But these processes are producing more widespread effects in recent
(45) warmer conditions. For example, the permafrost areas in central Alaska have been trending upward in temperature, and now nearly all of it is only –0.5 to –2.0°C. Annual air temperatures above freezing are now occurring across large portions of the
(50) permafrost regions, and are certain to thaw the permafrost if sustained. The only questions are exactly where (the sequence of microsites) and how fast. Calculations indicate that a substantial fraction of existing permafrost has started or will start the
(55) thaw process (which may take decades or centuries to complete to the greatest depths) in the next several decades.

Linear infrastructure (roads, pipelines, railroads, etc.) are at most risk from thawing permafrost,
(60) because such developments must proceed from point A to point B at some location, making it nearly impossible to avoid permafrost disruption. Developments and structures can be engineered to minimize thaw or even keep ground mate-
(65) rial frozen. But such engineering features have substantial costs and are not easily retrofitted. Permafrost and other cold soils hold an amount of carbon that, if it were entirely combusted, would double atmospheric CO_2 content. Warming and/or
(70) thawing of the cold or permafrost soils is beginning to move this carbon into the atmosphere in a variety of ways. Some of the largest wildland fires or burning seasons on record have occurred in the Arctic and Subarctic in direct response to increasing
(75) temperatures and drying.

GO ON TO THE NEXT PAGE ⟶

31. As it is used in line 22, the word *sporadic* most nearly means:

    A. occasional.

    B. plant-producing.

    C. continuous.

    D. melting.

32. If the geothermal gradient remains below cold surface temperatures, which of the following observations would a researcher expect to find?

    F. The permafrost would thaw.

    G. The frozen water content would melt.

    H. The permafrost would be intact.

    J. Dry permafrost would form.

33. The passage mentions all of the following dangers caused by permafrost thaw EXCEPT:

    A. shrinking populations of indigenous species.

    B. challenges to linear infrastructure.

    C. wildland fires.

    D. increased atmospheric carbon.

34. According to the passage, the discontinuous permafrost zone:

    F. contains sporadic masses of permafrost.

    G. is found in the coldest regions.

    H. is at most risk of permafrost thaw.

    J. is affected by local factors.

35. The author notes that "predictive models can be used to look back and forth in time with confidence" (lines 34–36) to make the point that:

    A. predictive models date back farther than 1970.

    B. predictive models are a reliable gauge of increasing temperature trends in permafrost.

    C. there is no way to predict temperature trends in permafrost.

    D. permafrost thawing is widespread at the southernmost areas of the United States, Canada, and Central Asia.

36. The passage states that which of the following activities contributes to thawing in warmer permafrost regions?

    F. Linear infrastructure development

    G. Carbon combustion

    H. Road and building construction

    J. Melting frozen water content

37. According to the passage, permafrost occurs at temperatures ranging from:

    A. 0 to –2°C.

    B. –0.5 to –2.0°C.

    C. near 0 to –10 or more °C.

    D. –10 to –20°C.

GO ON TO THE NEXT PAGE

38. With which of the following statements would the author most likely agree?

   F. It is feasible to engineer structures to keep the ground material frozen.

   G. Permafrost thawing will likely continue over the next several decades.

   H. Temperature trends in permafrost are exaggerated.

   J. Scientists can accurately predict where and how quickly permafrost thaw will occur.

39. The main idea of lines 39–57 is that:

   A. Alaskan permafrost has been increasing in temperature.

   B. warmer conditions exacerbate effects of natural events and surface-disturbing activities.

   C. all existing permafrost has or will begin thawing in the next several decades.

   D. warmer permafrost regions are impervious to road and building construction.

40. How does information about the permafrost zones function in the passage?

   F. It shows that permafrost can occur in a range of temperatures.

   G. It indicates where thawing is most likely.

   H. It explains where ice-rich and dry permafrost is found.

   J. It reveals where the richest carbon deposits exist.

SCIENCE TEST

35 Minutes—40 Questions

Directions: There are several passages in this test. Each passage is followed by several questions. After reading a passage, choose the best answer to each question and fill in the corresponding oval on your Answer Grid. You may refer to the passages as often as necessary. You are NOT permitted to use a calculator on this test.

PASSAGE I

In the 1920s, scientists developed numerous models of the atom, most of which posited a central nucleus surrounded by electrons:

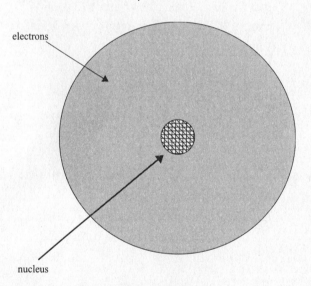

Figure 1

The protons and neutrons in the atom's nucleus have positive and neutral charges, respectively, whereas electrons have a negative charge. In the process of becoming ionized, an atom gains or loses electrons, thereby obtaining an overall positive or negative charge. Additionally, after atoms have become energized, they release such energy in the form of light. Electrons are thought to be responsible for this process.

In the 1920s, two scientists debated the way in which electrons surround an atom's nucleus.

SCIENTIST 1: BOHR MODEL

Electrons move around an atom's nucleus in precise, planet-like orbits. Any given orbit can only hold a certain number of electrons. Once the orbit is filled with electrons, the next level orbit must be used. For this reason, some atoms will be larger (have a larger radius) than others.

Additionally, if electrons become energized, they will "jump" from one orbit to the next. When they return to their normal energy level, they emit energy in the form of light. This accounts for the fact that excited atoms emit very specific and well-defined colors of light. If the position of electrons is not specified, the precise wavelengths of light that are emitted cannot be explained.

SCIENTIST 2: ELECTRON CLOUD MODEL

The precise location of electrons cannot be detected. Electrons move around a nucleus in a cloud. In this cloud, certain regions have a higher probability of containing electrons than others. The cloud extends all around the nucleus in 3 dimensions. The uncertainty of any one electron's position and the nature of its existence as a charged particle contribute to an understanding of the wave-particle nature of matter and energy.

GO ON TO THE NEXT PAGE ⟶

Though this model is seemingly at odds with a number of assumptions about the stability of matter in larger-scale reality, it is anchored to a concept called the *wavefunction*. The wavefunction helps specify the distinct shape of the probability clouds surrounding a nucleus. This assures that the position of the electrons is not entirely random.

1. Which of the following statements is most consistent with the electron cloud model?

   A. Electrons orbit the nucleus of an atom in fixed paths.

   B. Electrons are found in the nucleus of an atom.

   C. Electrons exhibit almost random patterns of movement around a nucleus.

   D. Electrons have a fixed position outside the nucleus.

2. By referring to the fact that the position of an electron follows the wavefunction, the scientist supporting the electron cloud model implies which of the following?

   F. The probability of an electron's position depends on its orbit.

   G. The color of emitted light depends on the charge of an atom.

   H. Protons and neutrons are also subject to the wave-particle duality.

   J. Electron configuration affects an atom's shape and corresponding properties.

3. According to the passage, a similarity between the Bohr model and the electron cloud model is that:

   A. electrons do not have a fixed position.

   B. the charge of electrons is based on probability.

   C. protons and neutrons are composed of many smaller particles.

   D. the atom is indivisible.

4. According to Scientist 1, which of the following observations provides the strongest evidence that electrons do NOT lie in a probability cloud surrounding the nucleus?

   F. Electrons have a fixed position around the nucleus.

   G. The light emitted by energized electrons is specific and predictable.

   H. Electrons behave according to the wavefunction.

   J. The charge of electrons is constant.

5. After the 1920s, it was observed that a single electron will exhibit patterns of motion that imply both that it is a distinct particle and also that the path it takes correlates to a probability. Which model does this observation support?

   A. The electron cloud model, because it confirms the wave-particle duality.

   B. The electron cloud model, because it shows that an electron travels in a distinct path.

   C. The Bohr model, because it shows that electrons travel in orbits.

   D. The Bohr model, because it confirms that electrons behave according to probability.

6. The scientist who describes the electron cloud model implies that the Bohr model is *weakened* by observing that:

   F. electrons have a greater chance of lying in specific areas around the nucleus than others.

   G. electrons behave like photons.

   H. the precise position of electrons cannot be known.

   J. the orbits of electrons are not circular.

GO ON TO THE NEXT PAGE ⇨

7. Which of the following diagrams is most consistent with the Bohr model of the atom?

A.

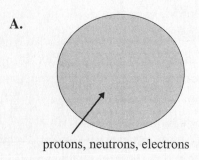

protons, neutrons, electrons

B.

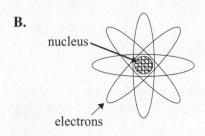

nucleus

electrons

C.

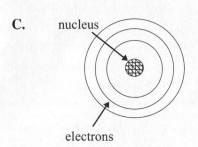

nucleus

electrons

D.

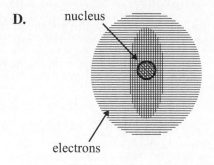

nucleus

electrons

PASSAGE II

Scientists noted an increase in acid rainfall and reports of respiratory ailments in a certain community. They suspected that both of these outcomes were due to increased levels of airborne pollutants, such as carbon monoxide and sulfur dioxide, entering the atmosphere in that community. Common sources of gaseous pollutants are factories, motor vehicles, or industrial processes that burn fossil fuels and release byproducts of their reactions into the air. To determine the sources of these pollutants, scientists conducted the following experiments.

EXPERIMENT 1

The scientists found that one likely source of pollutant gases was a network of highways located near the community. Sampling stations at ground level were set up near two major highways so that air samples could be recorded daily. The results of these measurements are shown in Table 1.

Table 1

Date	Carbon monoxide level (parts per million)	Sulfur dioxide level (parts per million)
Highway 1		
January 6	2.3	0.002
January 7	3.2	0.002
January 8	2.9	0.003
January 9	2.6	0.002
January 10	2.1	0.004
Highway 2		
January 6	3.4	0.004
January 7	3.8	0.006
January 8	4.9	0.004
January 9	3.4	0.003
January 10	3.2	0.002

EXPERIMENT 2

Scientists also suspected that another source of pollutants was from the community's power plant, an older coal-burning plant. Air samples were recorded from the tops of two different monitoring

GO ON TO THE NEXT PAGE ⟩

towers near the power plant's two main smoke-stacks, which emit most of the byproducts created in the electricity-generating process. The results are shown in Table 2.

Table 2

Date	Ozone level (parts per million)	Carbon monoxide level (parts per million)	Sulfur dioxide level (parts per million)
Tower 1			
January 6	0.05	3.3	0.005
January 7	0.06	3.2	0.006
January 8	0.11	3.3	0.009
January 9	0.15	4.3	0.013
January 10	0.10	4.2	0.009
Tower 2			
January 6	0.04	2.0	0.004
January 7	0.05	2.9	0.005
January 8	0.06	3.0	0.008
January 9	0.05	2.8	0.006
January 10	0.04	2.1	0.004

8. How is the design of Experiment 1 different from the design of Experiment 2, in terms of sampling methods?

F. In Experiment 1, sampling was done weekly, while in Experiment 2, sampling was done every day.

G. In Experiment 1, air was sampled at ground level, while in Experiment 2, air was sampled at the tops of two towers.

H. In Experiment 1, ozone levels were sampled, while in Experiment 2, ozone levels were not sampled.

J. In Experiment 1, only carbon monoxide was sampled, while in Experiment 2, only sulfur dioxide was sampled.

9. In order to obtain more information about the relationship between carbon monoxide, sulfur dioxide, and respiratory ailments, which of the following experiments should be carried out next?

A. Studying how asthma is affected by changes in temperature throughout the year.

B. Assessing the rates of respiratory illness in communities with varying average levels of carbon monoxide and sulfur dioxide.

C. Adding large amounts of carbon monoxide and sulfur dioxide to the air surrounding Highway 1.

D. Encouraging carpools to decrease traffic levels in the highways around this community.

10. Scientists suspected that sulfur dioxide emissions from the power plant were contributing to acid rain, which in turn was affecting the acidity of lakes in the surrounding countryside. In order to test this hypothesis, which of the following should the scientists do next?

F. Sample sulfur dioxide levels near the power plant's smaller smokestacks.

G. Measure the number of respiratory ailments suffered by people living near the lakes.

H. Increase the amount of coal burned by the power plant.

J. Measure the acidity of the water at a number of lakes with varying levels of atmospheric sulfur dioxide.

GO ON TO THE NEXT PAGE

11. What hypothesis concerning respiratory ailments were the scientists testing in Experiment 1?

   A. Pollutants from vehicular highway traffic cause an increase in respiratory ailments.

   B. Emissions from coal-burning power plants cause a decrease in respiratory ailments.

   C. Rainfall in the communities located near the highways causes a decrease in respiratory ailments.

   D. Acid rain tends to deposit pollutants into areas where highway traffic is least frequent.

12. Given the results of Experiments 1 and 2, all of the following actions would reduce levels of airborne pollutants EXCEPT:

   F. building more highways in the areas surrounding the community.

   G. placing limits on the amount of highway traffic near the community.

   H. reducing the amount of coal burned at the power plant.

   J. installing filters in the power plant's smokestacks that remove sulfur dioxide from the plant's emissions.

13. As carbon monoxide emissions are carried away from their sources, they tend to diffuse (become less concentrated). Which of the following would be the most likely approximate carbon monoxide level near Highway 1 on January 7 if the sampling station were set up closer to the roadway?

   A. 1.0 parts per million

   B. 2.0 parts per million

   C. 3.0 parts per million

   D. 4.0 parts per million

14. Which of the following is true for Experiment 2?

   I.   Ozone levels and sulfur dioxide levels increased then decreased in both towers.

   II. Carbon monoxide levels in Tower 2 were always greater than those in Tower 1.

   III. January 9 showed the highest emissions for all byproducts in both towers.

   F. I only

   G. II only

   H. I and II only

   J. I, II, and III

PASSAGE III

Students performed the following experiments to determine the melting point of several materials. They used the following equation to calculate the boiling point of various solutions:

$$T = K_b \times m \times i,$$

where

$$K_b = 0.512 \times \frac{degrees \times kg}{mol}$$

$$m = molality = \frac{mol\ solute}{kg\ solvent}$$

i = number of ions present per molecule of solute

EXPERIMENT 1

In order to prepare various solutions of sodium chloride (NaCl), 100.00 g of H_2O were added to a beaker. A known quantity of NaCl was dissolved

GO ON TO THE NEXT PAGE

into the water and the resulting boiling point of the solution was recorded. This procedure was repeated with different amounts of NaCl as shown on Table 1.

Table 1

Solution	Mass of H_2O (g)	Amount of NaCl (mol)	Boiling point (°C)
1	100.00	0	100.00
2	100.00	0.085	100.88
3	100.00	0.171	101.75
4	100.00	0.257	102.63
5	100.00	0.342	103.50

EXPERIMENT 2

In order to prepare various solutions of calcium chloride ($CaCl_2$), 100.00 g of H_2O were added to a beaker. A known quantity of $CaCl_2$ was dissolved into the water and resulting boiling point of the solution was recorded. This procedure was repeated with different amounts of $CaCl_2$ as shown on Table 2.

Table 2

Solution	Mass of H_2O (g)	Amount of $CaCl_2$ (mol)	Boiling point (°C)
6	100.00	0.270	104.15
7	100.00	0.360	105.53
8	100.00	0.450	106.91
9	100.00	0.541	108.29
10	100.00	0.631	109.67

EXPERIMENT 3

Each solution from Experiments 1 and 2 was brought to a boil. A small sample of material was placed in each solution. If the material melted, a "Y" was marked in Table 3. If the material did not melt, an "N" was marked in Table 3. This procedure was repeated for all eight materials.

Table 3

Material	Solution									
	1	2	3	4	5	6	7	8	9	10
1	Y	Y	Y	Y	Y	Y	Y	Y	Y	Y
2	N	Y	Y	Y	Y	Y	Y	Y	Y	Y
3	N	N	Y	Y	Y	Y	Y	Y	Y	Y
4	N	N	N	N	Y	Y	Y	Y	Y	Y
5	N	N	N	N	N	Y	Y	Y	Y	Y
6	N	N	N	N	N	N	N	Y	Y	Y
7	N	N	N	N	N	N	N	N	N	Y
8	N	N	N	N	N	N	N	N	N	N

GO ON TO THE NEXT PAGE

15. If the students wanted to increase the boiling point (T), what should they increase in the experiment?

      I. K_b

      II. Amount of NaCl

      III. Amount of $CaCl_2$

  A. I only

  B. I and II only

  C. II and III only

  D. I, II, and III

16. In Experiment 1, what was the boiling point of the solution with 0.171 mols of NaCl?

  F. 100°C

  G. 100.88°C

  H. 101.75°C

  J. 109.67°C

17. Based on Experiments 1–3, the melting point of Material 5 is most likely:

  A. less than 100°C.

  B. between 102.63°C and 103.50°C.

  C. between 103.50°C and 104.15°C.

  D. greater than 109.67°C.

18. If, in Experiment 2, a sixth solution had been prepared using 0.721 mol $CaCl_2$, the boiling point would be closest to which of the following?

  F. 108.75°C

  G. 111.07°C

  H. 113.72°C

  J. 115.02°C

19. A ninth material was submerged in Solutions 1–6 as in Experiment 3. Which of the following is NOT a possible set of results for the table data for this material?

	Solution					
	1	2	3	4	5	6
A.	Y	Y	Y	Y	N	N
B.	Y	Y	Y	Y	Y	Y
C.	N	N	N	N	Y	Y
D.	N	N	N	N	N	N

20. Which of the following best explains why the students recorded data for their solutes in mol rather than g or kg?

  F. The H_2O was already measured in kg.

  G. The units for mass are less accurate.

  H. The change in boiling point depends on molality.

  J. The melting point of the various materials does not depend on the mass of the materials.

21. Would a student be supported by Experiments 1–3 if she claimed that Material 7 had a lower melting point than Material 8?

  A. Yes, because in Solution 10, Material 7 melted and Material 8 did not.

  B. Yes, because in Solution 10, Material 8 melted and Material 7 did not.

  C. No, because the melting point of Material 8 cannot be determined from the data in Experiments 1–3.

  D. No, because the melting point of Material 7 cannot be determined from the data in Experiments 1–3.

GO ON TO THE NEXT PAGE

PASSAGE IV

Rural areas have their own climate that differs from large cities and the adjacent suburban areas. A scientist performed the following studies to learn more about a rural climate.

STUDY 1

Air temperatures, in degrees Celsius (°C), were recorded hourly over a 24-hour period at 3 sites: a rural site, the center of a large city (the urban site), and an adjacent suburban site. This was done on 30 consecutive days during the spring and 30 consecutive days during the fall. Each hourly temperature was averaged over the given season. The results are in Figure 1.

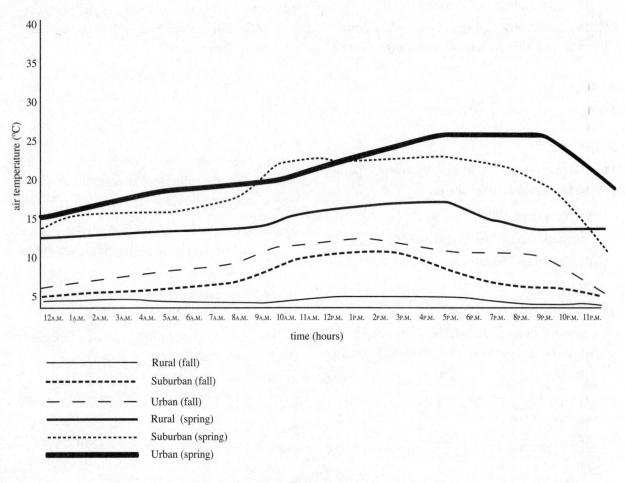

Figure 1

STUDY 2

A site at the suburban site was selected where a concrete parking lot was located next to a large grassy park. Starting at 9 am, air temperature readings were taken at three locations above the parking lot and at three locations above the grassy park. Air temperature readings were taken every hour until 3 PM. The results are in Table 2.

GO ON TO THE NEXT PAGE ⟶

Table 1

| Time (hours) | Air temperature reading (°C) | | | | | |
| | Parking lot | | | Grassy Park | | |
	Site 1	Site 2	Site 3	Site 1	Site 2	Site 3
9 A.M.	13	13	14	9	9	9
10 A.M.	15	14	14	9	10	9
11 A.M.	17	17	17	10	10	9
12 P.M.	20	19	19	11	11	10
1 P.M.	22	21	20	12	11	11
2 P.M.	22	22	21	13	12	12
3 P.M.	23	24	23	13	13	12

STUDY 3

Weather instruments were used to measure the wind direction on 30 days at various altitudes above the 3 sites used in Study 1. The wind velocities, in kilometers per hour (km/hr), were used to generate the wind profiles shown in Figure 3.

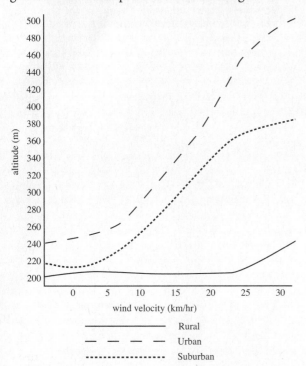

Figure 2

STUDY 4

The scientist kept track of the cloud cover and the daily precipitation in the rural area and the suburban area. It was found that the rural area had 5% fewer cloudy or hazy days than the suburban site and 5% less precipitation than the suburban site. Air quality measurements showed that the suburban air had 10 times more dust particles than the rural air.

22. According to Study 1, during which of the following time periods does the suburban site always have a higher temperature than an urban site on a spring day?

    F. between 3 A.M. and 6 A.M.

    G. between 6 A.M. and 9 A.M.

    H. between 9 A.M. and 12 P.M.

    J. between 3 P.M. and 6 P.M.

23. Water vapor needs solid "nuclei" for it to condense into water droplets and form clouds. According to Study 4, which of the following is the best explanation why the rural site had 5% less rain than the suburban site?

    A. The wind velocity was higher at the suburban site than the rural site.

    B. There were more dust particles in the air at the suburban site to become nuclei for water droplets.

    C. There were fewer clouds at the suburban site.

    D. Rain needs dust particles to form.

GO ON TO THE NEXT PAGE

24. Based on Study 3, if a weather balloon ascending from an altitude of 240 m to an altitude of 340 m measures a 20 km/hr increase in wind velocity, it is most likely over which type of area?

F. Rural
G. Suburban
H. Urban
J. It cannot be determined from the data

25. If the results of Study 1 are indicative of any suburban area, what can be said about seasonal climates in suburban areas?

A. The average temperature range in the fall is smaller than the average temperature range in the suburbs in the spring.
B. The average temperature range in a suburban area is much greater in the fall than in the spring.
C. The maximum temperature in the spring in a suburban area is the same as the maximum temperature in the fall.
D. the minimum temperature in the spring in a suburban area is the same as the minimum temperature in the fall in the same areas.

26. According to Study 1, the spring time temperature difference in a suburban site at 3 A.M. and 3 P.M. is approximately

F. 3°C
G. 8°C
H. 10°C
J. 15°C

27. According to Study 3, wind velocity in suburban areas increases:

A. less rapidly with altitude than rural sites.
B. at the same rate with altitude as the wind velocities in rural sites.
C. at the same rate with altitude as the wind velocities in urban areas.
D. less rapidly with altitude than urban sites.

28. Based on the findings in Study 1 and the results of Study 2, which of the following would most likely lower air temperature in urban areas?

F. Implementing tougher environmental measures to reduce pollution
G. Creating urban parks with grass and trees
H. Regulating the height of buildings to decrease wind
J. Increasing the amount of parking available

GO ON TO THE NEXT PAGE

PASSAGE V

The movement of planets in the solar system and objects around them is governed by the force of gravity. Gravitational effects are determined by considering many factors, such as a planet's mass and the distance between bodies. Table 1 lists the masses and radii for several planets.

Table 1

Planet	Mass (kg)	Radius (km)
Saturn	5.69×10^{26}	60,268
Jupiter	1.90×10^{27}	71,492
Earth	5.98×10^{24}	6,378
Venus	4.87×10^{24}	6,051
Mercury	3.3×10^{23}	2,440

Figure 1 shows the acceleration due to gravity of an object at various distances from the center of 3 planets.

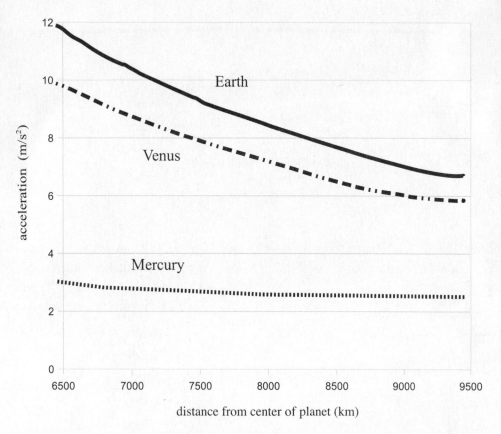

Figure 1

GO ON TO THE NEXT PAGE

Perihelion is the point in a planet's orbit at which it is closest to the sun. Figure 2 shows how the orbital velocity of the same 3 planets varies as each planet approaches and recedes from perihelion (a negative distance means the planet is approaching perihelion, positive means the planet is receding).

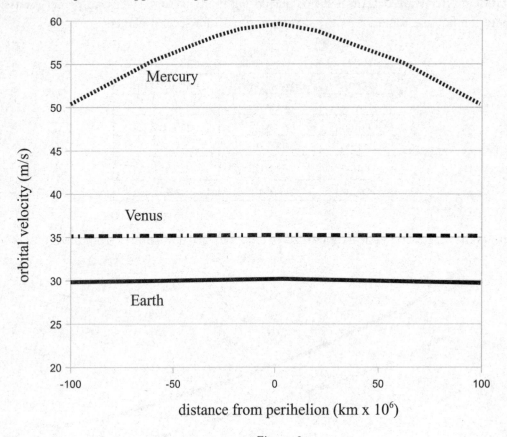

Figure 2

29. According to Figure 2, as Mercury approaches perihelion and then recedes from it, its orbital velocity:

   A. increases, then decreases.
   B. decreases, then increases.
   C. decreases only.
   D. increases only.

30. Suppose that a planet was found to have a mass between that of Saturn and Jupiter. Based on Table 1, which of the following would be a possible radius for the planet?

   F. 2,240 km
   G. 6,197 km
   H. 63,452 km
   J. 87,128 km

GO ON TO THE NEXT PAGE

31. Which of the planets listed on Table 1 has the greatest mass?

    A. Saturn

    B. Jupiter

    C. Earth

    D. Mercury

32. According to Figure 2, the orbital velocity of Mercury 75×10^6 km away from perihelion (approaching) is closest to the orbital velocity of which of the following?

    F. The orbital velocity of Mercury 100×10^6 km away from perihelion, receding.

    G. The orbital velocity of Mercury 75×10^6 km away from perihelion, receding.

    H. The orbital velocity of Mercury 50×10^6 km away from perihelion, receding.

    J. The orbital velocity of Mercury 50×10^6 km away from perihelion, approaching.

33. According to Figure 1, does an object fall faster towards Earth or towards Venus from a distance of 8,000 km?

    A. Venus, because the acceleration due to gravity from Venus is higher.

    B. Venus, because the acceleration due to gravity from Venus is lower.

    C. Earth, because the acceleration due to gravity from Earth is higher.

    D. Earth, because the acceleration due to gravity from Earth is lower.

34. If a planet were found to have a mass of 8.5×10^{23} kg and a radius of 5,423 km, which of the following would be its predicted orbital velocity, in m/s, at perihelion?

    F. 60

    G. 45

    H. 30

    J. 15

GO ON TO THE NEXT PAGE

PASSAGE VI

The following chemical equation represents a typical acid-base reaction:

$$HCl + NaOH \rightarrow H_2O + NaCl$$

Table 1 lists common pH indicators and the pH ranges over which a distinct color change occurs:

Table 1

Indicator	pH Range
Methyl yellow	2.9 – 4.0
Bromocresol green	3.8 – 5.4
Methyl red	4.4 – 6.2
Phenol red	6.8 – 8.4
Phenolphthalein	8.3 – 10.0
Alizarine	10.1 – 12.0

In the process of acid-base titration, the *equivalence point* is the point at which equal concentrations of an acid and base are present. When an acid or base is added to a solution at its equivalence point, changes in pH are typically much more drastic than they are at other points in the titration process. Figure 1 shows the pH of Solution A and Solution B versus the amount of an NaOH solution added.

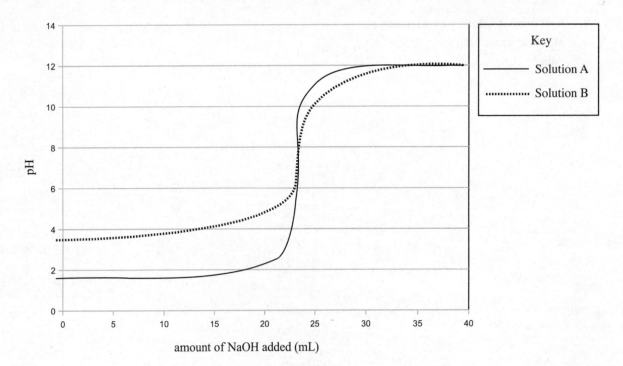

Figure 1

Figure 2 shows the reaction rate for Solutions A and B (as a percentage of the reaction rate at their equivalence point) versus the amount of NaOH solution added:

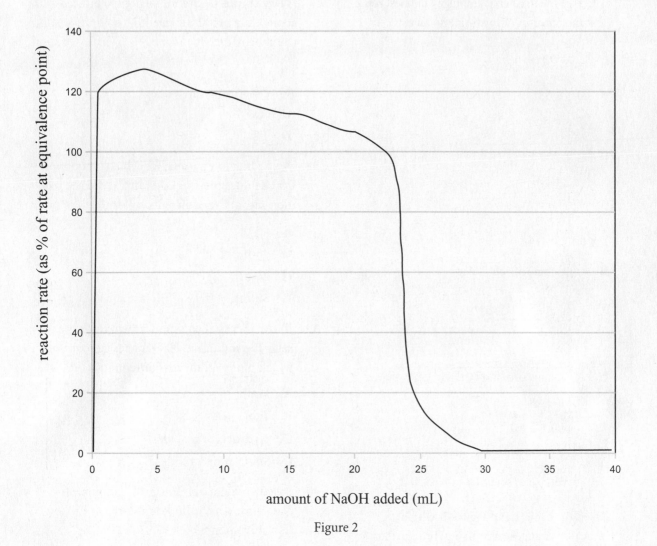

amount of NaOH added (mL)

Figure 2

GO ON TO THE NEXT PAGE

35. If the experimental setup were reversed and Solution A were titrated into a beaker of NaOH, which of the following graphs would best represent the corresponding titration curve?

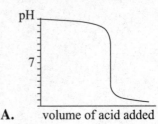

A.

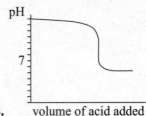

B.

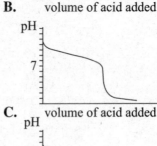

C.

D.

36. Based on Table 1 and Figure 1, which indicator changes color in a pH range that includes the equivalence point of Solution A?

F. Bromocresol green

G. Methyl red

H. Phenol red

J. Alizarine

37. If the chemical reaction associated with the chemical equation shown in the passage takes place completely (with negligible unused reactants), the pH of the resulting solution should be approximately:

A. 0.

B. 2.

C. 7.

D. 14.

38. According to Figure 2, for which amount of NaOH does the reaction rate exceed the reaction rate at the equivalence point?

F. 0 mL

G. 5 mL

H. 25 mL

J. 30 mL

39. In the chemical equation shown in the passage, the sodium in NaOH becomes part of which of the following compound?

A. Water

B. Table salt

C. Hydrochloric acid

D. Sodium hydroxide

40. Based on Figures 1 and 2, the amount of NaOH for which the reaction rate is highest also corresponds to:

F. the equivalence point of Solution A.

G. the equivalence point of Solution B.

H. a high pH in Solution A.

J. a low pH in Solution B.

WRITING TEST

40 Minutes

Directions: This is a test of your writing skills. You will have forty (40) minutes to write an essay in English. Before you begin planning and writing your essay, read the writing prompt carefully to understand exactly what you are being asked to do. Your essay will be evaluated on the evidence it provides of your ability to do the following:

- Express judgments by evaluating the three perspectives given in the prompt, taking a position on an issue, and explaining the relationship among all four ideas
- Develop a position by using logical reasoning and by supporting your ideas
- Maintain a focus on the topic throughout the essay
- Organize ideas in a logical way
- Use language clearly and effectively according to the conventions of standard written English

You may use the unlined pages in this test booklet to plan your essay. These pages will not be scored. *You must write your essay in pencil on the lined pages in the answer folder.* Your writing on those lined pages will be scored. You may not need all the lined pages, but to ensure you have enough room to finish, do NOT skip lines. You may write corrections or additions neatly between the lines of your essay, but do NOT write in the margins of the lined pages. *Illegible essays cannot be scored, so you must write (or print) clearly.*

If you finish before time is called you may review your work. Lay your pencil down immediately when time is called.

DO NOT OPEN THIS BOOKLET UNTIL TOLD TO DO SO.

GO ON TO THE NEXT PAGE

WILDERNESS AREAS

As Earth's population soars, cities are constantly expanding outward, and exponentially more natural resources are needed to supply human demand. Wilderness areas such as deserts, forests, grasslands, and tundra serve as land and natural resource reserves, offer noise, light, and air pollution buffers to neighboring cities, and harbor innumerable plant and animal species, many of which are becoming threatened, endangered, or even extinct. Should nations pass laws to preserve remaining wilderness areas in their natural state, even if these areas might be otherwise developed for economic gain? Given that land use rights can severely limit the growth capacity of a local or national economy, governments need to address at what point does potential development outweigh irreparable harm to these natural environments.

Read and carefully consider these perspectives. Each discusses the importance of protecting wilderness areas.

Perspective One	Perspective Two	Perspective Three
Nations should pass immediate and robust legislation to preserve all remaining wilderness areas, regardless of size or location. This type of legislation will help ensure that these areas will be left undisturbed, with little to no human interaction. Natural ecosystems will be able to thrive and many species may eventually no longer be threatened or endangered.	Nations should evaluate wilderness areas and the nearby economic growth to determine whether areas will be left undisturbed or whether they should be developed to support the economy. The goal should be a balance between the number of areas that may be developed to support growth and those that must be retained in their natural state to promote biodiversity and a healthy ecosystem.	Nations should not enact federal legislation, but instead should delegate to local jurisdictions the responsibility of making sound decisions about their own wilderness areas. National governments should provide guidance to promote balance throughout the country, but the localities will ultimately decide what is in the best interest of their communities.

ESSAY TASK

Write a unified, coherent essay in which you evaluate multiple perspectives regarding the government's role in preserving wilderness areas. In your essay, be sure to:

- analyze and evaluate the perspectives given
- state and develop your own perspective on the issue
- explain the relationship between your perspective and those given

Your perspective may be in full agreement with any of the others, in partial agreement, or wholly different. Whatever the case, support your ideas with logical reasoning and detailed, persuasive examples.

GO ON TO THE NEXT PAGE ⇨

PLANNING YOUR ESSAY

You may wish to consider the following as you think critically about the task:

Strengths and weaknesses of the three given perspectives

- What insights do they offer, and what do they fail to consider?
- Why might they be persuasive to others, or why might they fail to persuade?

Your own knowledge, experience, and values

- What is your perspective on this issue, and what are its strengths and weaknesses?
- How will you support your perspective in your essay?

_____

_____

_____

_____

_____

_____

_____

_____

_____

_____

_____

_____

_____

_____

_____

_____

_____

GO ON TO THE NEXT PAGE

GO ON TO THE NEXT PAGE

Answer Grid and Essay Practice Test Comment Forms

ACT Practice Test One
ANSWER SHEET

ENGLISH TEST

1. Ⓐ Ⓑ Ⓒ Ⓓ   11. Ⓐ Ⓑ Ⓒ Ⓓ   21. Ⓐ Ⓑ Ⓒ Ⓓ   31. Ⓐ Ⓑ Ⓒ Ⓓ   41. Ⓐ Ⓑ Ⓒ Ⓓ   51. Ⓐ Ⓑ Ⓒ Ⓓ   61. Ⓐ Ⓑ Ⓒ Ⓓ   71. Ⓐ Ⓑ Ⓒ Ⓓ
2. Ⓕ Ⓖ Ⓗ Ⓙ   12. Ⓕ Ⓖ Ⓗ Ⓙ   22. Ⓕ Ⓖ Ⓗ Ⓙ   32. Ⓕ Ⓖ Ⓗ Ⓙ   42. Ⓕ Ⓖ Ⓗ Ⓙ   52. Ⓕ Ⓖ Ⓗ Ⓙ   62. Ⓕ Ⓖ Ⓗ Ⓙ   72. Ⓕ Ⓖ Ⓗ Ⓙ
3. Ⓐ Ⓑ Ⓒ Ⓓ   13. Ⓐ Ⓑ Ⓒ Ⓓ   23. Ⓐ Ⓑ Ⓒ Ⓓ   33. Ⓐ Ⓑ Ⓒ Ⓓ   43. Ⓐ Ⓑ Ⓒ Ⓓ   53. Ⓐ Ⓑ Ⓒ Ⓓ   63. Ⓐ Ⓑ Ⓒ Ⓓ   73. Ⓐ Ⓑ Ⓒ Ⓓ
4. Ⓕ Ⓖ Ⓗ Ⓙ   14. Ⓕ Ⓖ Ⓗ Ⓙ   24. Ⓕ Ⓖ Ⓗ Ⓙ   34. Ⓕ Ⓖ Ⓗ Ⓙ   44. Ⓕ Ⓖ Ⓗ Ⓙ   54. Ⓕ Ⓖ Ⓗ Ⓙ   64. Ⓕ Ⓖ Ⓗ Ⓙ   74. Ⓕ Ⓖ Ⓗ Ⓙ
5. Ⓐ Ⓑ Ⓒ Ⓓ   15. Ⓐ Ⓑ Ⓒ Ⓓ   25. Ⓐ Ⓑ Ⓒ Ⓓ   35. Ⓐ Ⓑ Ⓒ Ⓓ   45. Ⓐ Ⓑ Ⓒ Ⓓ   55. Ⓐ Ⓑ Ⓒ Ⓓ   65. Ⓐ Ⓑ Ⓒ Ⓓ   75. Ⓐ Ⓑ Ⓒ Ⓓ
6. Ⓕ Ⓖ Ⓗ Ⓙ   16. Ⓕ Ⓖ Ⓗ Ⓙ   26. Ⓕ Ⓖ Ⓗ Ⓙ   36. Ⓕ Ⓖ Ⓗ Ⓙ   46. Ⓕ Ⓖ Ⓗ Ⓙ   56. Ⓕ Ⓖ Ⓗ Ⓙ   66. Ⓕ Ⓖ Ⓗ Ⓙ
7. Ⓐ Ⓑ Ⓒ Ⓓ   17. Ⓐ Ⓑ Ⓒ Ⓓ   27. Ⓐ Ⓑ Ⓒ Ⓓ   37. Ⓐ Ⓑ Ⓒ Ⓓ   47. Ⓐ Ⓑ Ⓒ Ⓓ   57. Ⓐ Ⓑ Ⓒ Ⓓ   67. Ⓐ Ⓑ Ⓒ Ⓓ
8. Ⓕ Ⓖ Ⓗ Ⓙ   18. Ⓕ Ⓖ Ⓗ Ⓙ   28. Ⓕ Ⓖ Ⓗ Ⓙ   38. Ⓕ Ⓖ Ⓗ Ⓙ   48. Ⓕ Ⓖ Ⓗ Ⓙ   58. Ⓕ Ⓖ Ⓗ Ⓙ   68. Ⓕ Ⓖ Ⓗ Ⓙ
9. Ⓐ Ⓑ Ⓒ Ⓓ   19. Ⓐ Ⓑ Ⓒ Ⓓ   29. Ⓐ Ⓑ Ⓒ Ⓓ   39. Ⓐ Ⓑ Ⓒ Ⓓ   49. Ⓐ Ⓑ Ⓒ Ⓓ   59. Ⓐ Ⓑ Ⓒ Ⓓ   69. Ⓐ Ⓑ Ⓒ Ⓓ
10. Ⓕ Ⓖ Ⓗ Ⓙ   20. Ⓕ Ⓖ Ⓗ Ⓙ   30. Ⓕ Ⓖ Ⓗ Ⓙ   40. Ⓕ Ⓖ Ⓗ Ⓙ   50. Ⓕ Ⓖ Ⓗ Ⓙ   60. Ⓕ Ⓖ Ⓗ Ⓙ   70. Ⓕ Ⓖ Ⓗ Ⓙ

MATH TEST

1. Ⓐ Ⓑ Ⓒ Ⓓ Ⓔ   11. Ⓐ Ⓑ Ⓒ Ⓓ Ⓔ   21. Ⓐ Ⓑ Ⓒ Ⓓ Ⓔ   31. Ⓐ Ⓑ Ⓒ Ⓓ Ⓔ   41. Ⓐ Ⓑ Ⓒ Ⓓ Ⓔ   51. Ⓐ Ⓑ Ⓒ Ⓓ Ⓔ
2. Ⓕ Ⓖ Ⓗ Ⓙ Ⓚ   12. Ⓕ Ⓖ Ⓗ Ⓙ Ⓚ   22. Ⓕ Ⓖ Ⓗ Ⓙ Ⓚ   32. Ⓕ Ⓖ Ⓗ Ⓙ Ⓚ   42. Ⓕ Ⓖ Ⓗ Ⓙ Ⓚ   52. Ⓕ Ⓖ Ⓗ Ⓙ Ⓚ
3. Ⓐ Ⓑ Ⓒ Ⓓ Ⓔ   13. Ⓐ Ⓑ Ⓒ Ⓓ Ⓔ   23. Ⓐ Ⓑ Ⓒ Ⓓ Ⓔ   33. Ⓐ Ⓑ Ⓒ Ⓓ Ⓔ   43. Ⓐ Ⓑ Ⓒ Ⓓ Ⓔ   53. Ⓐ Ⓑ Ⓒ Ⓓ Ⓔ
4. Ⓕ Ⓖ Ⓗ Ⓙ Ⓚ   14. Ⓕ Ⓖ Ⓗ Ⓙ Ⓚ   24. Ⓕ Ⓖ Ⓗ Ⓙ Ⓚ   34. Ⓕ Ⓖ Ⓗ Ⓙ Ⓚ   44. Ⓕ Ⓖ Ⓗ Ⓙ Ⓚ   54. Ⓕ Ⓖ Ⓗ Ⓙ Ⓚ
5. Ⓐ Ⓑ Ⓒ Ⓓ Ⓔ   15. Ⓐ Ⓑ Ⓒ Ⓓ Ⓔ   25. Ⓐ Ⓑ Ⓒ Ⓓ Ⓔ   35. Ⓐ Ⓑ Ⓒ Ⓓ Ⓔ   45. Ⓐ Ⓑ Ⓒ Ⓓ Ⓔ   55. Ⓐ Ⓑ Ⓒ Ⓓ Ⓔ
6. Ⓕ Ⓖ Ⓗ Ⓙ Ⓚ   16. Ⓕ Ⓖ Ⓗ Ⓙ Ⓚ   26. Ⓕ Ⓖ Ⓗ Ⓙ Ⓚ   36. Ⓕ Ⓖ Ⓗ Ⓙ Ⓚ   46. Ⓕ Ⓖ Ⓗ Ⓙ Ⓚ   56. Ⓕ Ⓖ Ⓗ Ⓙ Ⓚ
7. Ⓐ Ⓑ Ⓒ Ⓓ Ⓔ   17. Ⓐ Ⓑ Ⓒ Ⓓ Ⓔ   27. Ⓐ Ⓑ Ⓒ Ⓓ Ⓔ   37. Ⓐ Ⓑ Ⓒ Ⓓ Ⓔ   47. Ⓐ Ⓑ Ⓒ Ⓓ Ⓔ   57. Ⓐ Ⓑ Ⓒ Ⓓ Ⓔ
8. Ⓕ Ⓖ Ⓗ Ⓙ Ⓚ   18. Ⓕ Ⓖ Ⓗ Ⓙ Ⓚ   28. Ⓕ Ⓖ Ⓗ Ⓙ Ⓚ   38. Ⓕ Ⓖ Ⓗ Ⓙ Ⓚ   48. Ⓕ Ⓖ Ⓗ Ⓙ Ⓚ   58. Ⓕ Ⓖ Ⓗ Ⓙ Ⓚ
9. Ⓐ Ⓑ Ⓒ Ⓓ Ⓔ   19. Ⓐ Ⓑ Ⓒ Ⓓ Ⓔ   29. Ⓐ Ⓑ Ⓒ Ⓓ Ⓔ   39. Ⓐ Ⓑ Ⓒ Ⓓ Ⓔ   49. Ⓐ Ⓑ Ⓒ Ⓓ Ⓔ   59. Ⓐ Ⓑ Ⓒ Ⓓ Ⓔ
10. Ⓕ Ⓖ Ⓗ Ⓙ Ⓚ   20. Ⓕ Ⓖ Ⓗ Ⓙ Ⓚ   30. Ⓕ Ⓖ Ⓗ Ⓙ Ⓚ   40. Ⓕ Ⓖ Ⓗ Ⓙ Ⓚ   50. Ⓕ Ⓖ Ⓗ Ⓙ Ⓚ   60. Ⓕ Ⓖ Ⓗ Ⓙ Ⓚ

READING TEST

1. Ⓐ Ⓑ Ⓒ Ⓓ   6. Ⓕ Ⓖ Ⓗ Ⓙ   11. Ⓐ Ⓑ Ⓒ Ⓓ   16. Ⓕ Ⓖ Ⓗ Ⓙ   21. Ⓐ Ⓑ Ⓒ Ⓓ   26. Ⓕ Ⓖ Ⓗ Ⓙ   31. Ⓐ Ⓑ Ⓒ Ⓓ   36. Ⓕ Ⓖ Ⓗ Ⓙ
2. Ⓕ Ⓖ Ⓗ Ⓙ   7. Ⓐ Ⓑ Ⓒ Ⓓ   12. Ⓕ Ⓖ Ⓗ Ⓙ   17. Ⓐ Ⓑ Ⓒ Ⓓ   22. Ⓕ Ⓖ Ⓗ Ⓙ   27. Ⓐ Ⓑ Ⓒ Ⓓ   32. Ⓕ Ⓖ Ⓗ Ⓙ   37. Ⓐ Ⓑ Ⓒ Ⓓ
3. Ⓐ Ⓑ Ⓒ Ⓓ   8. Ⓕ Ⓖ Ⓗ Ⓙ   13. Ⓐ Ⓑ Ⓒ Ⓓ   18. Ⓕ Ⓖ Ⓗ Ⓙ   23. Ⓐ Ⓑ Ⓒ Ⓓ   28. Ⓕ Ⓖ Ⓗ Ⓙ   33. Ⓐ Ⓑ Ⓒ Ⓓ   38. Ⓕ Ⓖ Ⓗ Ⓙ
4. Ⓕ Ⓖ Ⓗ Ⓙ   9. Ⓐ Ⓑ Ⓒ Ⓓ   14. Ⓕ Ⓖ Ⓗ Ⓙ   19. Ⓐ Ⓑ Ⓒ Ⓓ   24. Ⓕ Ⓖ Ⓗ Ⓙ   29. Ⓐ Ⓑ Ⓒ Ⓓ   34. Ⓕ Ⓖ Ⓗ Ⓙ   39. Ⓐ Ⓑ Ⓒ Ⓓ
5. Ⓐ Ⓑ Ⓒ Ⓓ   10. Ⓕ Ⓖ Ⓗ Ⓙ   15. Ⓐ Ⓑ Ⓒ Ⓓ   20. Ⓕ Ⓖ Ⓗ Ⓙ   25. Ⓐ Ⓑ Ⓒ Ⓓ   30. Ⓕ Ⓖ Ⓗ Ⓙ   35. Ⓐ Ⓑ Ⓒ Ⓓ   40. Ⓕ Ⓖ Ⓗ Ⓙ

SCIENCE TEST

1. Ⓐ Ⓑ Ⓒ Ⓓ   6. Ⓕ Ⓖ Ⓗ Ⓙ   11. Ⓐ Ⓑ Ⓒ Ⓓ   16. Ⓕ Ⓖ Ⓗ Ⓙ   21. Ⓐ Ⓑ Ⓒ Ⓓ   26. Ⓕ Ⓖ Ⓗ Ⓙ   31. Ⓐ Ⓑ Ⓒ Ⓓ   36. Ⓕ Ⓖ Ⓗ Ⓙ
2. Ⓕ Ⓖ Ⓗ Ⓙ   7. Ⓐ Ⓑ Ⓒ Ⓓ   12. Ⓕ Ⓖ Ⓗ Ⓙ   17. Ⓐ Ⓑ Ⓒ Ⓓ   22. Ⓕ Ⓖ Ⓗ Ⓙ   27. Ⓐ Ⓑ Ⓒ Ⓓ   32. Ⓕ Ⓖ Ⓗ Ⓙ   37. Ⓐ Ⓑ Ⓒ Ⓓ
3. Ⓐ Ⓑ Ⓒ Ⓓ   8. Ⓕ Ⓖ Ⓗ Ⓙ   13. Ⓐ Ⓑ Ⓒ Ⓓ   18. Ⓕ Ⓖ Ⓗ Ⓙ   23. Ⓐ Ⓑ Ⓒ Ⓓ   28. Ⓕ Ⓖ Ⓗ Ⓙ   33. Ⓐ Ⓑ Ⓒ Ⓓ   38. Ⓕ Ⓖ Ⓗ Ⓙ
4. Ⓕ Ⓖ Ⓗ Ⓙ   9. Ⓐ Ⓑ Ⓒ Ⓓ   14. Ⓕ Ⓖ Ⓗ Ⓙ   19. Ⓐ Ⓑ Ⓒ Ⓓ   24. Ⓕ Ⓖ Ⓗ Ⓙ   29. Ⓐ Ⓑ Ⓒ Ⓓ   34. Ⓕ Ⓖ Ⓗ Ⓙ   39. Ⓐ Ⓑ Ⓒ Ⓓ
5. Ⓐ Ⓑ Ⓒ Ⓓ   10. Ⓕ Ⓖ Ⓗ Ⓙ   15. Ⓐ Ⓑ Ⓒ Ⓓ   20. Ⓕ Ⓖ Ⓗ Ⓙ   25. Ⓐ Ⓑ Ⓒ Ⓓ   30. Ⓕ Ⓖ Ⓗ Ⓙ   35. Ⓐ Ⓑ Ⓒ Ⓓ   40. Ⓕ Ⓖ Ⓗ Ⓙ

Name

EID

Name

EID

Name _____

EID _____

_____

_____

_____

_____

_____

_____

_____

_____

_____

_____

_____

_____

_____

_____

_____

_____

_____

_____

_____

_____

_____

TEST PREP AND
ADMISSIONS

ACT Essay Practice Test Comments

There are four separate score domains for the ACT Essay: Ideas and Analysis, Development and Support, Organization, and Language Use. Each domain is scored on a scale of 1 to 6. Two readers assign a score for each domain, and the scores are added together to generate a raw score that is between 8 and 48. The raw score is then converted to a scaled score that will be between 1 and 36. Here are some comments from your Kaplan grader based on these criteria to help you improve your essay writing.

Ideas and analysis	☐ This essay specifically discusses each of the three perspectives. The essay presents a fourth perspective and analyzes the relationship among all perspectives. ☐ Discuss each of the three perspectives before presenting a fourth perspective. Then analyze the relationship among all perspectives. ☐ Specifically discuss each of the three perspectives. Present a fourth perspective and discuss the relationship among all perspectives. ☐ Read the prompt again; this essay is off-topic.
Development and support	☐ The examples given provide strong support for your position and effectively provide context for your argument. ☐ Provide specific, relevant examples that provide additional insight and context. ☐ Develop examples more fully. ☐ Provide examples that are more specific and not overly general. ☐ Explain more fully how your examples relate to your position.
Maintains focus	☐ This essay maintains focus well. ☐ Maintain focus on the specific issue, not just the general topic. ☐ Maintain focus on the issue throughout. ☐ Use a topic sentence for each paragraph to help maintain focus.
Organization	☐ The ideas in the essay are well organized. ☐ Create a plan before you begin to write; avoid repeating ideas. ☐ Start a new paragraph to address a new point. ☐ Use transitions to lead the reader through your argument. ☐ Write a stronger conclusion; remember to budget your time.
Language use	☐ Spelling **and** ☐ grammar usage are satisfactory. ☐ Use of vocabulary **and** ☐ sentence structure are varied. ☐ Build a stronger vocabulary for Test Day; avoid repeating the same words. ☐ Review punctuation rules. ☐ Use more varied sentence structure. ☐ Proofread; remember to budget your time.

Additional Comments:

Administrative Purposes:

Student Name: _____   ID Number: _____

Test Number: 1   2   3   4

Essay grade: 0   1   2   3   4   5   6

(this score is doubled on your Practice Test results)

ACT Practice Test Two
ANSWER SHEET

ENGLISH TEST

1. (A)(B)(C)(D) 11. (A)(B)(C)(D) 21. (A)(B)(C)(D) 31. (A)(B)(C)(D) 41. (A)(B)(C)(D) 51. (A)(B)(C)(D) 61. (A)(B)(C)(D) 71. (A)(B)(C)(D)
2. (F)(G)(H)(J) 12. (F)(G)(H)(J) 22. (F)(G)(H)(J) 32. (F)(G)(H)(J) 42. (F)(G)(H)(J) 52. (F)(G)(H)(J) 62. (F)(G)(H)(J) 72. (F)(G)(H)(J)
3. (A)(B)(C)(D) 13. (A)(B)(C)(D) 23. (A)(B)(C)(D) 33. (A)(B)(C)(D) 43. (A)(B)(C)(D) 53. (A)(B)(C)(D) 63. (A)(B)(C)(D) 73. (A)(B)(C)(D)
4. (F)(G)(H)(J) 14. (F)(G)(H)(J) 24. (F)(G)(H)(J) 34. (F)(G)(H)(J) 44. (F)(G)(H)(J) 54. (F)(G)(H)(J) 64. (F)(G)(H)(J) 74. (F)(G)(H)(J)
5. (A)(B)(C)(D) 15. (A)(B)(C)(D) 25. (A)(B)(C)(D) 35. (A)(B)(C)(D) 45. (A)(B)(C)(D) 55. (A)(B)(C)(D) 65. (A)(B)(C)(D) 75. (A)(B)(C)(D)
6. (F)(G)(H)(J) 16. (F)(G)(H)(J) 26. (F)(G)(H)(J) 36. (F)(G)(H)(J) 46. (F)(G)(H)(J) 56. (F)(G)(H)(J) 66. (F)(G)(H)(J)
7. (A)(B)(C)(D) 17. (A)(B)(C)(D) 27. (A)(B)(C)(D) 37. (A)(B)(C)(D) 47. (A)(B)(C)(D) 57. (A)(B)(C)(D) 67. (A)(B)(C)(D)
8. (F)(G)(H)(J) 18. (F)(G)(H)(J) 28. (F)(G)(H)(J) 38. (F)(G)(H)(J) 48. (F)(G)(H)(J) 58. (F)(G)(H)(J) 68. (F)(G)(H)(J)
9. (A)(B)(C)(D) 19. (A)(B)(C)(D) 29. (A)(B)(C)(D) 39. (A)(B)(C)(D) 49. (A)(B)(C)(D) 59. (A)(B)(C)(D) 69. (A)(B)(C)(D)
10. (F)(G)(H)(J) 20. (F)(G)(H)(J) 30. (F)(G)(H)(J) 40. (F)(G)(H)(J) 50. (F)(G)(H)(J) 60. (F)(G)(H)(J) 70. (F)(G)(H)(J)

MATH TEST

1. (A)(B)(C)(D)(E) 11. (A)(B)(C)(D)(E) 21. (A)(B)(C)(D)(E) 31. (A)(B)(C)(D)(E) 41. (A)(B)(C)(D)(E) 51. (A)(B)(C)(D)(E)
2. (F)(G)(H)(J)(K) 12. (F)(G)(H)(J)(K) 22. (F)(G)(H)(J)(K) 32. (F)(G)(H)(J)(K) 42. (F)(G)(H)(J)(K) 52. (F)(G)(H)(J)(K)
3. (A)(B)(C)(D)(E) 13. (A)(B)(C)(D)(E) 23. (A)(B)(C)(D)(E) 33. (A)(B)(C)(D)(E) 43. (A)(B)(C)(D)(E) 53. (A)(B)(C)(D)(E)
4. (F)(G)(H)(J)(K) 14. (F)(G)(H)(J)(K) 24. (F)(G)(H)(J)(K) 34. (F)(G)(H)(J)(K) 44. (F)(G)(H)(J)(K) 54. (F)(G)(H)(J)(K)
5. (A)(B)(C)(D)(E) 15. (A)(B)(C)(D)(E) 25. (A)(B)(C)(D)(E) 35. (A)(B)(C)(D)(E) 45. (A)(B)(C)(D)(E) 55. (A)(B)(C)(D)(E)
6. (F)(G)(H)(J)(K) 16. (F)(G)(H)(J)(K) 26. (F)(G)(H)(J)(K) 36. (F)(G)(H)(J)(K) 46. (F)(G)(H)(J)(K) 56. (F)(G)(H)(J)(K)
7. (A)(B)(C)(D)(E) 17. (A)(B)(C)(D)(E) 27. (A)(B)(C)(D)(E) 37. (A)(B)(C)(D)(E) 47. (A)(B)(C)(D)(E) 57. (A)(B)(C)(D)(E)
8. (F)(G)(H)(J)(K) 18. (F)(G)(H)(J)(K) 28. (F)(G)(H)(J)(K) 38. (F)(G)(H)(J)(K) 48. (F)(G)(H)(J)(K) 58. (F)(G)(H)(J)(K)
9. (A)(B)(C)(D)(E) 19. (A)(B)(C)(D)(E) 29. (A)(B)(C)(D)(E) 39. (A)(B)(C)(D)(E) 49. (A)(B)(C)(D)(E) 59. (A)(B)(C)(D)(E)
10. (F)(G)(H)(J)(K) 20. (F)(G)(H)(J)(K) 30. (F)(G)(H)(J)(K) 40. (F)(G)(H)(J)(K) 50. (F)(G)(H)(J)(K) 60. (F)(G)(H)(J)(K)

READING TEST

1. (A)(B)(C)(D) 6. (F)(G)(H)(J) 11. (A)(B)(C)(D) 16. (F)(G)(H)(J) 21. (A)(B)(C)(D) 26. (F)(G)(H)(J) 31. (A)(B)(C)(D) 36. (F)(G)(H)(J)
2. (F)(G)(H)(J) 7. (A)(B)(C)(D) 12. (F)(G)(H)(J) 17. (A)(B)(C)(D) 22. (F)(G)(H)(J) 27. (A)(B)(C)(D) 32. (F)(G)(H)(J) 37. (A)(B)(C)(D)
3. (A)(B)(C)(D) 8. (F)(G)(H)(J) 13. (A)(B)(C)(D) 18. (F)(G)(H)(J) 23. (A)(B)(C)(D) 28. (F)(G)(H)(J) 33. (A)(B)(C)(D) 38. (F)(G)(H)(J)
4. (F)(G)(H)(J) 9. (A)(B)(C)(D) 14. (F)(G)(H)(J) 19. (A)(B)(C)(D) 24. (F)(G)(H)(J) 29. (A)(B)(C)(D) 34. (F)(G)(H)(J) 39. (A)(B)(C)(D)
5. (A)(B)(C)(D) 10. (F)(G)(H)(J) 15. (A)(B)(C)(D) 20. (F)(G)(H)(J) 25. (A)(B)(C)(D) 30. (F)(G)(H)(J) 35. (A)(B)(C)(D) 40. (F)(G)(H)(J)

SCIENCE TEST

1. (A)(B)(C)(D) 6. (F)(G)(H)(J) 11. (A)(B)(C)(D) 16. (F)(G)(H)(J) 21. (A)(B)(C)(D) 26. (F)(G)(H)(J) 31. (A)(B)(C)(D) 36. (F)(G)(H)(J)
2. (F)(G)(H)(J) 7. (A)(B)(C)(D) 12. (F)(G)(H)(J) 17. (A)(B)(C)(D) 22. (F)(G)(H)(J) 27. (A)(B)(C)(D) 32. (F)(G)(H)(J) 37. (A)(B)(C)(D)
3. (A)(B)(C)(D) 8. (F)(G)(H)(J) 13. (A)(B)(C)(D) 18. (F)(G)(H)(J) 23. (A)(B)(C)(D) 28. (F)(G)(H)(J) 33. (A)(B)(C)(D) 38. (F)(G)(H)(J)
4. (F)(G)(H)(J) 9. (A)(B)(C)(D) 14. (F)(G)(H)(J) 19. (A)(B)(C)(D) 24. (F)(G)(H)(J) 29. (A)(B)(C)(D) 34. (F)(G)(H)(J) 39. (A)(B)(C)(D)
5. (A)(B)(C)(D) 10. (F)(G)(H)(J) 15. (A)(B)(C)(D) 20. (F)(G)(H)(J) 25. (A)(B)(C)(D) 30. (F)(G)(H)(J) 35. (A)(B)(C)(D) 40. (F)(G)(H)(J)

Name

EID

Name

EID

Name _____

EID _____

_____

_____

_____

_____

_____

_____

_____

_____

_____

_____

_____

_____

_____

_____

_____

_____

_____

_____

_____

_____

_____

KAPLAN

TEST PREP AND
ADMISSIONS

ACT Essay Practice Test Comments

There are four separate score domains for the ACT Essay: Ideas and Analysis, Development and Support, Organization, and Language Use. Each domain is scored on a scale of 1 to 6. Two readers assign a score for each domain, and the scores are added together to generate a raw score that is between 8 and 48. The raw score is then converted to a scaled score that will be between 1 and 36. Here are some comments from your Kaplan grader based on these criteria to help you improve your essay writing.

Ideas and analysis	☐ This essay specifically discusses each of the three perspectives. The essay presents a fourth perspective and analyzes the relationship among all perspectives. ☐ Discuss each of the three perspectives before presenting a fourth perspective. Then analyze the relationship among all perspectives. ☐ Specifically discuss each of the three perspectives. Present a fourth perspective and discuss the relationship among all perspectives. ☐ Read the prompt again; this essay is off-topic.
Development and support	☐ The examples given provide strong support for your position and effectively provide context for your argument. ☐ Provide specific, relevant examples that provide additional insight and context. ☐ Develop examples more fully. ☐ Provide examples that are more specific and not overly general. ☐ Explain more fully how your examples relate to your position.
Maintains focus	☐ This essay maintains focus well. ☐ Maintain focus on the specific issue, not just the general topic. ☐ Maintain focus on the issue throughout. ☐ Use a topic sentence for each paragraph to help maintain focus.
Organization	☐ The ideas in the essay are well organized. ☐ Create a plan before you begin to write; avoid repeating ideas. ☐ Start a new paragraph to address a new point. ☐ Use transitions to lead the reader through your argument. ☐ Write a stronger conclusion; remember to budget your time.
Language use	☐ Spelling **and** ☐ grammar usage are satisfactory. ☐ Use of vocabulary **and** ☐ sentence structure are varied. ☐ Build a stronger vocabulary for Test Day; avoid repeating the same words. ☐ Review punctuation rules. ☐ Use more varied sentence structure. ☐ Proofread; remember to budget your time.

Additional Comments:

Administrative Purposes:

Student Name: _____   ID Number: _____

Test Number: 1   2   3   4

Essay grade: 0   1   2   3   4   5   6

(this score is doubled on your Practice Test results)

ACT Practice Test Three
ANSWER SHEET

ENGLISH TEST

1. Ⓐ Ⓑ Ⓒ Ⓓ	11. Ⓐ Ⓑ Ⓒ Ⓓ	21. Ⓐ Ⓑ Ⓒ Ⓓ	31. Ⓐ Ⓑ Ⓒ Ⓓ	41. Ⓐ Ⓑ Ⓒ Ⓓ	51. Ⓐ Ⓑ Ⓒ Ⓓ	61. Ⓐ Ⓑ Ⓒ Ⓓ	71. Ⓐ Ⓑ Ⓒ Ⓓ
2. Ⓕ Ⓖ Ⓗ Ⓙ	12. Ⓕ Ⓖ Ⓗ Ⓙ	22. Ⓕ Ⓖ Ⓗ Ⓙ	32. Ⓕ Ⓖ Ⓗ Ⓙ	42. Ⓕ Ⓖ Ⓗ Ⓙ	52. Ⓕ Ⓖ Ⓗ Ⓙ	62. Ⓕ Ⓖ Ⓗ Ⓙ	72. Ⓕ Ⓖ Ⓗ Ⓙ
3. Ⓐ Ⓑ Ⓒ Ⓓ	13. Ⓐ Ⓑ Ⓒ Ⓓ	23. Ⓐ Ⓑ Ⓒ Ⓓ	33. Ⓐ Ⓑ Ⓒ Ⓓ	43. Ⓐ Ⓑ Ⓒ Ⓓ	53. Ⓐ Ⓑ Ⓒ Ⓓ	63. Ⓐ Ⓑ Ⓒ Ⓓ	73. Ⓐ Ⓑ Ⓒ Ⓓ
4. Ⓕ Ⓖ Ⓗ Ⓙ	14. Ⓕ Ⓖ Ⓗ Ⓙ	24. Ⓕ Ⓖ Ⓗ Ⓙ	34. Ⓕ Ⓖ Ⓗ Ⓙ	44. Ⓕ Ⓖ Ⓗ Ⓙ	54. Ⓕ Ⓖ Ⓗ Ⓙ	64. Ⓕ Ⓖ Ⓗ Ⓙ	74. Ⓕ Ⓖ Ⓗ Ⓙ
5. Ⓐ Ⓑ Ⓒ Ⓓ	15. Ⓐ Ⓑ Ⓒ Ⓓ	25. Ⓐ Ⓑ Ⓒ Ⓓ	35. Ⓐ Ⓑ Ⓒ Ⓓ	45. Ⓐ Ⓑ Ⓒ Ⓓ	55. Ⓐ Ⓑ Ⓒ Ⓓ	65. Ⓐ Ⓑ Ⓒ Ⓓ	75. Ⓐ Ⓑ Ⓒ Ⓓ
6. Ⓕ Ⓖ Ⓗ Ⓙ	16. Ⓕ Ⓖ Ⓗ Ⓙ	26. Ⓕ Ⓖ Ⓗ Ⓙ	36. Ⓕ Ⓖ Ⓗ Ⓙ	46. Ⓕ Ⓖ Ⓗ Ⓙ	56. Ⓕ Ⓖ Ⓗ Ⓙ	66. Ⓕ Ⓖ Ⓗ Ⓙ	
7. Ⓐ Ⓑ Ⓒ Ⓓ	17. Ⓐ Ⓑ Ⓒ Ⓓ	27. Ⓐ Ⓑ Ⓒ Ⓓ	37. Ⓐ Ⓑ Ⓒ Ⓓ	47. Ⓐ Ⓑ Ⓒ Ⓓ	57. Ⓐ Ⓑ Ⓒ Ⓓ	67. Ⓐ Ⓑ Ⓒ Ⓓ	
8. Ⓕ Ⓖ Ⓗ Ⓙ	18. Ⓕ Ⓖ Ⓗ Ⓙ	28. Ⓕ Ⓖ Ⓗ Ⓙ	38. Ⓕ Ⓖ Ⓗ Ⓙ	48. Ⓕ Ⓖ Ⓗ Ⓙ	58. Ⓕ Ⓖ Ⓗ Ⓙ	68. Ⓕ Ⓖ Ⓗ Ⓙ	
9. Ⓐ Ⓑ Ⓒ Ⓓ	19. Ⓐ Ⓑ Ⓒ Ⓓ	29. Ⓐ Ⓑ Ⓒ Ⓓ	39. Ⓐ Ⓑ Ⓒ Ⓓ	49. Ⓐ Ⓑ Ⓒ Ⓓ	59. Ⓐ Ⓑ Ⓒ Ⓓ	69. Ⓐ Ⓑ Ⓒ Ⓓ	
10. Ⓕ Ⓖ Ⓗ Ⓙ	20. Ⓕ Ⓖ Ⓗ Ⓙ	30. Ⓕ Ⓖ Ⓗ Ⓙ	40. Ⓕ Ⓖ Ⓗ Ⓙ	50. Ⓕ Ⓖ Ⓗ Ⓙ	60. Ⓕ Ⓖ Ⓗ Ⓙ	70. Ⓕ Ⓖ Ⓗ Ⓙ	

MATH TEST

1. Ⓐ Ⓑ Ⓒ Ⓓ Ⓔ	11. Ⓐ Ⓑ Ⓒ Ⓓ Ⓔ	21. Ⓐ Ⓑ Ⓒ Ⓓ Ⓔ	31. Ⓐ Ⓑ Ⓒ Ⓓ Ⓔ	41. Ⓐ Ⓑ Ⓒ Ⓓ Ⓔ	51. Ⓐ Ⓑ Ⓒ Ⓓ Ⓔ
2. Ⓕ Ⓖ Ⓗ Ⓙ Ⓚ	12. Ⓕ Ⓖ Ⓗ Ⓙ Ⓚ	22. Ⓕ Ⓖ Ⓗ Ⓙ Ⓚ	32. Ⓕ Ⓖ Ⓗ Ⓙ Ⓚ	42. Ⓕ Ⓖ Ⓗ Ⓙ Ⓚ	52. Ⓕ Ⓖ Ⓗ Ⓙ Ⓚ
3. Ⓐ Ⓑ Ⓒ Ⓓ Ⓔ	13. Ⓐ Ⓑ Ⓒ Ⓓ Ⓔ	23. Ⓐ Ⓑ Ⓒ Ⓓ Ⓔ	33. Ⓐ Ⓑ Ⓒ Ⓓ Ⓔ	43. Ⓐ Ⓑ Ⓒ Ⓓ Ⓔ	53. Ⓐ Ⓑ Ⓒ Ⓓ Ⓔ
4. Ⓕ Ⓖ Ⓗ Ⓙ Ⓚ	14. Ⓕ Ⓖ Ⓗ Ⓙ Ⓚ	24. Ⓕ Ⓖ Ⓗ Ⓙ Ⓚ	34. Ⓕ Ⓖ Ⓗ Ⓙ Ⓚ	44. Ⓕ Ⓖ Ⓗ Ⓙ Ⓚ	54. Ⓕ Ⓖ Ⓗ Ⓙ Ⓚ
5. Ⓐ Ⓑ Ⓒ Ⓓ Ⓔ	15. Ⓐ Ⓑ Ⓒ Ⓓ Ⓔ	25. Ⓐ Ⓑ Ⓒ Ⓓ Ⓔ	35. Ⓐ Ⓑ Ⓒ Ⓓ Ⓔ	45. Ⓐ Ⓑ Ⓒ Ⓓ Ⓔ	55. Ⓐ Ⓑ Ⓒ Ⓓ Ⓔ
6. Ⓕ Ⓖ Ⓗ Ⓙ Ⓚ	16. Ⓕ Ⓖ Ⓗ Ⓙ Ⓚ	26. Ⓕ Ⓖ Ⓗ Ⓙ Ⓚ	36. Ⓕ Ⓖ Ⓗ Ⓙ Ⓚ	46. Ⓕ Ⓖ Ⓗ Ⓙ Ⓚ	56. Ⓕ Ⓖ Ⓗ Ⓙ Ⓚ
7. Ⓐ Ⓑ Ⓒ Ⓓ Ⓔ	17. Ⓐ Ⓑ Ⓒ Ⓓ Ⓔ	27. Ⓐ Ⓑ Ⓒ Ⓓ Ⓔ	37. Ⓐ Ⓑ Ⓒ Ⓓ Ⓔ	47. Ⓐ Ⓑ Ⓒ Ⓓ Ⓔ	57. Ⓐ Ⓑ Ⓒ Ⓓ Ⓔ
8. Ⓕ Ⓖ Ⓗ Ⓙ Ⓚ	18. Ⓕ Ⓖ Ⓗ Ⓙ Ⓚ	28. Ⓕ Ⓖ Ⓗ Ⓙ Ⓚ	38. Ⓕ Ⓖ Ⓗ Ⓙ Ⓚ	48. Ⓕ Ⓖ Ⓗ Ⓙ Ⓚ	58. Ⓕ Ⓖ Ⓗ Ⓙ Ⓚ
9. Ⓐ Ⓑ Ⓒ Ⓓ Ⓔ	19. Ⓐ Ⓑ Ⓒ Ⓓ Ⓔ	29. Ⓐ Ⓑ Ⓒ Ⓓ Ⓔ	39. Ⓐ Ⓑ Ⓒ Ⓓ Ⓔ	49. Ⓐ Ⓑ Ⓒ Ⓓ Ⓔ	59. Ⓐ Ⓑ Ⓒ Ⓓ Ⓔ
10. Ⓕ Ⓖ Ⓗ Ⓙ Ⓚ	20. Ⓕ Ⓖ Ⓗ Ⓙ Ⓚ	30. Ⓕ Ⓖ Ⓗ Ⓙ Ⓚ	40. Ⓕ Ⓖ Ⓗ Ⓙ Ⓚ	50. Ⓕ Ⓖ Ⓗ Ⓙ Ⓚ	60. Ⓕ Ⓖ Ⓗ Ⓙ Ⓚ

READING TEST

1. Ⓐ Ⓑ Ⓒ Ⓓ	6. Ⓕ Ⓖ Ⓗ Ⓙ	11. Ⓐ Ⓑ Ⓒ Ⓓ	16. Ⓕ Ⓖ Ⓗ Ⓙ	21. Ⓐ Ⓑ Ⓒ Ⓓ	26. Ⓕ Ⓖ Ⓗ Ⓙ	31. Ⓐ Ⓑ Ⓒ Ⓓ	36. Ⓕ Ⓖ Ⓗ Ⓙ
2. Ⓕ Ⓖ Ⓗ Ⓙ	7. Ⓐ Ⓑ Ⓒ Ⓓ	12. Ⓕ Ⓖ Ⓗ Ⓙ	17. Ⓐ Ⓑ Ⓒ Ⓓ	22. Ⓕ Ⓖ Ⓗ Ⓙ	27. Ⓐ Ⓑ Ⓒ Ⓓ	32. Ⓕ Ⓖ Ⓗ Ⓙ	37. Ⓐ Ⓑ Ⓒ Ⓓ
3. Ⓐ Ⓑ Ⓒ Ⓓ	8. Ⓕ Ⓖ Ⓗ Ⓙ	13. Ⓐ Ⓑ Ⓒ Ⓓ	18. Ⓕ Ⓖ Ⓗ Ⓙ	23. Ⓐ Ⓑ Ⓒ Ⓓ	28. Ⓕ Ⓖ Ⓗ Ⓙ	33. Ⓐ Ⓑ Ⓒ Ⓓ	38. Ⓕ Ⓖ Ⓗ Ⓙ
4. Ⓕ Ⓖ Ⓗ Ⓙ	9. Ⓐ Ⓑ Ⓒ Ⓓ	14. Ⓕ Ⓖ Ⓗ Ⓙ	19. Ⓐ Ⓑ Ⓒ Ⓓ	24. Ⓕ Ⓖ Ⓗ Ⓙ	29. Ⓐ Ⓑ Ⓒ Ⓓ	34. Ⓕ Ⓖ Ⓗ Ⓙ	39. Ⓐ Ⓑ Ⓒ Ⓓ
5. Ⓐ Ⓑ Ⓒ Ⓓ	10. Ⓕ Ⓖ Ⓗ Ⓙ	15. Ⓐ Ⓑ Ⓒ Ⓓ	20. Ⓕ Ⓖ Ⓗ Ⓙ	25. Ⓐ Ⓑ Ⓒ Ⓓ	30. Ⓕ Ⓖ Ⓗ Ⓙ	35. Ⓐ Ⓑ Ⓒ Ⓓ	40. Ⓕ Ⓖ Ⓗ Ⓙ

SCIENCE TEST

1. Ⓐ Ⓑ Ⓒ Ⓓ	6. Ⓕ Ⓖ Ⓗ Ⓙ	11. Ⓐ Ⓑ Ⓒ Ⓓ	16. Ⓕ Ⓖ Ⓗ Ⓙ	21. Ⓐ Ⓑ Ⓒ Ⓓ	26. Ⓕ Ⓖ Ⓗ Ⓙ	31. Ⓐ Ⓑ Ⓒ Ⓓ	36. Ⓕ Ⓖ Ⓗ Ⓙ
2. Ⓕ Ⓖ Ⓗ Ⓙ	7. Ⓐ Ⓑ Ⓒ Ⓓ	12. Ⓕ Ⓖ Ⓗ Ⓙ	17. Ⓐ Ⓑ Ⓒ Ⓓ	22. Ⓕ Ⓖ Ⓗ Ⓙ	27. Ⓐ Ⓑ Ⓒ Ⓓ	32. Ⓕ Ⓖ Ⓗ Ⓙ	37. Ⓐ Ⓑ Ⓒ Ⓓ
3. Ⓐ Ⓑ Ⓒ Ⓓ	8. Ⓕ Ⓖ Ⓗ Ⓙ	13. Ⓐ Ⓑ Ⓒ Ⓓ	18. Ⓕ Ⓖ Ⓗ Ⓙ	23. Ⓐ Ⓑ Ⓒ Ⓓ	28. Ⓕ Ⓖ Ⓗ Ⓙ	33. Ⓐ Ⓑ Ⓒ Ⓓ	38. Ⓕ Ⓖ Ⓗ Ⓙ
4. Ⓕ Ⓖ Ⓗ Ⓙ	9. Ⓐ Ⓑ Ⓒ Ⓓ	14. Ⓕ Ⓖ Ⓗ Ⓙ	19. Ⓐ Ⓑ Ⓒ Ⓓ	24. Ⓕ Ⓖ Ⓗ Ⓙ	29. Ⓐ Ⓑ Ⓒ Ⓓ	34. Ⓕ Ⓖ Ⓗ Ⓙ	39. Ⓐ Ⓑ Ⓒ Ⓓ
5. Ⓐ Ⓑ Ⓒ Ⓓ	10. Ⓕ Ⓖ Ⓗ Ⓙ	15. Ⓐ Ⓑ Ⓒ Ⓓ	20. Ⓕ Ⓖ Ⓗ Ⓙ	25. Ⓐ Ⓑ Ⓒ Ⓓ	30. Ⓕ Ⓖ Ⓗ Ⓙ	35. Ⓐ Ⓑ Ⓒ Ⓓ	40. Ⓕ Ⓖ Ⓗ Ⓙ

Name

EID

Name

EID

Name

EID

KAPLAN

TEST PREP AND
ADMISSIONS

ACT Essay Practice Test Comments

There are four separate score domains for the ACT Essay: Ideas and Analysis, Development and Support, Organization, and Language Use. Each domain is scored on a scale of 1 to 6. Two readers assign a score for each domain, and the scores are added together to generate a raw score that is between 8 and 48. The raw score is then converted to a scaled score that will be between 1 and 36. Here are some comments from your Kaplan grader based on these criteria to help you improve your essay writing.

Ideas and analysis	☐ This essay specifically discusses each of the three perspectives. The essay presents a fourth perspective and analyzes the relationship among all perspectives. ☐ Discuss each of the three perspectives before presenting a fourth perspective. Then analyze the relationship among all perspectives. ☐ Specifically discuss each of the three perspectives. Present a fourth perspective and discuss the relationship among all perspectives. ☐ Read the prompt again; this essay is off-topic.
Development and support	☐ The examples given provide strong support for your position and effectively provide context for your argument. ☐ Provide specific, relevant examples that provide additional insight and context. ☐ Develop examples more fully. ☐ Provide examples that are more specific and not overly general. ☐ Explain more fully how your examples relate to your position.
Maintains focus	☐ This essay maintains focus well. ☐ Maintain focus on the specific issue, not just the general topic. ☐ Maintain focus on the issue throughout. ☐ Use a topic sentence for each paragraph to help maintain focus.
Organization	☐ The ideas in the essay are well organized. ☐ Create a plan before you begin to write; avoid repeating ideas. ☐ Start a new paragraph to address a new point. ☐ Use transitions to lead the reader through your argument. ☐ Write a stronger conclusion; remember to budget your time.
Language use	☐ Spelling **and** ☐ grammar usage are satisfactory. ☐ Use of vocabulary **and** ☐ sentence structure are varied. ☐ Build a stronger vocabulary for Test Day; avoid repeating the same words. ☐ Review punctuation rules. ☐ Use more varied sentence structure. ☐ Proofread; remember to budget your time.

Additional Comments:

Administrative Purposes:

Student Name: _____   ID Number: _____

Test Number: 1   2   3   4

Essay grade: 0   1   2   3   4   5   6

(this score is doubled on your Practice Test results)

ACT Practice Test Four
ANSWER SHEET

ENGLISH TEST

1. Ⓐ Ⓑ Ⓒ Ⓓ	11. Ⓐ Ⓑ Ⓒ Ⓓ	21. Ⓐ Ⓑ Ⓒ Ⓓ	31. Ⓐ Ⓑ Ⓒ Ⓓ	41. Ⓐ Ⓑ Ⓒ Ⓓ	51. Ⓐ Ⓑ Ⓒ Ⓓ	61. Ⓐ Ⓑ Ⓒ Ⓓ	71. Ⓐ Ⓑ Ⓒ Ⓓ
2. Ⓕ Ⓖ Ⓗ Ⓙ	12. Ⓕ Ⓖ Ⓗ Ⓙ	22. Ⓕ Ⓖ Ⓗ Ⓙ	32. Ⓕ Ⓖ Ⓗ Ⓙ	42. Ⓕ Ⓖ Ⓗ Ⓙ	52. Ⓕ Ⓖ Ⓗ Ⓙ	62. Ⓕ Ⓖ Ⓗ Ⓙ	72. Ⓕ Ⓖ Ⓗ Ⓙ
3. Ⓐ Ⓑ Ⓒ Ⓓ	13. Ⓐ Ⓑ Ⓒ Ⓓ	23. Ⓐ Ⓑ Ⓒ Ⓓ	33. Ⓐ Ⓑ Ⓒ Ⓓ	43. Ⓐ Ⓑ Ⓒ Ⓓ	53. Ⓐ Ⓑ Ⓒ Ⓓ	63. Ⓐ Ⓑ Ⓒ Ⓓ	73. Ⓐ Ⓑ Ⓒ Ⓓ
4. Ⓕ Ⓖ Ⓗ Ⓙ	14. Ⓕ Ⓖ Ⓗ Ⓙ	24. Ⓕ Ⓖ Ⓗ Ⓙ	34. Ⓕ Ⓖ Ⓗ Ⓙ	44. Ⓕ Ⓖ Ⓗ Ⓙ	54. Ⓕ Ⓖ Ⓗ Ⓙ	64. Ⓕ Ⓖ Ⓗ Ⓙ	74. Ⓕ Ⓖ Ⓗ Ⓙ
5. Ⓐ Ⓑ Ⓒ Ⓓ	15. Ⓐ Ⓑ Ⓒ Ⓓ	25. Ⓐ Ⓑ Ⓒ Ⓓ	35. Ⓐ Ⓑ Ⓒ Ⓓ	45. Ⓐ Ⓑ Ⓒ Ⓓ	55. Ⓐ Ⓑ Ⓒ Ⓓ	65. Ⓐ Ⓑ Ⓒ Ⓓ	75. Ⓐ Ⓑ Ⓒ Ⓓ
6. Ⓕ Ⓖ Ⓗ Ⓙ	16. Ⓕ Ⓖ Ⓗ Ⓙ	26. Ⓕ Ⓖ Ⓗ Ⓙ	36. Ⓕ Ⓖ Ⓗ Ⓙ	46. Ⓕ Ⓖ Ⓗ Ⓙ	56. Ⓕ Ⓖ Ⓗ Ⓙ	66. Ⓕ Ⓖ Ⓗ Ⓙ	
7. Ⓐ Ⓑ Ⓒ Ⓓ	17. Ⓐ Ⓑ Ⓒ Ⓓ	27. Ⓐ Ⓑ Ⓒ Ⓓ	37. Ⓐ Ⓑ Ⓒ Ⓓ	47. Ⓐ Ⓑ Ⓒ Ⓓ	57. Ⓐ Ⓑ Ⓒ Ⓓ	67. Ⓐ Ⓑ Ⓒ Ⓓ	
8. Ⓕ Ⓖ Ⓗ Ⓙ	18. Ⓕ Ⓖ Ⓗ Ⓙ	28. Ⓕ Ⓖ Ⓗ Ⓙ	38. Ⓕ Ⓖ Ⓗ Ⓙ	48. Ⓕ Ⓖ Ⓗ Ⓙ	58. Ⓕ Ⓖ Ⓗ Ⓙ	68. Ⓕ Ⓖ Ⓗ Ⓙ	
9. Ⓐ Ⓑ Ⓒ Ⓓ	19. Ⓐ Ⓑ Ⓒ Ⓓ	29. Ⓐ Ⓑ Ⓒ Ⓓ	39. Ⓐ Ⓑ Ⓒ Ⓓ	49. Ⓐ Ⓑ Ⓒ Ⓓ	59. Ⓐ Ⓑ Ⓒ Ⓓ	69. Ⓐ Ⓑ Ⓒ Ⓓ	
10. Ⓕ Ⓖ Ⓗ Ⓙ	20. Ⓕ Ⓖ Ⓗ Ⓙ	30. Ⓕ Ⓖ Ⓗ Ⓙ	40. Ⓕ Ⓖ Ⓗ Ⓙ	50. Ⓕ Ⓖ Ⓗ Ⓙ	60. Ⓕ Ⓖ Ⓗ Ⓙ	70. Ⓕ Ⓖ Ⓗ Ⓙ	

MATH TEST

1. Ⓐ Ⓑ Ⓒ Ⓓ Ⓔ	11. Ⓐ Ⓑ Ⓒ Ⓓ Ⓔ	21. Ⓐ Ⓑ Ⓒ Ⓓ Ⓔ	31. Ⓐ Ⓑ Ⓒ Ⓓ Ⓔ	41. Ⓐ Ⓑ Ⓒ Ⓓ Ⓔ	51. Ⓐ Ⓑ Ⓒ Ⓓ Ⓔ
2. Ⓕ Ⓖ Ⓗ Ⓙ Ⓚ	12. Ⓕ Ⓖ Ⓗ Ⓙ Ⓚ	22. Ⓕ Ⓖ Ⓗ Ⓙ Ⓚ	32. Ⓕ Ⓖ Ⓗ Ⓙ Ⓚ	42. Ⓕ Ⓖ Ⓗ Ⓙ Ⓚ	52. Ⓕ Ⓖ Ⓗ Ⓙ Ⓚ
3. Ⓐ Ⓑ Ⓒ Ⓓ Ⓔ	13. Ⓐ Ⓑ Ⓒ Ⓓ Ⓔ	23. Ⓐ Ⓑ Ⓒ Ⓓ Ⓔ	33. Ⓐ Ⓑ Ⓒ Ⓓ Ⓔ	43. Ⓐ Ⓑ Ⓒ Ⓓ Ⓔ	53. Ⓐ Ⓑ Ⓒ Ⓓ Ⓔ
4. Ⓕ Ⓖ Ⓗ Ⓙ Ⓚ	14. Ⓕ Ⓖ Ⓗ Ⓙ Ⓚ	24. Ⓕ Ⓖ Ⓗ Ⓙ Ⓚ	34. Ⓕ Ⓖ Ⓗ Ⓙ Ⓚ	44. Ⓕ Ⓖ Ⓗ Ⓙ Ⓚ	54. Ⓕ Ⓖ Ⓗ Ⓙ Ⓚ
5. Ⓐ Ⓑ Ⓒ Ⓓ Ⓔ	15. Ⓐ Ⓑ Ⓒ Ⓓ Ⓔ	25. Ⓐ Ⓑ Ⓒ Ⓓ Ⓔ	35. Ⓐ Ⓑ Ⓒ Ⓓ Ⓔ	45. Ⓐ Ⓑ Ⓒ Ⓓ Ⓔ	55. Ⓐ Ⓑ Ⓒ Ⓓ Ⓔ
6. Ⓕ Ⓖ Ⓗ Ⓙ Ⓚ	16. Ⓕ Ⓖ Ⓗ Ⓙ Ⓚ	26. Ⓕ Ⓖ Ⓗ Ⓙ Ⓚ	36. Ⓕ Ⓖ Ⓗ Ⓙ Ⓚ	46. Ⓕ Ⓖ Ⓗ Ⓙ Ⓚ	56. Ⓕ Ⓖ Ⓗ Ⓙ Ⓚ
7. Ⓐ Ⓑ Ⓒ Ⓓ Ⓔ	17. Ⓐ Ⓑ Ⓒ Ⓓ Ⓔ	27. Ⓐ Ⓑ Ⓒ Ⓓ Ⓔ	37. Ⓐ Ⓑ Ⓒ Ⓓ Ⓔ	47. Ⓐ Ⓑ Ⓒ Ⓓ Ⓔ	57. Ⓐ Ⓑ Ⓒ Ⓓ Ⓔ
8. Ⓕ Ⓖ Ⓗ Ⓙ Ⓚ	18. Ⓕ Ⓖ Ⓗ Ⓙ Ⓚ	28. Ⓕ Ⓖ Ⓗ Ⓙ Ⓚ	38. Ⓕ Ⓖ Ⓗ Ⓙ Ⓚ	48. Ⓕ Ⓖ Ⓗ Ⓙ Ⓚ	58. Ⓕ Ⓖ Ⓗ Ⓙ Ⓚ
9. Ⓐ Ⓑ Ⓒ Ⓓ Ⓔ	19. Ⓐ Ⓑ Ⓒ Ⓓ Ⓔ	29. Ⓐ Ⓑ Ⓒ Ⓓ Ⓔ	39. Ⓐ Ⓑ Ⓒ Ⓓ Ⓔ	49. Ⓐ Ⓑ Ⓒ Ⓓ Ⓔ	59. Ⓐ Ⓑ Ⓒ Ⓓ Ⓔ
10. Ⓕ Ⓖ Ⓗ Ⓙ Ⓚ	20. Ⓕ Ⓖ Ⓗ Ⓙ Ⓚ	30. Ⓕ Ⓖ Ⓗ Ⓙ Ⓚ	40. Ⓕ Ⓖ Ⓗ Ⓙ Ⓚ	50. Ⓕ Ⓖ Ⓗ Ⓙ Ⓚ	60. Ⓕ Ⓖ Ⓗ Ⓙ Ⓚ

READING TEST

1. Ⓐ Ⓑ Ⓒ Ⓓ	6. Ⓕ Ⓖ Ⓗ Ⓙ	11. Ⓐ Ⓑ Ⓒ Ⓓ	16. Ⓕ Ⓖ Ⓗ Ⓙ	21. Ⓐ Ⓑ Ⓒ Ⓓ	26. Ⓕ Ⓖ Ⓗ Ⓙ	31. Ⓐ Ⓑ Ⓒ Ⓓ	36. Ⓕ Ⓖ Ⓗ Ⓙ
2. Ⓕ Ⓖ Ⓗ Ⓙ	7. Ⓐ Ⓑ Ⓒ Ⓓ	12. Ⓕ Ⓖ Ⓗ Ⓙ	17. Ⓐ Ⓑ Ⓒ Ⓓ	22. Ⓕ Ⓖ Ⓗ Ⓙ	27. Ⓐ Ⓑ Ⓒ Ⓓ	32. Ⓕ Ⓖ Ⓗ Ⓙ	37. Ⓐ Ⓑ Ⓒ Ⓓ
3. Ⓐ Ⓑ Ⓒ Ⓓ	8. Ⓕ Ⓖ Ⓗ Ⓙ	13. Ⓐ Ⓑ Ⓒ Ⓓ	18. Ⓕ Ⓖ Ⓗ Ⓙ	23. Ⓐ Ⓑ Ⓒ Ⓓ	28. Ⓕ Ⓖ Ⓗ Ⓙ	33. Ⓐ Ⓑ Ⓒ Ⓓ	38. Ⓕ Ⓖ Ⓗ Ⓙ
4. Ⓕ Ⓖ Ⓗ Ⓙ	9. Ⓐ Ⓑ Ⓒ Ⓓ	14. Ⓕ Ⓖ Ⓗ Ⓙ	19. Ⓐ Ⓑ Ⓒ Ⓓ	24. Ⓕ Ⓖ Ⓗ Ⓙ	29. Ⓐ Ⓑ Ⓒ Ⓓ	34. Ⓕ Ⓖ Ⓗ Ⓙ	39. Ⓐ Ⓑ Ⓒ Ⓓ
5. Ⓐ Ⓑ Ⓒ Ⓓ	10. Ⓕ Ⓖ Ⓗ Ⓙ	15. Ⓐ Ⓑ Ⓒ Ⓓ	20. Ⓕ Ⓖ Ⓗ Ⓙ	25. Ⓐ Ⓑ Ⓒ Ⓓ	30. Ⓕ Ⓖ Ⓗ Ⓙ	35. Ⓐ Ⓑ Ⓒ Ⓓ	40. Ⓕ Ⓖ Ⓗ Ⓙ

SCIENCE TEST

1. Ⓐ Ⓑ Ⓒ Ⓓ	6. Ⓕ Ⓖ Ⓗ Ⓙ	11. Ⓐ Ⓑ Ⓒ Ⓓ	16. Ⓕ Ⓖ Ⓗ Ⓙ	21. Ⓐ Ⓑ Ⓒ Ⓓ	26. Ⓕ Ⓖ Ⓗ Ⓙ	31. Ⓐ Ⓑ Ⓒ Ⓓ	36. Ⓕ Ⓖ Ⓗ Ⓙ
2. Ⓕ Ⓖ Ⓗ Ⓙ	7. Ⓐ Ⓑ Ⓒ Ⓓ	12. Ⓕ Ⓖ Ⓗ Ⓙ	17. Ⓐ Ⓑ Ⓒ Ⓓ	22. Ⓕ Ⓖ Ⓗ Ⓙ	27. Ⓐ Ⓑ Ⓒ Ⓓ	32. Ⓕ Ⓖ Ⓗ Ⓙ	37. Ⓐ Ⓑ Ⓒ Ⓓ
3. Ⓐ Ⓑ Ⓒ Ⓓ	8. Ⓕ Ⓖ Ⓗ Ⓙ	13. Ⓐ Ⓑ Ⓒ Ⓓ	18. Ⓕ Ⓖ Ⓗ Ⓙ	23. Ⓐ Ⓑ Ⓒ Ⓓ	28. Ⓕ Ⓖ Ⓗ Ⓙ	33. Ⓐ Ⓑ Ⓒ Ⓓ	38. Ⓕ Ⓖ Ⓗ Ⓙ
4. Ⓕ Ⓖ Ⓗ Ⓙ	9. Ⓐ Ⓑ Ⓒ Ⓓ	14. Ⓕ Ⓖ Ⓗ Ⓙ	19. Ⓐ Ⓑ Ⓒ Ⓓ	24. Ⓕ Ⓖ Ⓗ Ⓙ	29. Ⓐ Ⓑ Ⓒ Ⓓ	34. Ⓕ Ⓖ Ⓗ Ⓙ	39. Ⓐ Ⓑ Ⓒ Ⓓ
5. Ⓐ Ⓑ Ⓒ Ⓓ	10. Ⓕ Ⓖ Ⓗ Ⓙ	15. Ⓐ Ⓑ Ⓒ Ⓓ	20. Ⓕ Ⓖ Ⓗ Ⓙ	25. Ⓐ Ⓑ Ⓒ Ⓓ	30. Ⓕ Ⓖ Ⓗ Ⓙ	35. Ⓐ Ⓑ Ⓒ Ⓓ	40. Ⓕ Ⓖ Ⓗ Ⓙ

Name _____

EID _____

_____

_____

_____

_____

_____

_____

_____

_____

_____

_____

_____

_____

_____

_____

_____

_____

_____

_____

_____

_____

_____

_____

Name

EID

Name

EID

KAPLAN

TEST PREP AND
ADMISSIONS

ACT Essay Practice Test Comments

There are four separate score domains for the ACT Essay: Ideas and Analysis, Development and Support, Organization, and Language Use. Each domain is scored on a scale of 1 to 6. Two readers assign a score for each domain, and the scores are added together to generate a raw score that is between 8 and 48. The raw score is then converted to a scaled score that will be between 1 and 36. Here are some comments from your Kaplan grader based on these criteria to help you improve your essay writing.

Ideas and analysis	☐ This essay specifically discusses each of the three perspectives. The essay presents a fourth perspective and analyzes the relationship among all perspectives. ☐ Discuss each of the three perspectives before presenting a fourth perspective. Then analyze the relationship among all perspectives. ☐ Specifically discuss each of the three perspectives. Present a fourth perspective and discuss the relationship among all perspectives. ☐ Read the prompt again; this essay is off-topic.
Development and support	☐ The examples given provide strong support for your position and effectively provide context for your argument. ☐ Provide specific, relevant examples that provide additional insight and context. ☐ Develop examples more fully. ☐ Provide examples that are more specific and not overly general. ☐ Explain more fully how your examples relate to your position.
Maintains focus	☐ This essay maintains focus well. ☐ Maintain focus on the specific issue, not just the general topic. ☐ Maintain focus on the issue throughout. ☐ Use a topic sentence for each paragraph to help maintain focus.
Organization	☐ The ideas in the essay are well organized. ☐ Create a plan before you begin to write; avoid repeating ideas. ☐ Start a new paragraph to address a new point. ☐ Use transitions to lead the reader through your argument. ☐ Write a stronger conclusion; remember to budget your time.
Language use	☐ Spelling **and** ☐ grammar usage are satisfactory. ☐ Use of vocabulary **and** ☐ sentence structure are varied. ☐ Build a stronger vocabulary for Test Day; avoid repeating the same words. ☐ Review punctuation rules. ☐ Use more varied sentence structure. ☐ Proofread; remember to budget your time.

Additional Comments:

Administrative Purposes:

Student Name: _____   ID Number: _____

Test Number: 1   2   3   4

Essay grade: 0   1   2   3   4   5   6

(this score is doubled on your Practice Test results)